Uruguay was once the most stable democracy in Latin America, but in 1973 the military seized power for the first time. Political parties did not disappear, however, even though they were made illegal. By the 1980s Uruguay's generals were anxious to find a way to withdraw from power. Yet they continued to insist on certain guarantees as the price for holding elections. The issue of whether to make any concessions to the military came to divide the country's three major parties: the Blancos, the Colorados, and the Left. Nevertheless, the latter two parties eventually did agree to a pact in July 1984. The military agreed to return to the barracks and the politicians made an implicit commitment not to prosecute them for their past human rights violations.

CAMBRIDGE LATIN AMERICAN STUDIES

GENERAL EDITOR
SIMON COLLIER

ADVISORY COMMITTEE
MALCOLM DEAS, STUART SCHWARTZ, ARTURO VALENZUELA

72

NEGOTIATING DEMOCRACY

For a list of other books in the
Cambridge Latin American Studies series,
please see page 265.

NEGOTIATING DEMOCRACY

POLITICIANS AND GENERALS IN URUGUAY

CHARLES GUY GILLESPIE

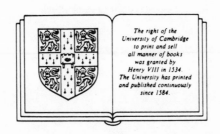

The right of the
University of Cambridge
to print and sell
all manner of books
was granted by
Henry VIII in 1534.
The University has printed
and published continuously
since 1584.

CAMBRIDGE UNIVERSITY PRESS

Cambridge

New York   Port Chester   Melbourne   Sydney

Published by the Press Syndicate of the University of Cambridge
The Pitt Building, Trumpington Street, Cambridge CB2 1RP
40 West 20th Street, New York, NY 10011, USA
10 Stamford Road, Oakleigh, Melbourne 3166, Australia

© Cambridge University Press 1991

First published 1991

Printed in the United States of America

Library of Congress Cataloging-in-Publication Data
Gillespie, Charles. 1959–1991
Negotiating democracy : politicians and generals in Uruguay /
Charles Guy Gillespie.
    p.   cm. – (Cambridge Latin American studies ; 72)
        Includes bibliographical references.
                ISBN 0–521–40152–6
    1. Political parties – Uruguay.   2. Uruguay – Politics and
government – 1973–   3. Civil–military relations – Uruguay.   I. Title.
                        II. Series.
                JL3698.A1G5   1991
320.9895 – dc20   90–28839
                                                          CIP

British Library Cataloguing in Publication Data
Gillespie, Charles Guy
Negotiating democracy – (Cambridge Latin American
            studies, 72).
        1. Uruguay. Politics
            I. Title.
            320.9895

        ISBN 0–521–40152–6 hardback

For Richard Goodkin

Contents

Foreword

This work is a major contribution to comparative politics that many colleagues and friends expected to be the first of many by an outstanding young scholar. The study of Uruguayan politics was put on the map of Latin-American Studies by Charles Gillespie, not only by the present monograph, but by numerous articles and papers in collective books and by the work and enthusiasm he put into organizing a memorable conference on Uruguay at the Wilson Center for Scholars in Washington in 1984. He brought together scholars, intellectuals, and politicians from Uruguay and interested persons from the United States. His influence on the development of political science in that small Southern Cone democracy was enormous.

The present book contributes significantly to the study of transitions from authoritarian regimes to democracy. This theme has attracted more and more intellectual attention, renewed by the changes in Eastern Europe. To date no single monograph on these transitions in South America has been so well researched, providing so much insight into the political development of a country from democracy to authoritarianism and back to democracy. There is no comparable work, not only for any Latin-American country, but also for most countries that have experienced such changes since the seventies. We who work in that subject must turn to Gillespie's contribution. The study combines a wide range of methodological approaches, from historical, institutional, and legal analysis to the use of electoral data and personal interviews. In the course of extended fieldwork, living in the center of Montevideo and across from the Artigas monument, Charlie Gillespie became fully acquainted with intellectuals, scholars, and politicians during the critical years of the transition. This is a work based on a very personal experience of the process it studies.

Charlie came from a British-Irish family. Born in London in 1958, he obtained a BA from Oxford in 1980, where he studied at Magdalen College. After working for the *Economist* he came to Yale, where in 1987 he received a Ph.D. in Political Science with distinction. He was a Prize Teaching Fellow at Yale College from 1982 to 1983 and was awarded fellowships from the Tinker Foundation, the Interamerican Foundation, and the SSRC. His thesis was awarded the dissertation Prize of the New England Council on Latin-American Studies (1988). While at Yale, Charlie taught British and Western European politics. His academic career took him first to Amherst College and later to the University of Wisconsin at Madison, where he impressed students and colleagues with tireless devotion to his task under trying circumstances.

Just before his untimely death he did important research on Paraguay, where he went to observe the 1989 elections as member of the delegation of the Latin-American Studies Association. His next big project was to be a study of the ideological change toward democracy among Latin-American intellectuals from their earlier critical writings and thought. This would have been a major and much-needed contribution, on which he had already done much work. It was inspiring to see him continue his scholarly work until a tragic end.

Those who, like myself, were associated with him as teachers, classmates, colleagues, and students, will miss his scholarly contributions, but, even more, we will miss a sensitive person full of life, energy, and enthusiasm — and a true friend.

Juan Linz

Acknowledgments

This book is the product of seven years of work. During that time I have had the help of a great number of professors and friends at Yale University, at the University of Wisconsin, Madison, and in Uruguay. In its final form it owes more to Juan Linz than to anyone else, and I am profoundly grateful for the time and great effort he devoted to helping me improve it. His commitment to his graduate students is legendary and extraordinarily generous. More than once I felt that I was abusing his intellectual time and hospitality; whatever inadequacies may remain in the final product are my own responsibility. To Alfred Stepan I owe a debt of gratitude for encouraging me in the early stages of the project and helping me get to Uruguay. Among my friends and colleagues, Luis Eduardo González (both at CIESU and at Yale) has been an inspiration and a model of patience in responding to a barrage of questions, ranging from the painstakingly detailed to the monumentally broad. Juan Rial helped me greatly in Montevideo, particularly when it came to deciding whom I should interview, and he was most generous with his hospitality. Rodolfo Goncebate very kindly shared his questionnaire on Argentine politicians developed with Juan Linz. I have used many of his questions here. Margaret Keck provided invaluable assistance in sharpening my ideas and editing the first part of the manuscript.

Among Uruguayan social scientists whom I should like to thank for exchanging ideas, information, and help are Carlos Filgueira, César Aguiar, María del Huerto Amarillo, Horacio Martorelli, Romeo Pérez, Martín Gargiulo, Gerónimo De Sierra, Luis Costa Bonino, Rolando Francò, and Pablo Mieres. There were, of course, many more who helped me, to whom I apologize for not having the space to list them individually. I would like, however, to add a general note of thanks to the Centro de Informaciones y Estudios Sobre el Uruguay (CIESU), where I taught an introductory course in political science. I am particularly grateful for the contribution CIESU made in having my questionnaire typed and retyped and in publishing my early essays as working papers. I am also grateful to the Centro Interdisciplinario de Estudios Sobre el Desarrollo Uruguayo

(CIEDUR) for the invitation to participate in various seminars on the transition during 1984.

My earliest work on the breakdown of Uruguayan democracy has been incorporated into parts of Chapter 3. At different times it has benefited from the comments of David Mayhew, Robert Lane, Robert Dahl, Edy Kaufman, Howard Handelman, M. H. J. Finch, and Milton Vanger. The data analysis, especially in Chapters 3, 5, and 8, required a great deal of patient advice from Greg Herek, John Mark Hansen, and Luis González – though not all of it may have sunk in. Parts of Chapters 6–8 have benefited from the comments (at different stages) of Robert Kaufman, Scott Michael, Michael Coppedge, and Ben Ross Schneider. Part of Chapter 9 draws on an essay that appeared in a volume edited by Paul Drake and Eduardo Silva, *Elections and Democratization in Latin America, 1980–85*; both Paul Drake and David Collier made useful suggestions at that time. All my work on the Uruguayan transition has benefited from my close collaboration with Louis Goodman during the planning of the 1984 conference on Uruguay at the Wilson Center Latin American Program in Washington, D.C.

The company and friendship of Uruguayan journalists and editors as the dramatic events of 1984 unfolded were especially valuable. Particularly kind to me were Miguel Arregui, Carlos Jones, and Jorge Otero. Carmen Ariztegui and the other librarians at *El Día* were also a great help in providing materials and checking facts on many occasions. The staff of the Biblioteca del Palacio Montevideo, the Intendencia Municipal de Montevideo, and the Dirección General de Estadísticas y Censos all gave of their time. Valuable opinion data were generously provided by Luis Alberto Ferreira of Gallup Uruguay and César Aguiar and Agustin Canzani of Equipos Consultores.

Funds for fieldwork and write-up were provided by the Inter-American Foundation and by the Social Science Research Council under grants from the American Council of Learned Societies and the Ford Foundation.

To my parents and Richard Goodkin I wish to repeat the thanks I am not always able to put into words. I am also deeply grateful for the kindness and dedication of the nurses and doctors of St. Mary's Hospital in London and the University of Wisconsin Hospital in Madison. My greatest debt, however, is to the Uruguayan politicians whom I interviewed, as well as the militants who showed me how the parties organized themselves at the grass roots and welcomed a *gringo* to their meetings and conventions. Perhaps the most touching moments came when an old woman outside the Colorado Convention promised me her family would give me their votes, when I joined the euphoric Blanco campaign bus as it careened through the back-country roads from village to village while children threw white flower petals on Juan Raúl Ferreira, and when I was repeatedly introduced to a bemused Base Committee of the Broad Front as *compañero*. For all the warmth and spirit that they shared in times of great difficulty and hope I thank them all.

1

Introduction: Political parties, theories of regime change, and the Uruguayan case

This book examines a crucial case of democratic breakdown and rebirth that took place over the past generation in what was formerly the most stable democracy in Latin America. Uruguay's plunge into authoritarian rule seriously undermined the case for "Uruguayan exceptionalism" vis-à-vis the rest of Latin America that had pervaded the classic literature on the country.[1] Yet if stable authoritarianism was to become the dominant regime type among Latin America's more advanced nations in the late twentieth century – as some pessimists predicted – Uruguay represented inhospitable soil, given its long democratic record.

There has never been a functioning democracy without political parties, and yet, ironically, parties usually play a key role in democratic breakdowns. Nowhere was that more true than in Uruguay, notwithstanding the widely held view that its democratic system fell victim to one or another kind of external assault during the 1960s and early 1970s. Uruguay experienced two decades of declining domestic production after the end of the Korean War boom, but despite increasing social strife, its democracy held up. Few democracies have faced such a deadly challenge.[2] Uruguay's traditional parties, the Blancos and the Colorados, had long been firmly entrenched in the state, using its resources to strengthen themselves vis-à-vis rival power groups: foreign capital, domestic economic elites, and popular movements. However, their reliance on the historical "relative autonomy" of the political system weakened those parties once state resources began to dwindle as a result of prolonged economic stagnation. The distribution of favors as a means of vote-getting by these parties was in decline, but its replacement by more programmatic "outbidding" only contributed even more to the growing fiscal crisis. Ideological and charismatic appeals by new politicians also exacerbated the spiral of conflict and authoritarian reaction.

1 See, for example, Fitzgibbon (1954).
2 Gillespie and González (1989).

Samuel Huntington's discussion of the dangers of party decay bears a chilling relevance to military intervention in Uruguay:

> The susceptibility of a political system to military intervention varies inversely with the strength of its political parties. . . . The decline in party strength, the fragmentation of leadership, the evaporation of mass support, the decay of organizational structure, the shift of political leaders from party to bureaucracy, the rise of personalism, all herald moments when colonels occupy the Capitol. Military coups do not destroy parties; they ratify the deterioration which has already occurred.[3]

By the time of the 1973 coup, Uruguay's parties and their leaders were exhausted, devoid of constructive solutions and unable to unite to prevent the military takeover. Thus, it was all the more surprising that only a decade after their legal "suspension" by the military in 1973, Uruguay's traditional parties had been reborn and were leading the opposition to the military regime in cooperation with the illegal Left. One goal of this book is to explore the extent of that revival and its consequences. This study sets out to place political parties at the center of theoretical attention under an authoritarian regime during its installation, erosion, and demise.

The importance of parties in regime change is well known, but has been less well studied than might have been expected. Uruguay, however, afforded a fascinating case for study in the early 1980s. After 12 years of military rule, the country underwent a process of negotiated military withdrawal and elections that culminated in democratic restoration.

Only in rare circumstances do modern military institutions lose their monopoly over the means of coercion, let alone suffer violent overthrow. The student of transitions must therefore focus on a range of semivoluntary decisions to hand power to elected civilians, ranging from guided institutionalization, through negotiated withdrawal, to abdication. Uruguay's transition constituted a crucial case for comparative politics in that it grew out of a broad stalemate between the regime and the opposition. Unlike the case of Brazil, internal pressures for reform were weak, and, unlike the case of Argentina, the regime was not experiencing an internal crisis sufficient to topple it from power. Uruguay was thus situated *analytically as well as geographically* in between these two neighboring cases – one of deliberate liberalization, the other of disastrous collapse.

Apart from their role in promoting regime change and stability, political parties must be seen as the sine qua non for democracy in the modern nation-state – even in small polities such as Uruguay. They recruit leaders and contribute to the political education of the public, tasks also performed by other institutions, such as functional interest associations.

3 Huntington (1968, p. 409).

However, there are three further tasks that parties are uniquely equipped to perform in democracies: aggregation of interests, articulation of coherent political choices, and protection of pluralism. Parties both protect the "parts" of the polity and integrate them; without parties, elections degenerate into meaningless plebiscites, and interest conflicts are unmediated. The more time passes, the more it seems that parties in one form or another are necessary for pluralism, and pluralism for democracy.

Debate on regime change in Latin America: the neglect of parties

A variety of theories of political change based on simple predictions that economic development would produce democracy were laid belatedly to rest in the 1970s. Yet analysis of the new bureaucratic authoritarian regimes in Latin America had not proceeded far when the pressure of events in the 1980s shifted attention to the question of authoritarian erosion and crisis.[4] Starting with Brazil's political "opening" in 1974 and the extraordinary defeat of the new authoritarian constitution in Uruguay's 1980 plebiscite, debates over democratic transitions began to reveal three gaps in the literature:

1 overemphasis on the onset of bureaucratic authoritarianism, which led to neglect of the subsequent problems of institutionalization,
2 the downplaying of political institutions, and especially parties, and a tendency to reduce political phenomena to economic causes,[5] and
3 lack of attention to the Uruguayan case, which, because of the weight of political institutions and democratic political culture, shows the inadequacy of a focus on the alliance between the state and fractions of the bourgeoisie.

This study aims to address these three inadequacies by analyzing the roles of political parties in resisting authoritarianism and providing political alternatives to military rule in Uruguay. Above all, it attempts to

---

4 O'Donnell (1979b) defined bureaucratic authoritarianism not as a state but as a regime based on a "system of political exclusion of a previously activated popular sector."

5 To be fair to O'Donnell, it was partly the "consumption" of his work that led to this often economistic interpretation of authoritarianism. His earliest writing had brilliantly analyzed the "impossible game" of politics in Argentina from 1955 to 1966. See Chapter 4 of his *Modernization and Bureaucratic-Authoritarianism* (1973). In his "middle period," typified by the essay "Reflections on the Patterns of Change in the Bureaucratic-Authoritarian State" (1978), O'Donnell focused more and more on alliances among the state and bourgeois class fractions. The centering of subsequent debate on accumulation rather than legitimation, and the implications for such elite economic alliances, is clear in the volume edited by Collier: *The New Authoritarianism in Latin America* (1979). The difficulties of using the same theories to explain authoritarian crises were to become increasingly evident, and O'Donnell's work moved in new directions.

show that an understanding of the failure of democracy, as well as the prospects for overcoming authoritarianism, must be rooted in an analysis of the behavior of political parties. In particular, it emphasizes the role of competitive party strategies in determining both the path and the timing of democratic transitions and the subsequent prospects for democratic consolidation.[6]

Political parties not only can help to erode authoritarian regimes by their strategies of resistance but also can provide the key to the question of how a particular authoritarian regime is to be superseded. The manner in which power passes from authoritarian rulers to oppositions can vary greatly, ranging from revolutionary overthrow, through abdication born of crisis, to negotiated transaction, and even voluntary democratization "from above." These alternatives correspond to what Stepan has called *paths*.[7] The timing of regime changes is also an important problem, involving far more than the question of how long citizens must endure a particular tyranny. Over time, the range of alternatives open to political actors narrows, and "historic opportunities" may be missed. For example, a regime may attempt to liberalize "too late," or seek negotiations at a time when the opposition has become too radicalized, thus reducing the likelihood of peaceful change. The possible paths of regime change are thus closely related to *timing*, and both of these strongly affect the likelihood that liberal democracy will emerge and be consolidated.[8]

As this study will show, the parties' tactics were in the end the determining factors in the timing and manner of democratic transition in Uruguay. Military calculations of the costs and benefits of remaining in office, versus handing power to elected leaders, were strongly influenced by the parties' strategies of opposition. They were also influenced by the environment in which the military ruled: an absence of legitimacy, economic failure, and party tactics that controlled disruptive popular mobilizations. However, it was the parties' decision to negotiate with the Uruguayan commanders in chief that made possible a relatively peaceful transfer of power to civilians and constrained those political actors who sought more radical alternatives to what became known as the "Naval Club pact."

The focus of this study on parties as critical actors during phases of regime change was not chosen on the basis of any a priori assumption that they are the only potential political actors that matter, but derived from sustained observations of the unfolding of events in Uruguay. During

6 By "consolidation" I mean not the achievement of a "steady state" of perfect democracy, but rather a situation of regime resilience that permits a permanent process of adaptation, innovation, and responses to challenges.

7 Stepan (1986).

8 This discussion of timing owes much to an unpublished essay by Linz (1985).

the period of the authoritarian regime, I was struck by the peculiar vacuum in which technocratic decisions were being made, as well as the very limited articulation of political demands by most of the economic elite (with the exception of the ranchers).[9] That comparative reticence on the part of the economic elite to assume a leading political role was even more evident as the transition to democracy began. Neither open displays of support for the authoritarian regime nor clear denunciations of it were common.

Popular movements, and especially trade unions, provided a far more active and vocal presence in demanding the return of democracy. Union activity reemerged from clandestinity to a state of de facto toleration in 1984, as did so-called new social movements, such as human-rights organizations, women's groups, and residents' associations. Yet, as the mode of Uruguay's transition to democracy crystallized, the limited ability of such popular movements and organizations to influence the course of events became clear.[10] In this way, the value of a focus on party elites, seemingly the weakest of political actors at the height of military rule, was confirmed. So, too, was the necessity of following the political outlook of the officer corps, though here information was much harder to come by.

Studying Uruguayan parties under authoritarianism

Uruguay's traditional parties, the Colorados and the Blancos, are notoriously loosely structured and informally organized.[11] Although they still account for two-thirds of the electorate, neither has a clearly defined membership or a highly developed party apparatus. Rather, they consist of career politicians, some with distinguished family histories and political lineages, who form an array of competing factions with certain common inheritances and outlooks.[12]

This study is centered on a set of more than seventy formal interviews with elite members of Uruguay's political parties, conducted mainly in

9 The evidence is set out in the first part of Chapter 6.

10 The evidence is discussed at the beginning of Chapter 7.

11 Although definitions of what constitutes a "party" vary, here we are mainly concerned with organizations that put up candidates for public office. Though occasionally there are dissenting voices, most would agree that despite highly developed internal factions, Uruguay's Colorados and Blancos are single political parties. Comparativists unfamiliar with Uruguay have sometimes been misled on this point. The alliance of leftist groups known as the Broad Front is more correctly seen as a coalition of independent parties, but for brevity I shall refer to it as "a party."

12 Some parties with very "loose" and unstructured organizations have historically shown a remarkable capacity for survival, for instance, the British Conservative party. The substance of parties' strength sometimes seems to reside in the electorate and its ingrained political subcultures, rather than in bureaucratic organizations. Strong party identifications may be just as enduring as a bureaucratic apparatus under authoritarian regimes.

Montevideo during 1984 and 1985.[13] These were supplemented by count-less informal conversations with politicians in their homes and offices, during conventions, and in the corridors of the National Assembly. The interviews included both of the traditional parties, with all of their major Montevideo factions, the parties of the Left, and some smaller parties, such as the Civic Union. Normally, one could not reach an adequate understanding of the Left parties, which are membership-based, without interviewing middle-level activists; however, such activists did not re-establish strong control over their leaders during the democratic transition.[14] Some sectors of the Left did not even have active membership cadres. Therefore, the elite-interview-based strategy of investigation was appropriate for an understanding of all parties during the transition.

Given the factionalized nature of the traditional parties and the com-plexity of the Left coalition, particular emphasis was placed on inter-viewing leaders from every sector and current of opinion.[15] The interviewees in almost all cases were past or future executive or legislative officeholders, members of party or faction executive committees, estab-lished "bosses" of political clubs, or influential leaders of more modern components of party organization, such as program committees, youth groups, and labor fronts. Interviewees were first chosen on the basis of clear historical salience or media attention, and subsequently by means of the "snowball" technique. Among those whom I interviewed were presidential contenders, or their running mates, from the three major parties in both the 1971 and 1984 elections.[16] Until recently there had been no other study of Uruguayan political elites of comparable scope.[17]

Once excluded from power, political parties face a host of dangers, including atrophy of their organizations, loss of relevance to new social groups and issues, and general decline into marginality. In their struggle to adapt to changing circumstances, the degree to which the authoritarian regime attempts to restructure the state and society will determine the

---

13 The Appendix lists the respondents to the questionnaire, and the first part of the Bibliography details the names and the dates for the interviewees quoted.

14 This was not true of one sizable leftist party that encountered less repression, the Christian Democrats. Revealingly, they experienced major internal conflict leading to the ouster of their longtime leader.

15 Both open-ended questions and pointed questions were used. The questions were developed with the guidance of Juan Linz, many of them repeating studies of parties and elites in other countries, including Rodolfo Goncebate's study of Argentina. Two versions of the questionnaire were used, one long and one shorter, and hence the variation in the number of respondents on each question.

16 Interviews were granted on the understanding that answers would not be attributed to individuals.

17 A complementary study of Uruguayan legislators undertaken in 1985 and 1986 provided an opportunity to test the validity of my findings, and happily it produced broadly comparable results (González 1988). González used a more rigidly defined set of interviewees: the universe of legislators elected in 1984.

depth of the challenge faced by parties. At the height of the regime's power, their strategies must necessarily be largely defensive and reactive. However, they need not be passive: The closure of representative institutions may even act as a stimulus to seek new spheres for political activity and organized resistance. Chapter 5 examines the struggle between military attempts to reengineer the party system from above and opposition efforts to revitalize it from below.

The existing theoretical literature on how parties fare under military regimes is rather meager. Bearing in mind the distinction between the impact of the regime on parties and their limited capacity to adapt to the new conditions (both of which determine their relative capacity to survive), we note the following arguments:

1   The impact of the regime will depend on the degree to which it succeeds in implementing a project for the transformation of society and political economy, rather than on simple repression.[18]
2   Insofar as the regime does have a foundational dimension, parties should harness new social movements and political arenas for the articulation of strategies of survival and opposition.[19]

The Uruguayan military regime in comparative perspective

Though it succumbed to military intervention in the same year as did Chile (1973), for Uruguay the abrogation of democracy, and particularly the de facto installation of permanent military government, was far more *sui generis*.[20] In fact, Uruguay constituted a limiting case of the "new authoritarianism" that swept Argentina and Chile at about the same time. The degree of political polarization and revolutionary threat preceding the coup was lower than in those other cases,[21] and the success of the military in creating a political support space in the face of the traditional parties was minimal. The party system was subject neither to the disintegration that occurred in Chile nor to the creation of new parties "from above" that went on in Brazil.

In 1980 the Chilean dictator, General Pinochet, won a plebiscite on a

18 Garretón (1979).
19 Garretón (1981).
20 For those who might not see the Chilean coup as any less aberrant, it should be pointed out that the Chilean military were heavily involved in politics in the 1920s and 1930s. In Uruguay, the modern military had never been involved in politics. When President Terra carried out an institutional coup in 1933, he dispatched the fire brigade to carry it out! One of the keys to military subordination had been the deliberate policy of Colorado governments to underpay the armed forces, to deprive them of prestige, and to award privileges to the police force.
21 Remmer and Merkx (1982).

new authoritarian constitution. In the same year, political parties orchestrated the defeat of a similar project in Uruguay, and their victory by a ratio of 3:2 was admitted by the military – indeed a unique event under an authoritarian regime! Although Argentina abruptly moved toward democracy at a faster pace than did Uruguay in the wake of the South Atlantic war, it did so in a far more improvised and disorderly fashion, under the weight of an internal crisis of the military. Uruguay's leaders were not deflated by such strategic defeats.

Uruguay's transition to democracy was unlike that of Brazil in that it was completed after only one decade of military intervention, rather than two. It should also be stressed that it was really a case of redemocratization, whereas prior experience of democracy in Brazil, and to some extent even in Argentina, had been far more sporadic and unstable.[22] During that time, Uruguay had experienced nothing like the rapid social changes (particularly industrialization and urbanization) seen in Brazil. By 1973, Uruguay had long been predominantly urban and literate. It lacked a peasantry, but possessed a large middle class and a population almost exclusively descended from European immigrants. Export-oriented growth policies notwithstanding, Uruguay has increasingly come to appear to be a prematurely "postindustrial" society, with a rapidly aging population that puts increasing strain on the country's once-vaunted welfare state.

On a darker note, Uruguay's transition was peculiar in that the country began moving toward democracy while still under conditions of relatively high political repression.[23] As late as June 1984, leading Blanco politicians were arrested and detained, and many former party leaders remained banned from political activity, along with all leftist parties of the Broad Front. The press continued to be censored and periodically closed, sometimes indefinitely.[24] It was illegal to mention the name of the exiled Blanco leader Wilson Ferreira Aldunate, quote his statements, or print his photograph.

From 1980 onwards, the military attempted to engineer wider political participation without real liberalization: *inclusion* without *contestation*, to use the terms of Robert Dahl.[25] Yet there probably can be no such thing

---

22 Indeed, Dahl (1985, pp. 38–44) has made the striking statement that Uruguay may represent the only case to date anywhere in the world of a strongly institutionalized democracy breaking down.

23 The last deaths from torture for political motives in Brazil (those of Vladimir Herzog and Manoel Fiel Filho) occurred in 1975; in Uruguay, the Roszlik case, discussed in Chapter 7, occurred in May 1984.

24 Though opposition weeklies began to appear with the 1980 plebiscite, a brief attempt was made to introduce prior censorship in late 1983 and early 1984. Until then, fear among those in the news media had led them to censor themselves.

25 These dimensions of democracy were elaborated by Dahl (1971).

as a regime that is even moderately "inclusionary" or "accountable" while it remains completely unliberalized. Freedom of expression and association was not guaranteed, and those who were judged to have overstepped the arbitrary and ill-defined bounds of the permissible were subject to being deprived of other rights, such as being detained without trial. These bounds were extremely narrow when compared, for example, with those set by the Brazilian authoritarian regime after President Geisel initiated the policy of *distensão* (relaxation). In Brazil the military regime passed an amnesty, whereas the Uruguayan generals insisted that amnesty wait until the politicians had taken over.[26] The failure of the military's plans was rooted in both the low level of their mass support (unlike in Chile) and their determination to marginalize, rather than co-opt, the old political elite (unlike Brazil).

Explaining and promoting transitions to democracy

The most basic factor in the survival of a regime is its *legitimacy*.[27] Modern Latin American military regimes suffer from the absence of real legitimacy, defined as a capacity to invoke obedience from citizens and groups even when this clashes with their self-interests. Most of the time the military more or less lamely claim to be defending democracy from "subversion" or from "totalitarianism." Yet their pretended transitory nature, by definition, rules out institutionalized legitimacy. In fact, one way for authoritarian rule to give way to democratic transitions is through the launching of inadequate attempts at legitimation and institutionalization, particularly where this involves a project for limited liberalization that gets out of hand. As Chapter 4 shows, the vain search for legitimacy eventually undermined military rule in Uruguay, but that by no means determined an automatic or easy return to democracy.

Given the importance of analyses centering on *political economy* in explaining the advent of modern authoritarian rule in Latin America, it is not surprising that such analysis should be invoked to explain the crisis in Uruguay. In his later work on bureaucratic authoritarianism, O'Donnell began to argue that the "transnationalization" of economic activities weakened the state, while economic stabilization plans had early on hurt the

---

26 The Brazilian reciprocal amnesty was intended to free prisoners of conscience and spare the military from prosecution for human-rights violations. One thing differed between the two cases, however: Uruguay's Tupamaros guerrillas had first taken up arms against a democracy; Brazil's guerrillas fought against a military dictatorship.

27 Regimes that are performing quite poorly sometimes seem to survive for relatively long periods precisely because they are seen as being legitimate. One can also imagine the opposite circumstance: the collapse of a regime, even though it is performing well (i.e., is making effective decisions vis-à-vis challenges), because it is viewed as illegitimate.

national bourgeoisie's weakest elements. The military were divided over economic policies because of their nationalism and were not necessarily subject to free-enterprise profit "worship." O'Donnell thus concluded that bureaucratic authoritarianism was ultimately "a suboptimal form of bourgeois domination" lacking in the mediations for achieving consensus.[28] A process of erosion resulted "from the efforts of the dominant classes to satisfy their demands upon the state." In that way democracy was revived as an alternative *faute de mieux*. But whereas economic crises and loss of support from the economic elite are almost always seen in the crises of authoritarian regimes, they rarely determine the form or timing of a transition to democracy. The limited role of disastrous economic policies in undermining military rule in Uruguay is discussed in Chapter 6.

Other analyses of regime change have focused on *popular movements*. Although the modern form of exclusionary military rule in Latin America has demobilizing and atomizing impacts on both political and civil societies, some autonomous institutions manage to survive (plant-level unions, church groups, autonomous colleges, rural organizations, etc.), and new ones may be nurtured into life.[29] Insofar as the military and technocrats succeeded in redefining development models, even short-lived regimes engineered changes in social structure, notably increases in female participation in the labor force and increased growth of the informal sector. In many cases the response of the opposition was to attempt to promote new social movements. The industrial proletariat, under physical assault and in any case relatively small, seemed an unlikely agent of social transformation. The prototypical new movements included women's groups, shantytown dwellers, ecclesiastical base communities, and so on. The proponents of popular movements argued that they not only could contribute to authoritarian erosion but also could become major protagonists in the democratic transition. However, Chapter 7 shows why and how (rhetoric aside) that failed to occur in Uruguay.

A fourth approach to analyzing transitions focuses on *power-holding institutions*, particularly their interest in maintaining an authoritarian system. At what point will the military see it as being in their best interest to return to the barracks? Here a simple axiom has been propounded by Robert Dahl: Power-holders such as the military will opt for liberalization when the costs of repression exceed the costs of toleration.[30] Similar calculations presumably apply to full democratization. But what are the

28 O'Donnell (1979b).

29 This is particularly true where long-lasting authoritarian regimes successfully promote industrialization, urbanization, and other forms of modernization. For example, the successful organization of the São Paulo metalworkers was an unintended effect of the Brazilian military's policies to promote development.

30 Dahl (1971).

costs of repression for those who maintain a secure monopoly of the means of coercion? Alfred Stepan has emphasized the military's "bottom-line" commitment to surviving as a hierarchical institution, which requires a retreat to the barracks if factional disputes lead to irreconcilable internal conflicts. But the calculus of interests is also connected to the balance of forces between the military and the opposition, where the strategy of each is to raise the costs for the other.

A final type of analysis of transitions addresses not only the reasons why transitions to democracy occur but also how and when they will occur. The analysis of *opposition alliances and strategies* centers on such issues as coalition formation, tactics of negotiation, and willingness to enter pacts. Leaving aside insurrectionary strategies, these alliances are aimed at strengthening the bargaining position of the opposition. On the one hand, a pact within the opposition can raise the prestige of parties and other opposition movements relative to the military. The achievement of a pact will greatly raise the level of domestic challenge to the regime, undermining its capacity to divide and rule (if not atomize) civil society. Meanwhile, the military's attitude to withdrawal may be favorably affected by the possibility of a deal with a "responsible" opposition.

A number of hypotheses emerged in the debates of the late 1970s and early 1980s regarding what opposition parties can do and should do to promote transitions to democracy:

1 "Moderate" oppositions should resist co-optation by the regime, but should compromise with its "soft-liners." This requires both the defeat of opportunist and extremist civilian rivals and the maintenance of disciplined control over the opposition's own supporters.[31]
2 Parties do well to unite behind proposals for *procedural* democracy, postponing potentially divisive policy debates until after the transition.[32]
3 Workers' hopes for immediate economic gains must be reined in and definitely not encouraged by opposition parties.[33]

The natural and essentially democratic process whereby political competition is based on criticism can have an overall debilitating effect on the credibility and reputation of the opposition. Suspending that process for the duration of the transition tends to mitigate this danger. But under what conditions will political parties be able to form the requisite alliances and pursue the necessarily subtle strategies of opposition and negotiation? A host of difficulties, ranging from rivalries to ideologies, stand in the way of such processes. Where the social and economic systems are at stake,

31 O'Donnell (1979a).
32 Stepan (1980).
33 Przeworski (1986).

to what extent are procedural and substantive compromises separable? Consider, for example, issues such as the system of land tenure or the level of state intervention in the economy.[34] Prescriptions for restraint by the opposition can raise equally heated debates. Might not the lowering of popular expectations weaken the momentum behind the return to democracy? More important, the question of how such restraint is to be achieved remains to be addressed. Finally, what legitimate democratic interests get sacrificed in the process? These questions are addressed in the core of this book, principally in Chapters 6–8.

Parties and initial democratic consolidation

The problem of democratic restoration does not end with the calling of elections. Although this study does not attempt to delve into the long-term prospects for democratic consolidation, the "founding elections" and early policies of the new democratic government will crucially influence the chances for democratic survival. At this stage, too, parties appear crucial. Among the existing hypotheses about the political processes central to consolidation we find the following:

1 Political actors must show a propensity to learn from past mistakes and retain a "historical memory" of crises.[35]
2 Party cohesion, functional to democratic stabilization and the strengthening of democratic institutions, can be promoted through engineering from above (e.g., via adaptation of electoral systems) or participation from below, which promotes "deeper" democracy by renovating leadership and programs.[36]
3 Party-system characteristics play a major role in democratic consolidation. The electoral struggle must produce a tendency toward competition for the middle ground, while the party system must also incorporate democratic options from the left and the right of the political spectrum.[37]

Here again, dilemmas immediately arise. The emphasis on constitutional reengineering and partisan renewal in the interest of strengthening democracy conflicts with the supposition that traditional forms possess intrinsically superior legitimacy of an ascriptive rather than rational kind. If relative policy consensus among parties is a positive factor during the phase of military withdrawal, might not "too much" consensus stand in the way of policy renewal and adaptation in the era of democratic con-

34 As the 1985 *acuerdo* among opposition parties in Chile eloquently demonstrated in its clauses guaranteeing not only the private property of individuals but also that of joint-stock firms, the line between democratic procedures and political substance can disappear.
35 Linz (1982).
36 See González (1985a).
37 Gillespie (1986b).

solidation? This raises the question of how and when parties may safely return to the spirited political competition that is, after all, the reason for democracy.

The behavior of parties and their leaders during democratic crises ultimately determines the capacity of any democratic system to sustain itself.[38] The loyalty of political leaders to democratic principles is clearly of the utmost importance. More than abstract commitment to ideals, they must show a willingness to defend existing democratic institutions as valuable, even though normally imperfect, expressions of popular will and guarantors of freedom. The problem is, of course, immensely complicated by the competing conceptions held by different political actors regarding what democracy should be. The survival of democratic regimes in crisis may come to depend not only on the degree of antisystem opposition they face but also on the extent to which parties and politicians commit themselves to governing, with all the costs and compromises this may entail.

An outline of the book

Part I of this study discusses the crisis and survival of Uruguay's political parties and their relation to authoritarianism. Chapter 2 introduces the uninitiated reader to the parties and their leaders, and Chapter 3 examines the crisis of Uruguayan democracy and the role that political parties played in its breakdown. Chapter 4 outlines the specific characteristics and problems of the Uruguayan military technocratic regime, its political constraints and economic proclivities. Emphasis is placed on the regime's lack of legitimacy, but also on the fact that this was not a sufficient condition for a return to democracy.

Part II develops the core of the study: the crisis of military rule in Uruguay and the tortuous path to democratic transition. Chapter 5 examines the very different attempts made at renovation of Uruguayan political parties, both by the opposition and by the military after 1980, and the impact of those attempts on their leaders, activists, ideas, and aims. Against the background of declining regime performance and the increasing disaffection of the economic elite, Chapter 6 discusses the origins and interactions of party and military tactics in the failed "dialogue" from 1981 to 1983. The lesson of the Uruguayan case is that crises do not automatically produce transition. Chapter 7 then examines the rather brief attempt at mobilization of the radical opposition against the regime in late 1983 and early 1984 and the crisis of the Blancos' strategy of opposing compromise with the military. Chapter 8 describes the fun-

38 See Linz and Stepan (1978).

damental reasons for the other parties' decisions to enter the Naval Club pact, the conditions for their success in "negotiating democracy," and thus the ultimate form of the transition to democracy.

Part III of this study turns to the early process of democratic consolidation. In Chapter 9, interview data on changes within the parties and the campaign strategies they pursued in the November 1984 elections are combined with analysis of the electoral results to assess the extent to which parties had undergone a process of adaptation and renovation. Chapter 10 sketches the immediate challenges faced by the democratic system, speculates on the comparative costs and benefits of the negotiated path Uruguay traveled on its way back to civilian rule, and evaluates whether early trends in the party system were favorable to democratic consolidation. The Conclusion then draws together some of the lessons of this study regarding the relative importance of parties and the particular roles they may or may not choose to play in promoting or hindering regime changes, setting them in comparative perspective.

PART I

The crisis and survival of Uruguayan political parties

2

Politicians and parties in Uruguay:
origins and crisis

Uruguay's two so-called traditional parties, the Colorados and Blancos,[1] emerged during the civil wars that rent the republic almost immediately after its independence in 1828. In 1971, at the last elections held prior to the military intervention, the combined forces of the left achieved major inroads into the Colorado and Blanco vote. Yet the Left's 18% was slightly less than half that obtained by the Popular Unity party in Chile the previous year, and unlike the latter, it was built on a coalition that included the Christian Democrats. The survival of the traditional parties as the defining reference points of Uruguayan political culture is a curious fact that remains to be convincingly explained. They have weathered twenty-five years of almost continuous political crisis following a period of instability, best illustrated by the fact that Uruguay enacted no fewer than five constitutions between 1918 and 1967. In effect, the political parties in Uruguay have retained far more legitimacy than have the regimes.

During this century, Uruguay has experienced at least 50 years of democracy,[2] longer overall than Costa Rica's 41 years or Colombia and Venezuela's 32. Pessimistic cultural determinism is thus inapplicable to Uruguay, Latin America's most homogeneous, most Europeanized, and best educated nation.[3] The fact that the country was scarcely settled beyond

1 The more formal name for the Blancos is the National party. *Colorado* and *blanco* mean "red" and "white," and the colors refer purely to headbands worn by the combatants in the civil wars, not the colors of revolution and reaction.

2 If we are rigorously strict, and consider the period 1933 to 1942 – when Uruguay's elected president rewrote the nation's constitution following a pact with the most powerful opposition leader – to have constituted a nonpolyarchy, then democracy had survived for over three decades at the time of the 1973 coup. To this we might add the 15 years from 1918 to 1933 and the 6 years since March 1985.

3 It is the size of Britain without Wales, has 3 million inhabitants, and is Latin America's most urbanized nation (85%), as well as the one with the lowest annual population growth rate (0.7%) after Guyana and Surinam. In the early 1980s, literacy was 96.3%, the expectation of life was 70.3 years, infant mortality was 30.3 per 1,000 live births, and only 17% of the labor force was employed in agriculture. Though during most of this century it was one of the wealthiest countries

a thin coastal strip during the colonial period makes arguments focusing on colonial heritage irrelevant.[4] Uruguayan society and culture exhibit profoundly democratic structures and values, in marked contrast with neighboring Argentina's militarist, elitist, antidemocratic, and clerical traditions.[5] The similarities in their civil societies belie the existence of political societies that are wholly dissimilar.

The transition from civilian parliamentary government, dominated by various elites, to democracy was a slow process in Uruguay. This fact calls to mind Dahl's hypothesis that the historical sequence of regime liberalization before mass participation is more favorable than the reverse, or their simultaneous occurrence.[6] Competition among political elites and parliamentary practices had been the norm for four decades when the first elections on the basis of universal adult male suffrage were held in 1918. Earlier than in Chile, and without the rupture that occurred in Argentina, Uruguay was uniquely a case of early and stable inclusionary democratization in Latin America.[7]

Uruguay's traditional parties: the Colorados and the Blancos

History weighs heavily in Uruguayan politics. Uruguay's parties are the oldest in the southern cone of Latin America and among the oldest in the world. Although the structures of the traditional parties have been notoriously fluid, and their programs often inconsistent, there remain traditions and political identifications that, to the Uruguayan, are unmistakably Colorado and Blanco. Between 1865 and 1958, the Colorados were able to maintain control over the national government (though frequently that involved dictators in the nineteenth century). The National party survived as a party of protest, defending the periphery against the center (Montevideo), tending to side with export-oriented ranching interests against the increasing pressure of the urban industrial sector that grew under state protection. The Blancos rebelled in 1875, 1897, and

in Latin America, lack of petroleum resources and economic stagnation have caused it to fall to fifth place among mainland states in terms of gross national product (GNP) per capita. However, it still retains an income distribution that is one of the most favorable on the continent.

4 The authors who stress various kinds of burdensome institutional and cultural traditions include Silvert (1967). Uruguay's modern political institutions owe hardly anything to Imperial Spain.

5 The two countries, which were united until 1828, and even today remain highly interconnected by communications media, tourism, and migration, provide a striking example of the limits to which mass culture can be used to explain political systems.

6 Dahl (1971).

7 Cavarozzi (1978).

1904, although slowly the practice of coexistence emerged among the elite parties. Only in the twentieth century did democratization proceed by incorporation of the masses into politics. The process of rapid urbanization that brought as much as half of the population to the capital and the surrounding agricultural region provided President Batlle y Ordóñez (1903–7 and 1911–15) the social base needed to transform his urban patrician party into a mass political machine. It was on that basis that Colorado hegemony was reconstructed after the last bloody civil war (1903–4) put an end to Blanco risings.

Despite the relative homogeneity of Uruguayan society, there were clearly major differences in mentality between the leading Colorados and Blancos – and there still are today. With regard to recruitment and background, the Colorado cupula included a predominance of urban notables, a fair number of families descended from Italian and other immigrants, many lawyers (known in Uruguay as *doctores*), intellectuals, and people engaged in commerce. Such strata tended to be less well represented in the Blanco party, where traditional (*criollo*) elites, especially large landowners, retained a stronger position.[8] Batlle was a notable anticlerical who regularly scandalized even many in his own party with disrespectful attacks on the Catholic church.[9] Religious sentiment and churchgoing were far more common among Blancos. Thus, it would seem that in substantive terms, shared values were not prima facie characteristics of the political elite in Uruguay. According to Colorado historian Alberto Zum Felde, "one [party] represented the force of Europeanist innovation, the other the force of conservative nationalism."[10]

Batlle's principles became the dominant ideology of the Colorado party, and they continued to dominate Uruguayan politics long after his death in 1929. His progressive reforms made the popular description of Uruguay as the "Switzerland of South America" wholly unfitting: With respect to the rights accorded to women, labor, and other groups, as well as the provision of welfare benefits and state intervention in the process of economic growth, Uruguay was far ahead of the country whose system of government had inspired Batlle during a trip to Europe. Although *Ba-*

---

8 To take revealing biographical examples, the great Colorado leader José Batlle y Ordóñez considered himself a follower of Krausean philosophy, founded a liberal newspaper, and traveled widely in Europe. His arch opponent in the last civil war was a man who avoided the city at all costs and whose strength as a *caudillo* lay in his capacity to command a rebel army of rural workers. There is some doubt that Aparicio Saravia could write, and certainly his influence did not derive from the power of his pen.

9 A number of Catholic Colorados felt compelled to found a new party, the Civic Union, as a result of his policies, which included legalized divorce and the secularization of all public holidays.

10 Zum Felde (1967).

tllismo was not socialism, as both its proponents and its critics liked to claim, it was not far from modern "social democracy" in policy content (but not organization).[11]

Batlle and his followers created the modern Uruguayan state.[12] Prosperity allowed the government to bridge the tensions between the urban and the rural bourgeoisie and also to fulfill the expectations of the popular sector.[13] During the years from 1918 to 1933, Uruguay elected a nine-member National Council of Administration, alongside the presidency, to handle domestic affairs; three of those seats in what was often called the *colegiado* were reserved for the opposition – in practice, the Blancos. Though the agencies in charge of public works, police, postal services, and the key port of Montevideo proved more enduring than the *colegiado*, the principle of "coparticipation" (power sharing) became established. The spoils system in the public sector, within both traditional parties, prevented an overconcentration of state power, which in theory should have increased rapidly with the creation of state agencies, banks, and commercial enterprises.[14] Although defeated in the last civil war, the Blancos had not been destroyed; they adapted more or less successfully to the role of loyal opposition.

The electoral system: the double simultaneous vote

Uruguayan parties have always been subject to chronic internal conflict and factionalism, and Batlle never managed to take over the Colorado party completely. Conflicts among personalist leaders and squabbles over the spoils system were as important as ideological disputes in breeding this factionalism. However, the two-party system never quite broke down; breakaway parties were few and unsuccessful. That was despite the fact that Uruguay adopted a system of proportional representation in elections to the Senate and Chamber of Deputies, which normally favors the multiplication of parties. In the first place, two-party dominance was bolstered by the ban, under Uruguay's electoral law, on "ticket splitting": Each voter had to vote for local, legislative, and executive candidates all from

---

11 Batlle's success in winning the popular vote gave Uruguay a somewhat schizophrenic inheritance, as the Colorados remained entrenched in the state administration and never attempted to recruit a mass social movement or create links with unions on the lines of a social democratic party in the European tradition.

12 See Vanger (1963, 1980). The literature in Spanish is too vast to cite, but relevant authors include Real de Azúa (1964, 1984) and Barrán and Nahum (various years).

13 Hopes for land reform were, however, abandoned by the Batllists in the interest of peace with the Blanco leaders.

14 The concern that a centralized economy may not be propitious for pluralist democracy was not a problem in Uruguay.

the same party. Another explanation for the survival of the two-party system, however, was the emergence and refinement of a far more exotic electoral practice known as the *double simultaneous vote* (DSV), a system that survives to this day.[15]

Under the system of the double simultaneous vote, citizens must choose among many competing lists of candidates in their favored party (technically known as a *lema*). Each list corresponds to a different faction, and this allows the various Blanco and Colorado factions to persist side by side without splitting the parties. In fact, winning elections requires that they not split, however artificial their unity: For a time in the middle of this century, a movement known as the Independent National party broke away from the Blancos; only after they returned to the fold did the Blancos ever win an election.

The Blancos and Colorados usually run at least three candidates each in presidential elections. Under the system of the double simultaneous vote, the winning candidate for chief executive is the one with the most votes *in the party with the most votes*.[16] Thus, the Colorados won the 1971 election because they had 13,000 more votes than the Blancos, even though their leading candidate, Juan María Bordaberry, had fewer votes than the leading Blanco, Wilson Ferreira. In other words, strong rivals in your own party are an advantage if you are trying to win the presidential race. But they must not get too strong and overtake you, for then one of them will be elected with the help of your votes!

In order to maximize their representation in legislative elections (held at the same time as the presidential election), several factional lists in a given party may form alliances known as *sublemas*.[17] These support a single candidate for president and usually have the same list of names for the Senate, but each has a different candidate list for the Chamber of Deputies. As in the presidential race, the votes for all the lists in a *sublema* are pooled. Several small factions may in this way manage to win one seat in the lower house that they might otherwise not have won. Two or more larger factions may also win an extra congressional seat by forming a *sublema*.

The result of Batlle's compromise with opponents inside his own party and the odd method of vote counting in elections was ultimately the

15 This is frequently (but wrongly) referred to in popular speech as the *ley de lemas* (law of mottoes), after an act of 1910, though the mechanism is codified in various statutes.

16 Uruguay combines its double simultaneous vote with strict proportional representation. A concise explanation of the electoral law (from an opponent of the method) is available: Pérez Pérez (1971). In English, see Taylor (1955).

17 These alliances operate so that "spare" votes, left over after each list has been alotted its representatives, can be pooled rather than wasted; extra seats go to the list nearest to the minimum "quota" of votes for electing a senator or deputy.

frustration of his desire to build a cohesive programmatic party. Quite simply, the electoral law tends to punish parties of principle and reward alliances of convenience. Half a century later, the resulting factionalism would still be a source of political instability.

Party fragmentation and economic stagnation

As in other nations of Latin America, the disastrous short-term impact of the Great Depression was more than compensated for by the long-run boost to industrialization of the domestic economy necessitated by the sudden lack of foreign exchange to purchase manufactured imports. During the 1930s, the state took the initiative in developing basic industries such as oil refining and cement production. The decade after World War II, which saw rapid progress in import-substituting industrialization under the influence of the ideas of the United Nations Economic Commission for Latin America, represented the farthest logical development of the *Batllista* model.[18] That period of prosperity concluded shortly after the adoption of a fully collegial executive, instead of the presidency, in 1951.

In 1958 the Blanco party won control over the national government for the first time since 1865. The new National Council of Government[19] attempted in vain to shrink the oversized public sector that a majority of Uruguayans were briefly willing to blame for three decades of export stagnation. However, the simple arithmetic of voting made it doubtful that any government could be reelected on the basis of the cuts in public spending urged on by the International Monetary Fund (IMF). The overwhelming majority of Uruguayans lived in cities (nearly half of them in the capital) and depended to a greater or lesser extent on the public sector's transfer of resources from ranching to the urban economy. The middle classes, in particular, benefited from public-sector jobs, pensions, and a patchwork of welfare services.[20] As important was the patronage that *both* parties needed to win elections. After the "pork-barrel pact" of 1931, the Blancos began to match the Colorados in the extent of their urban clientelist vote-gathering machines. Indeed, they later acquired their own populist leader, Fernández Crespo, who dominated local politics in Montevideo during 1958–62.

Jobs and help in getting the bureaucracy to act were traded for the

---

18 See Hirschman's chapter "The Political Economy of Import Substituting Industrialization" (Hirschman 1969) on the general model, and see Millot, Silva, and Silva (1973) for the specifics of the Uruguayan case.

19 In 1951, Uruguay again revised its constitution and restored the *colegiado*, this time in pure form.

20 Indispensable for an understanding of the political economy of the imperfect welfare state is Finch (1981).

Table 2.1. *Numbers of civil servants and pensioners, 1930–69*

Group	1930	1932	1936	1955	1961	1969
Civil servants[a]	30,000	52,000	57,500	166,400	193,700	213,000
State pensioners	48,300	—[b]	73,300	196,700	278,000	429,700
Civil servants/voters	9.4%	32.4%	15.3%	18.9%	16.5%	17.3%
Pensioners/voters	15.5%	—	19.5%	22.4%	27.6%	34.9%

[a]Includes employees of state enterprises (*entes autónomos*).
[b]Data unavailable.
Source: Aguiar (1984).

votes of the newly arrived migrants from rural areas.[21] Party organizations resembled the urban machines that once dominated city politics in the United States, with the added dimension of a greater mass of competing factions in both parties, organized in literally hundreds of political clubs grouped around the personalist leaders of the various *barrios* of Montevideo.[22]

The sheer size of the Uruguayan state in relation to civil society, its domination of economic activity, and its even greater preponderance in terms of urban employment opportunities made the significance of patronage far greater than in North American cities at the height of machine politics. By the end of the 1960s, a majority of Uruguayan voters were dependent on the state for their income, as Table 2.1 shows. Contacts with politicians became indispensable to secure a pension, a job, or help in cutting through red tape.

The rise of new political leaders

It is, of course, insufficient to stress merely the clientelist nature of the traditional parties' appeal to the electorate.[23] For instance, the Blanco margin of victory was so large in 1958 (499,000 votes to 379,000) that it probably was unnecessary for them to have sought an alliance with the right-wing rural demagogue Benito Nardone. Any simple model of patronage voting cannot explain such a landslide shift of votes. What patronage *can* explain, however, is the utter failure of Blanco retrenchment policies to stick. By the time of the 1962 elections, total public employment had increased, and inflation was becoming a serious problem,

21 Colorado deputy Fa Robaina (1972) published a selection of requests he had received.
22 See Rama (1971), who states that Montevideo had 8,000 political clubs for just 42 deputies.
23 There exists a relatively well developed literature on the particularist nature of political participation in Uruguay based on surveys of voters before the 1971 elections (Biles 1972).

Table 2.2. *Major parties and factions at the beginning of the 1970s*

Party and main factions	Leaders	Major lists	Votes in 1971 Montevideo	Votes in 1971 Interior
Colorado lema			278,392	403,232
Unidad y Reforma	Sen. Jorge Batlle	"15"	88,498	154,306
Unión Colorada y Batllista	President (1968–72) Jorge Pacheco Areco	"6614," "123," etc.	163,314	216,201
Blanco lema			209,651	459,171
Por la Patria*	Sen. Wilson Ferreira	"903"	103,661	147,531
Movimiento Nacional de Rocha*	Sen. Carlos Julio Pereyra	"504"	38,161	72,990
Herrerismo*	General Aguerrondo, Martín Echegoyen	"904," "2" "874," "26"	38,388	190,181
Broad Front			212,406	91,869
Patria Grande	Sen. Enrique Erro	"4190"	57,385	13,559
FIDEL (Communist party)	Sen. Rodney Arismendi	"1001"	70,832	29,379
Partido Socialista	Sen. José Pedro Cardoso	"90"	23,409	12,518
Partido Democrata Cristiano*	Sen. Juan Pablo Terra	"808"	39,551	21,706
Lista 99*	Sen. Zelmar Michelini	"9988"	18,516	12,963

*Por la Patria, Movimiento de Rocha, and W. Beltrán's "Lista 400" formed a *sublema*, "Defensores de las Leyes," to back Ferreira for president.
*Herrerismo consisted of two *sublemas*, "Herrerismo-Ruralismo" and "Unidos a la Victoria," both backing General Aguerrondo for president.
*Christian Democrats and "List 99" formed a *sublema*, "Frente del Pueblo."
Sources: Corte Electoral, *Elecciones Generales 28 de noviembre de 1971*, and Julio Fabregat, *Elecciones Uruguayas* (Montevideo, 1972).

and yet real disposable incomes were rising, as they did before every election.[24] Significantly, although the Blancos narrowly won the election, there was a massive shift from their conservative factions to the more progressive factions, which took control of the National Council of Government.

As the crisis of Uruguayan democracy deepened throughout the 1960s, there emerged a new generation of political leaders (Table 2.2) whose appeal clearly was *not* just clientelistic. They covered a broad range: Jorge Pacheco Areco, who amassed the support of right-wing Colorados, playing

24 Finch (1979). An excellent survey of the crisis of the 1960s from economists and sociologists is available (Benvenuto et al. 1971). Data on the "political business cycle" come from González (1976).

effectively on authoritarian tendencies among the marginal and popular classes; General Líber Seregni, candidate of the leftist Broad Front in the 1971 elections; Senator Wilson Ferreira Aldunate, who built the largest Blanco *sublema* (cartel of lists), calling his faction Por la Patria (For the Fatherland). Senator Ferreira, often referred to by his first name, Wilson, built up a national following using weekly radio broadcasts in which he set out his new brand of liberal and democratic principles. He narrowly missed victory in the 1971 elections.[25]

The National party moved to the left, but meanwhile, in the Colorado party, the balance of factions was swinging in favor of the right. The death of the "honest-broker" president, General Oscar Gestido, in 1967 paved the way for the succession of his little-known vice-president, Jorge Pacheco Areco. The Unión Colorada y Batllista (UCB), which he took over, became the largest *sublema* within the Colorado party during the course of the same decade in which it had been founded. By then, the link with the ideals of Batllism was tenuous: The UCB and the more moderate "List 15" had been the principal motive forces behind the abandonment of the plural executive in 1966 and the adoption of a Gaullist-type constitution.[26] The older clientelist factions that resisted the creation of a strong presidency fared poorly in the elections.

The decade of the 1960s saw the beginning of an expansion of the leftist parties from their hitherto marginal role. An important influence was the Cuban revolution, and to some extent the radicalization of the world Catholic church, though Uruguay had long been a very secular society. The former event produced a radicalization of the Socialist party, and the latter led to a split in the Christian Democratic movement. Along with the communists (who first created an electoral front with the revealing acronym FIDEL), these parties and various other former leaders of traditional parties and extreme-left "groupuscules" formed the Frente Amplio, or Broad Front, for the 1971 elections. Outside of Montevideo the left's progress was minimal. Evidence suggests that their sociological support was not particularly working-class, despite their strong organizational links to the Convención Nacional de los Trabajadores (CNT) union federation, founded in 1962. Many working men and women made the reasonably rational decision to support militant trade unions, but to vote for the more moderate parties that might still be able to provide them with particularized benefits.

Because the Broad Front received 18.2% of the vote in the 1971

25 As explained earlier, the total votes for all Colorados being higher than those for the Blancos, Bordaberry became president. However, the Blancos accused the governing Colorados of fraud, and there were nagging inconsistencies in the results (Franco 1984). The vote discrepancy was more than twice the Colorados' margin of victory.

26 See Gillespie (1987b).

elections, some believed that a decade of economic scarcity (and sporadic austerity), coupled with mounting inflation, had led to growing dissatisfaction among workers. However, there is no evidence that the ideological polarization that accompanied the pre-coup crisis was paralleled by any dramatic rise in class voting. By far the best predictors of leftist voting were youth and years of formal education.[27] Much of the shift to the left probably can be ascribed to the defection of the Colorados' progressive faction, Zelmar Michelini's "List 99," to the Broad Front.[28] Along with an earlier breakaway faction from the Blanco party led by Senator Erro, this group had become disillusioned at the prospect that radical change could be effected by working within the traditional parties.

One final political movement that should be mentioned in the context of the radicalization of the 1960s was the Movimiento de Liberación Nacional–Tupamaros (MLN–Tupamaros). This consisted of a military wing, the Tupamaros proper, and a political wing. The latter eventually created so-called Tupamaros support committees in the university and various faculties. Originally founded by a renegade socialist, Raúl Sendic, the Tupamaros began working with the cane workers in the department of Artigas in the north in 1963. These workers several times marched on the capital to demand legislation to improve their wages and working conditions. Slowly, however, the Tupamaros turned to a strategy of direct action.[29] By 1970 they had developed into a highly organized urban guerrilla force that outclassed the police, fueling dangerous *foquista* illusions that Uruguay was ripe for revolution.[30]

The nature of Uruguayan parties

The coalition of most of Uruguay's leftist parties in the Broad Front after 1971 shared some characteristics with the situation of the two traditional parties, with their competing fractions. The Left encompassed a broad spectrum of ideologically radical and more moderate progressive doctrines, though that differed from the ideological fuzziness in most sectors of the

27 Graceras (1977).
28 Because all the polls wildly overestimated the support that the Left would get in the 1971 election, it is worth reading Guidobono's postmortem (1972).
29 A particularly insightful analysis of the Tupamaros has argued that the guerrillas deliberately sought to negate everything about the cozy old ways of Batllism: They were ultranationalist, religious rather than pragmatic in their fervor, antihedonistic and ascetic, heroic and adventurous rather than risk-averse, and universalist rather than particularist in their outlook (Costa Bonino 1985, pp. 62–8).
30 There are many books on the Tupamaros, and inevitably they rarely present a balanced view. The best works are by Gilio (1972), Labrousse (1973), and Porzecanski (1973). Brief, but very informative and analytic, is Gillespie (1980), who argues that the Uruguayan terrorists were better organized than those of Argentina and Brazil.

Table 2.3. *Structural characteristics of Uruguayan parties*

Characteristic	Traditional parties	Broad Front parties
Ideologization	Weak	Strong
Membership	Informal	Formal
Organization	Regional caucus	Mixed cell/branch
Structural articulation	Intermediate	High
Centralization	Intermediate	High
Participation	Marginal	Militant
Leadership selection	Competitive	Centralized
Leadership diversity	Low	Low
Leadership authority	Personalist factionalized	Bureaucratic consociational

Colorado and Blanco parties. There were also many personalistic leaders on the Left, though they were more circumscribed than their counterparts in the traditional parties by the participation of sub-elites, the formal functioning of the Broad Front, or (in the case of those allied to the communists) by the dictates of their sponsors. Despite the fact that the Broad Front was pluralist at the highest level, factionalism was not encouraged within its constituent parties.[31]

Above all, most leftist groups had a cadre of active militants who could be relied upon to undertake party work, turn up at meetings and demonstrations, and represent their party in union politics. Except during elections, the Colorados and Blancos were largely without unpaid helpers, and active participation at the grass roots was minimal. The contrasting structural characteristics of Uruguay's parties enumerated in Table 2.3 are modeled on the writings of Duverger and Janda.[32] It should be noted that they reflect the dominant patterns in the traditional parties and on the Left, respectively. The factions of the traditional parties were by no means all equally fluid in their organization. Nor were the different factions of the Broad Front all equally bureaucratic; they included tiny groupuscules, personalist bosses, and former leaders of the traditional parties as well.

Whereas the Blancos and Colorados tended to shun elaborate ideology, the parties of the Broad Front harnessed it to many tasks, though there

31 Both socialists and communists had serious internal splits at varying times, in all cases culminating in the expulsion of the minority. The only exceptions to this unity rule would be on the extreme left of the Front, where a bewildering number of groupuscules and veteran radicals formed a kind of "front within a front" known as the "Patria Grande" *sublema*, led by Senator Erro.

32 See, in particular, Janda and King (1985). I have omitted some of the characteristics (such as extraparliamentary origin, age) that Janda and King found to lack significance and have simplified others.

was a generalized tendency toward increasing ideologization during the late 1960s. (Strident anticommunism and economic neoliberalism seeped into the Colorado party, while antiimperialist ideas revived in the Blanco party and were joined by a new commitment to radical economic reforms.) The traditional parties had no formal membership, whereas the Left (apart from breakaway factions from the traditional parties) normally insisted on affiliation, dues paying, and even a period of probation for new members. However, only the communists had a really sizable membership.

Whereas the traditional parties relied on temporary clubs at election time and did not have permanent local branches, the Left retained its complex texture of branches and cells, as well as the newly created base committees set up in every city neighborhood to bring together militants from all the Broad Front. What Duverger calls "articulation" also varied between traditional and leftist parties. The former had their national conventions and executive bodies, but these met less and less frequently after the 1950s, as politics shifted more and more toward secret backroom dealing among personalist leaders. By contrast, on top of the far more formal organizational structure of its constituent parties, the Broad Front also had its plenum and presidency (consisting of General Líber Seregni and his staff of advisers). This greater articulation paralleled the comparative centralization of the Left.[33] Meanwhile, the loosely identifiable "members" of the traditional parties did not participate in the life of their groups to the same extent as did those on the Left. Frentistas were forever demonstrating, attending meetings, leafleting, or putting up posters, and they oriented their leisure activities toward political events such as concerts by left-wing musicians. They were also expected to become active in the trade-union movement.

It would be wrong, however, to overdraw the implications of the organizational differences between the traditional parties and the Left. Leadership selection was centralized at the level of parties in the Broad Front, but because it was an alliance, the competitive aspects typical of the traditional parties and their factionalism also emerged. The concentration of authority was less personalist and more bureaucratic, but the nature of Uruguay's electoral system having dictated the need for coalition, the Broad Front seemed also to reproduce a consociational (rather than majoritarian) pattern of decision making.

The Uruguayan political class: education, family, and business ties

The interviews with Uruguayan politicians conducted for this study help to clarify the sources of cohesion and differentiation within what has often

---

33 Weak in the interior, it was easier for the Left to remain centralized.

been characterized as a political class.[34] Perhaps it is not surprising that in a small country the politicians should come from similar backgrounds, be educated together (in the only university), and see their families intermarry, sometimes forming virtual political dynasties. The proportions of politicians interviewed who had relatives active in politics were extremely high for all parties, averaging 69% overall and going as high as 77% for the Colorados. The politicians' families also tended to be broadly similar in terms of economic status, with the overwhelming majority in all parties coming from families they characterized as in average or prosperous circumstances. Only 17% claimed to come from poor families, and 3% from wealthy backgrounds.

As could be expected for a nation as highly educated as Uruguay, 65% of all politicians surveyed were college graduates, and another 29% had some university education. The importance of university politics is evident when we note that 71% of Colorados, 81% of Frente members, and 89% of Blancos reported membership in political movements as students.

One interesting area of divergence in this apparently rather uniform picture concerns religion. Colorados were far less likely than Blancos or Frentistas to have attended a religious secondary school, in keeping with the party's long-standing secular and anticlerical tradition. Only 5% of Colorados had attended such schools, as compared with 50% of Blancos and 54% of Frentistas. Colorado politicians were also much less likely to be practicing Catholics: only 13%, as compared with 65% for Blancos and 30% for the Broad Front.

Perhaps because of the number who were exiled under the military regime, a higher proportion of Frentistas reported having lived or studied abroad: 50%, compared with 39% of Colorados and 22% of Blancos. A far more striking reflection of the impact of the dicatorship on politicians, though, was the startlingly high proportion from each party who reported having been detained for political reasons: 48% of Colorados, 57% of Blancos, and 68% of Frentistas.

In addition to the anticlerical divide, the historical differentiation between parties regarding their ties to the rural sector seems to persist to this day. Blancos were twice as likely to own ranches or to come from landowning families as were politicians of other parties. Although Colorados were somewhat more likely to be involved in business, commerce, or finance, it is striking that in no party were more than 14% of those interviewed involved in such activities. The great majority of politicians were drawn from the liberal professions: law, education, journalism, and other white-collar occupations.

In short, the historical portrait of a political class with a certain "relative

---

34 In this section, the biographical information regarding politicians interviewed is culled from the far more detailed discussion in Chapter 2 of my Ph.D. dissertation (Gillespie 1987a).

autonomy" from the country's economic elite and with deep roots in the middle classes of this middle-class nation holds up to this day.[35] The defining cleavages in the recruitment and background of politicians are the secular-versus-religious divide (with its concomitant influence over education) and rural/provincial-versus-metropolitan, even cosmopolitan, links. In Uruguay's middle-class society, with a strongly statist economy, capital and labor are not always the major political actors.

A crisis of Uruguayan political parties?

Nevertheless, ever sensitive to mass electoral pressures, Uruguayan parties became swamped under a tidal wave of sectoral and class demands as the economy began to deteriorate in the 1950s.[36] Those programmatic parties that attempted to compete for votes found that they were handicapped by their lack of equal access to political resources. The ability to manipulate the patronage networks of public enterprises and ministries gave incumbents a great electoral advantage. Yet that only added to the ideological stridency of the Left, and as the economic crisis worsened, incumbents were increasingly voted out of office.

Agreement among politicians is surprisingly high that Uruguay's parties were seriously flawed and decaying by the time the military intervened. One young Blanco asserted that "the National party used to be a mass of lists, each one led by a *caudillo* trying to get hold of jobs" for his supporters.[37] Table 2.4 clearly shows how the number of lists in elections continued to mushroom as the parties fragmented. The low levels of organization and structure in the traditional parties prevented them from implementing new developmental models that would have conflicted with clientelistic vote-gathering techniques. One Colorado leader expressed the view that "at the end of the 1960s the traditional parties were exhausted in terms of ideas and leaders. Yet the Frente had the same vices as the

35 However, if one were to include more politicians from the interior, one might find somewhat more links to business and, especially, ranching. Note, too, that many politicians, Blancos in particular, apparently list themselves as lawyers or members of some other profession, even though they have ranches.

36 Shefter (1977) has pointed out the consequences of the advent of mass political participation through universal suffrage before a centralized professional bureaucracy has been created: a tendency for political penetration of state agencies, and thus a party system characterized by clientelism and rampant factionalism. The opposite sequence, in which a corps of trained state administrators is set up before democratization of the political regime, produces more programmatic, ideological, and organized political parties.

37 Personal interview with a supporter of Wilson Ferreira, Montevideo, 13 July 1984. A perennial figure of the military regime argued that "though they had a democratic charter," the traditional parties "were run by one man or a group of men." Personal interview, Montevideo, 31 October 1984.

Table 2.4. *Increasing fragmentation of the traditional parties*

Parameter	1946	1958	1962	1966	1971
No. of lists for deputy					
Blancos	45	126	204	229	308
Colorados	108	151	146	230	246
Senators in major *sublema*					
Blancos	100%	55%	47%	31%	67%
Colorados	60%	58%	57%	38%	54%

Source: Aguiar (1984).

traditional parties. They took advantage of the double simultaneous vote without really defining a common position. Seregni was a Batllista in new packaging."[38]

The absence of cohesively organized and coherently programmatic parties was not alleviated by the creation of a strong presidency in 1967. The persistence of the double-simultaneous-vote electoral system made rational voting practically impossible. There could be little certainty which of the sectors of a favored party might end up benefiting from an individual's vote. In the 1971 elections, sincerely liberal and democratic Colorados contributed to the victory of Bordaberry, the man who would lead Uruguay into authoritarianism.[39] Equally, there were conservative Blancos who cast their ballots for a no-hope candidate out of sheer principle, although they knew their votes would be transferred to the progressive, Wilson Ferreira.[40] Historical traditions and the electoral laws prevented a reorganization of the party system to offer the electorate a clear choice between conservatism and reformism.

The immobilism of the party system in practical terms (notwithstanding the major factional swings) combined with the rapid deterioration of respect for civil liberties under Pacheco and Bordaberry's presidencies to create the ideal conditions for the terrorists to propagate their thesis that "bourgeois" democracy was a "sham."[41] That led proponents of change to resort to increasingly ideological denunciations of the system. Inevi-

---

38 Personal interview, Montevideo, 15 March 1985. The Wilsonistas would, of course, argue that Wilson Ferreira represented both new ideas and leadership, but he narrowly failed to win the 1971 election.

39 Moderate liberal Amílcar Vasconcellos received 48,844 votes in the presidential election, more than the discrepancy in the overall totals, and far more than the Colorado margin of victory.

40 General Aguerrondo, who has often been accused of antidemocratic tendencies, received 228,569 votes, almost enough to elect Ferreira!

41 The Broad Front was able to register its competing lists only as factions within the Christian Democratic party.

tably, and ironically, the electoral law also hampered coherence on the Left. Although the program of the Broad Front was simple reformism, the Left's rhetoric was revolutionary, and it frightened the upper class.

The actions of the Tupamaros guerrillas had a corrosive effect on the Uruguayan party system, eroding tolerance for opponents and creating a polarized ideological climate. Traditional politicians became more and more convinced that the guerrillas represented a threat to democracy. Eventually, Wilson Ferreira and most Blancos voted for President Bordaberry's draconian "Law of State Security and Public Order," in 1972, which suspended the normal time limit for holding suspected subversives and permitted their trial in military courts. The opposition of the Broad Front to that dangerous legal precedent was taken as evidence of their complicity with the guerrillas.

The long tenure of many of the political elite had inevitably produced some corruption, and the terrorists exposed such corruption publicly, as well as secretly to the military once captured. Political leaders anxious to appear above dirty politics began to court the military on all sides, a trend that began with the crop of generals nominated for the 1971 presidential election. Senators and deputies were subject to increasingly virulent attacks from the armed forces, who accused them of corruption and links with the terrorists. A so-called Commission for the Suppression of Economic Crimes was set up by the military, and Senator Batlle was briefly arrested on charges that he had profited from currency speculation on the basis of advance knowledge of a devaluation.[42]

Despite the crisis of democracy after 1968, in some ways Uruguay's two-party system was relatively stable: The Blancos and Colorados received 80% of the votes in the 1971 election. However, that apparently "stable" party system was neither sufficiently strong nor adaptable. Indeed, it suffered from all the problems Huntington mentioned, as discussed in Chapter 1: fragmentation of leadership, evaporation of mass support, decay of organization, a shift of leaders to the bureaucracy, and increasing personalism. By 1973, Uruguay's democracy was collapsing, despite one of the longest and most successful experiments with political freedom Latin America had ever seen.

---

42 Though he was released, the "List 15" senators and deputies no longer supported the Bordaberry government after late 1972.

3

The breakdown of democracy

Uruguay's democratic regime did not break down in a single event, but rather was eroded by stages. Democracy has at least two analytic dimensions: the degree of accountability of rulers and the degree of pluralistic toleration of opposition and dissent within political society.[1] After 1968 there was a twofold process of closing down representative institutions and political arenas (from the power-sharing executive, to the wage councils, to the National Assembly) and an escalating repression of opposition groups (from terrorists, to unions, to students, to leftists, to Colorados and Blancos).

Just before his sudden death in December 1967, President Gestido issued an executive order banning the Socialist party, which had openly advocated guerrilla warfare for "national liberation." He was succeeded by Vice-President Pacheco, who introduced nonparty technocrats into the cabinet, began to rule by emergency decree, and used the military to repress strikes. In July 1969 the Pacheco administration announced curbs on media coverage of terrorism. In September of 1971 the effort to repress the Tupamaros guerrillas led to suspension of the right of habeas corpus on the basis of a declaration of "internal war." The following year the National Assembly approved the Law of State Security and Public Order, permitting military trials of alleged subversives.

President Bordaberry was inaugurated in 1972 following the hotly contested elections of the previous year. However, the involvement of the military in politics, first in strikebreaking and then in the war against the guerrillas, produced unstoppable momentum for their final takeover of power. In February 1973 the army and air force rebelled against President Bordaberry and forced him to accept the creation of a National Security Council to oversee his actions. In June they closed Parliament and dissolved the CNT union confederation. The breakdown of democracy

---

1 These dimensions are similar to, but not identical with, those of "participation" and "contestation" in Dahl's *Polyarchy* (1971).

had become complete, as the regime had both drastically reduced its accountability and silenced or destroyed the bulk of the opposition.[2]

The five most salient aspects of Uruguay's crisis after 1968 (roughly in ascending order of the threat they posed to democracy) were (a) ideological extremism, (b) economic instability, (c) labor–industrial strife, (d) mounting violence, and (e) military "role expansion." Some of the links are obvious: The results of repeated financial crises, falling output, declining real wages, and galloping inflation were labor militancy and increasing ideological radicalism in politics. Other causal chains were more subtle, such as the influence of the Tupamaros on the thinking of the military. There have also been alleged cases of linkage that are spurious or doubtful, such as the military's equation of worker militancy with terrorist subversion.

Ideological extremism

Most of the politicians interviewed for this study believed that ideological extremism, primarily on the left, but also on the right, had been an important cause of the crisis of democracy, and ideological discourse became increasingly common in the traditional parties in the early 1970s (Table 3.1).[3] In spite of labor's continued alienation from the traditional parties, a moderate social-democratic left never became electorally viable, and revolutionary rhetoric flourished. The Uruguayan Left included such diverse groups as the Guevarist Socialist party, the Christian Democrats (strongly influenced by the Second Vatican Council), and the anarchist "Combative Tendency," which formed a militant movement within many unions. Although the Broad Front as a whole did not espouse a revolutionary socialist position, it included many politicians who did. In many cases the Left was ambiguous in its attitude to the terrorists' actions, tending to stress their "inevitability" as reactions to an oppressive government and economic system. Ironically, the Communist party, an im-

---

2 So long as a democratically elected executive merely takes steps to rule, without responding to the ongoing demands of political society (without systematically attacking it), there remains hope that this state of exception will be temporary. Once all dissent is repressed as well, one must speak of a fully authoritarian situation.

3 The data in the following tables are based on questionnaire interviews undertaken in 1984 and early 1985, both with politicians active prior to the breakdown of democracy and with those who had begun their political careers under authoritarianism. Although it cannot be claimed that the results are necessarily accurate reflections of the pre-1973 politicians' views, they were strongly corroborated by personal interviews with major political figures active at the time of the crisis. Politicians were chosen for interviews in rough proportion to their parties' vote shares in 1984. Nevertheless, the validity of the "All" column in the tables depends on the degree of confidence placed in the representativity of the universe of interviewees.

Table 3.1. *Political actors seen as responsible for disorder and violence*[a]

Group	Left (%) (n = 17)	Blancos (%) (n = 22)	Colorados (%) (n = 24)	All[b] (%) (n = 68)
(a) Extreme Left	47	86	100	81
(b) The government	100	59	33	59
(c) Extreme Right	76	45	42	51
(d) Police & military	65	18	29	34

[a]The question: "In your opinion, which groups were principally responsible for the disorder and violence which the country faced 1968–73?"
[b]Includes three leaders of the Civic Union, one Patriotic Union leader, and one nonpartisan high-ranking officer close to the military regime.

portant member of the Frente, took a far more moderate line, as did the Front's 1971 presidential candidate, the retired general Líber Seregni.

Ideological extremism was by no means the exclusive province of the Left; an outbreak almost as severe occurred on the right. Examples ranged from Benito Nardone, cofounder of the "ruralist movement" in the 1950s, who called even the Colorados communists, to a newly dominant fraction of the Colorados themselves, led by the authoritarian demagogue Jorge Pacheco Areco. Even further to the right of these were a proto-fascist group within the Blanco party and emerging paramilitary organizations.

Although the politicians interviewed cited ideological polarization among elites as a widespread problem, they did not see the process occurring to the same degree at a mass level. Although the level of ideological extremism was perceived to be strong during that period, often that was because those with the most polarized positions were also the most audible: politicians, the media, and the guerrillas. Nevertheless, among the intelligentsia, particularly in the universities and among students, radicalism grew in the early 1970s.

Economic crisis

Many commentators have been tempted to conclude from the severity of the economic crises that besieged Uruguay from the mid-1950s onward that these alone can explain the breakdown of democracy.[4] From 1955

4 One radical leader of the Socialist party bluntly blamed the coup on "the need to take the strict application of the International Monetary Fund's 'recipe' to its ultimate consequences" (personal interview, Montevideo, 1985). Perhaps it is only to be expected that right-wing Colorados, supporters of the former president, Pacheco, should disagree. A former Pachequista minister argued that "economic factors were not a serious factor in the breakdown of democracy: Pacheco brought

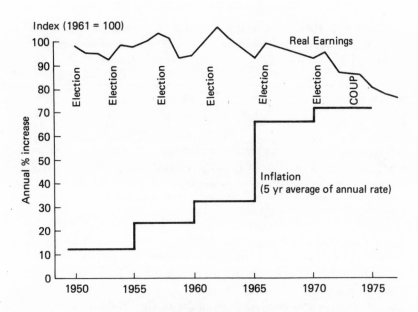

Figure 3.1. Elections, earnings, and inflation, 1950–77.

to 1970, real per capita gross domestic product (GDP) fell at a rate equivalent to 0.3% each year (and would have fallen much faster had it not been for the growing tide of emigration). Investment fell from around one-fifth of GDP in the 1950s to one-tenth in the 1960s. Inflation several times burst into three digits before sinking back under the impact of IMF austerity measures (in 1959 and 1968). During election years, however, governments regularly ran large fiscal deficits to try to ensure their re-election (20% of public spending in 1962, 29% in 1971). Real earnings always rose in such election years.

Although the crisis of import-substitution industrialization combined with trade deficits to produce economic stagnation, policy failures exacerbated the situation. Evidence suggests that stagnating export volumes were as much to blame for successive foreign-exchange crises as were adverse movements in the terms of trade. World prices for Uruguay's beef and wool were actually improving sharply at the height of the political crisis of 1973. Nevertheless, politicians differed radically on the importance they attributed to the economic crisis in Uruguay's democratic breakdown; whereas 90% of Broad Front members considered it a primary cause, only 30% of Blancos and 20% of Colorados did (Table 3.2).

growth and price stability by 1971." However, the expansionary preelection policies of 1971 brought a surge in inflation the following year.

Table 3.2. *Politicians' rankings of the relative importance of factors involved in the breakdown of democracy*[a]

| Factor | Perceived relative importance: percentage responding "most" or "second most" | | | |
	Left $n = 9$	Blancos $n = 14$	Colorados $n = 17$	All[b] $n = 47$
(a) The growing perception the armed forces had of their role in society, their idea of order and attitudes toward politicians and social forces	44	57	58	49
(b) The consequences of subversion by the guerrillas and the state of near civil war	0	36	68	47
(c) The economic crisis and the necessity to protect and/or make conditions for the economic system to work	89	29	21	34
(d) The causes were basically political: the inadequacies of parties and antagonism between political leaders	11	29	37	32
(e) [The breakdown] was due to the deep crisis of Uruguayan society and political culture, which goes back to the 1930s, if not the 19th century	44	14	0	19
(f) Changes in economic and social forces not channeled through democratic institutions (like parties), feeling one defended interests best by other means	22	21	21	19
(g) External factors, the interests of other powers, economic concerns linked to them and their conflicts, etc.	22	29	5	15

[a] The question: "In 1973 Uruguay experienced a crisis that led to a new system of government. Contradictory explanations have been given for this process. . . . What importance would you assign the following statements (ranking them from most important to least important)?"
[b] Includes three leaders of the Civic Union, one Patriotic Union leader, and one nonpartisan high-ranking officer close to the military regime.

Interestingly, the younger the politician, the more likely he or she was to subscribe to the economistic view.

Industrial conflict

Inextricably bound up in the vicious circle of stagnating output and inflation was the problem of escalating industrial militancy. According to Howard Handelman, real wages fell by 24% in the private sector and 40% in the public sector from 1957 to 1967.[5] The military claimed that 26 general strikes had been called by the Convención Nacional de los Trabajadores (CNT) union federation during 1972, following the inauguration of President Bordaberry in March.[6] Those strikes were not just industrial stoppages, but were calculated political attempts to alter government policies. The military alleged that the union federation was controlled by the Communist party, but they could not show that that contributed to strike activity. If anything, the communists pursued a cautious policy with regard to labor disruption and often found themselves criticized by the ultraleft for that very reason. Yet in 1968 President Pacheco used the constitutional mechanism of "prompt security measures" (emergency powers) to impose wage and price freezes and abolish the 25-year-old wage councils in which managers and workers negotiated pay in each industry.

There was a distinct radicalization among unions once the emergency powers were used to "militarize" strikers, a fate that befell workers in the state electricity and telephone utility (ANTEL) and oil corporation (ANCAP). Strikers were legally "called up" into the army and told to return to work. If they refused, they could be tried as "deserters" by military courts.[7] In 1969, militarization of strikers was used for the first time against private-sector employees – this time the bank workers.[8] The moderate Colorado senator Amílcar Vasconcellos denounced the measure as equal to "slavery."[9] Looking back, an old and respected Batllista Colorado member was frankly critical of Pacheco's handling of industrial unrest:

Pacheco over-rode the Constitution to rule by decree. Instead of responding to social challenges he repressed them, which was an extremist game to play. To ban the Socialist Party was unconstitutional, unnecessary and a cause of irritation. The correct way to have handled the union crisis would have been to unite the [Colorado] party and treat Parliament with more respect. Real wages had fallen very sharply in 1965, but the Government resisted union demands, being dominated by business sectors.[10]

5 Handelman (1984). For a different view of Uruguayan labor, see Cosse (1984).
6 Uruguay, Junta de Comandantes en Jefe (1978).
7 It was claimed that this was necessary because strikers might booby-trap sophisticated plants in such a way as to cause accidents if untrained military personnel attempted to run generators or refineries.
8 See the speech against the militarization by Senator Zelmar Michelini of the Colorado left (who later joined the Broad Front) in August 1969: Uruguay, Asamblea General, *Diario de Sesiones*, Vol. 51, p. 334; also cited by Amarillo (1985, p. 15).
9 Uruguay, Asamblea General, *Diario de Sesiones*, Vol. 51, p. 302; also cited by Amarillo (1985, p. 15).
10 Personal interview, Montevideo, 12 July 1984.

Table 3.3. *Social groups seen as responsible for crises*[a]

Group	Left (%) (n = 17)	Blancos (%) (n = 22)	Colorados (%) (n = 24)	All[b] (%) (n = 68)
(a) Businessmen	35	5	12	15
(b) The trade unions	0	5	29	14
(c) Students & youth	0	5	21	6
(d) Foreign subversives	0	9	4	6

[a]The question: "In your opinion, which groups were principally responsible for the disorder and violence which the country faced 1968–73?"
[b]Includes one Patriotic Union and three Civic Union leaders and a high-ranking military officer close to the regime.

It is unclear whether labor unrest alone (e.g., in the absence of the Tupamaros guerrilla activities) would have constituted a *sufficient* condition for the crisis of democracy. Experts argued at the end of 1970 that the power of the unions had been weakened by the Pacheco government.[11] The very militant bank workers went back to work with almost none of their demands met,[12] and the stream of general strikes was also a symptom of labor's declining power. What Handelman shows, however, is that labor militants had begun to scare managers and owners quite badly (especially when the factory occupations became violent and the Tupamaros began to kidnap businessmen). Uruguayan democracy became delegitimated in the eyes of businessmen for failing to protect their personal safety, liberty, and property, just as it appeared hollow to strike leaders who were detained in barracks by the military.[13]

The perceived importance of the industrial-relations crisis can be gauged from a question that asked politicians to state which political and social actors were most to blame for the crisis of 1968–73. The four groups mentioned were the unions, businessmen, students and youth, and foreign subversive elements.[14] Table 3.3 shows the results. Almost no Blancos

11 Using the "Delphi" principle, Gallup Uruguay asked experts whether unions had been strengthened or weakened during 1970: 30% thought they had been weakened, and 33% thought their power was unchanged; only 17% saw their power as having grown. *Informe Gallup 1971*, p. 14.
12 In 1973, unemployment was 9%; coupled with repressive government measures, that weakened the CNT's capacity to influence public policy.
13 The tone of industrial relations was illustrated by a founder of the bank-workers union (AEBU) and former deputy from the Socialist party, who wrote in a monthly encyclopedia that the president's assault on strikers "violently manifested the decision of the oligarchy to break a tacit agreement that regulated social relations" (D'Elía 1969). The content of union manifestos and publications was even more inflammatory.
14 Respondents could choose as many as they liked. The results for political actors are reported in Table 3.1.

blamed either unions or businessmen for the crisis (just 5% in each case). Of the Left leaders, none mentioned the unions, but more than one-third thought that businessmen had played a major role in generating social conflicts. Finally, almost as many Colorados blamed the unions, but only one in eight cited businessmen. Revealingly, the best predictors of those blaming business for the country's crisis were whether or not the politicians were businessmen themselves, and what sort of state role they favored in the economy, not the party to which they belonged. Also revealing was the fact that despite the greater hostility among Colorados, the best predictor for blaming the students was the interviewee's level of education: The less educated they were, the more politicians blamed students for disorder and violence. Finally, almost no politicians took seriously the military's oft-repeated claim that Uruguay had fallen victim to foreign subversive elements.

What is most striking about Table 3.3, if we compare it to Table 3.1, is the unmistakable tendency among all politicians to blame political actors, such as the extreme Left and Right, or the government, for disorder and violence far more frequently than they blame social actors such as unions or businessmen. Even Colorados blamed the unions less often than they blamed the government, and it was a Colorado administration![15] On the other hand, more Frentistas blamed the extreme Left than blamed businessmen, and more mentioned the extreme Right as being responsible for the crisis than the police or military. Whether or not they were correct in diagnosing the sources of disorder and violence as political rather than social, politicians clearly perceived the breakdown of democracy as stemming from a disorder of the polity.

Political violence

Along with the military's role expansion, guerrilla violence was one of the factors in the final breakdown of democracy ranked highest by politicians: Recall from Table 3.2 that 47% of interviewees ranked it either first or second. According to data compiled from newspapers, 1969 saw more armed violence against the government in Uruguay than in any other Latin American nation, whereas in the 1950s it had experienced the least among 20 countries examined.[16] For the Colorados it was the major cause of the democratic breakdown, and even though Broad Front

15 Whether they would have done so in 1972 is hard to say. Obviously, the decline of the Pachequistas relative to the Batllistas between 1971 and 1984 was one reason for this finding. Nevertheless, the constant friction between Parliament and the executive meant that dissatisfaction among Colorado politicians not actually in the government was high under both Pacheco (1968–72) and Bordaberry (from 1972 onward).
16 Duff and McCamant (1976, p. 184).

Table 3.4. *Public sympathy for the Tupamaros guerrillas in Montevideo[a]*

Level of justification	Party identification			Age			
	Left (%)	Blancos (%)	Colorados (%)	18–25 (%)	26–50 (%)	51+ (%)	All (%)
Very	45	13	6	20	18	12	17
A little	35	24	21	31	28	19	26
Not at all	10	41	58	31	35	45	38
No response	10	22	15	18	19	24	19
Total	100	100	100	100	100	100	100

[a] The question: "Given the political conditions in our country, are movements like the Tupamaros very justified, a little, or not at all justified?"
Source: Gallup Uruguay, *Informe de Opinión Pública*, No. 186–7, February 1972, Table 20.

leaders downplayed the responsibility of the Tupamaros for the coup, they often complained of right-wing violence against their headquarters during the 1971 election campaign.[17] The "Movement of National Liberation–Tupamaros" were Latin America's most successful urban guerrillas, and they won widespread sympathy, and support, especially among youth and on the Left (Table 3.4). Yet, despite a surprising amount of sympathy for the Tupamaros, the overwhelming majority of Uruguayans totally rejected armed revolution.[18] Most sympathizers hoped that the government would negotiate with the guerrillas, which it publicly refused to do.

There is no doubt that a growing climate of violence was promoted by the Tupamaros, who abandoned their original Robin Hood tactics with the decision to execute Dan Mitrione, a U.S. police adviser whom they kidnapped and held in a so-called people's prison during August 1970. The sophistication and success of the guerrillas in outwitting the Uruguayan police made the calls to bring in the armed forces increasingly difficult to resist.[19] However, the military claimed (truthfully) to have

17 One bitter leftist leader did, however, express the view that "Pacheco caused the guerrillas to mushroom and benefited politically as a result" (personal interview, Montevideo, 27 March 1985).
18 Even 88% of leftist supporters thought that the problems of the country should be solved while preserving law and order, as did 97% of Colorados and 99% of Blancos; see Gallup Uruguay, *Informe de Opinión Pública*, No. 178–9, October 1971, Table 41.
19 A former top air-force commander disagreed when offered the widely circulated view that the police were outgunned. He argued that "during the 1971 elections when sedition was at its height, the fight against it was still in the hands of the police and they did quite well, *but they were hamstrung by the legal system*" (personal interview, Montevideo, 13 December 1984). This would tend to suggest that the major motive for bringing in the military was to use military courts to try accused prisoners, so as to dispense with the niceties (and inefficiency) of Uruguayan legal procedure. The military argued that judges were subject to intimidation.

defeated the national-liberation movement during 1972, a year before they took power.[20] The eruption of political violence cannot therefore be seen as a sufficient condition for the democratic breakdown, though it made military role expansion unavoidable. As we shall see, it was the politicians' failure to control that process by maintaining a united front that sealed their fate.

Military intervention in politics

The final aspect of the crisis that needs to be considered is that of military role expansion – the factor that eventually determined what type of regime would replace Uruguay's liberal democracy. The armed forces had previously been unprestigious and apolitical, but the crisis of the 1960s coincided with exposure to national-security doctrines taught by U.S. advisers and teachers at the Army School of the Americas in Panama. Those doctrines made a fetish out of the need to contain Soviet expansionism in the Third World following the Cuban revolution.[21]

On 8 September 1971, President Pacheco decreed that the armed forces would intervene in the battle against the guerrilla movements, using his status as commander in chief to bypass Parliament. That immediately led to the creation of the Joint Chiefs of Staff, or Estado Mayor Conjunto, known as ESMACO.[22] Partly distracted by the election campaign, the political parties made no effort to oppose the decree. A recently promoted general, Gregorio Alvarez, who had been nominated on merit (rather than seniority or political connections), was given his first command as coordinator of the new organ. He immediately built up a team of young officers such as Abdón Raimúndez (army) and Jorge Martínez[23] (air force), and they, along with General Alvarez, were among the group that began to press for political intervention.

Conspiracies had existed in Uruguay since the Blanco administration of 1963–7, but the politicians had managed to appoint commanders in

---

20 Armed-forces propaganda subsequently alleged that having learned from its mistakes, the "military-political apparatus of sedition" was in "full process of reorganization and reactivation," allegedly with foreign aid (document of the Joint Chiefs of Staff, 12 December 1972, cited in Uruguay, Junta de Comandantes en Jefe, 1978). The absence of further terrorist acts would suggest otherwise.

21 National-security doctrine has been discussed by Arriagada (1980) and Comblin (1977).

22 According to Amarillo (1985, p. 20), General Alvarez had begun work on coordinating the campaign against the guerrillas from an ad hoc office at the School of Arms and Services.

23 Not to be confused with the army commander, César Martínez, who was ousted by the rebels during the February 1973 crisis.

chief who had remained loyal to the Constitution.[24] The crucial process that made military role expansion possible during the period after 1970 was the attrition of those high-ranking generals who owed their appointments to politicians. The influence of the Colorados in military circles was also damaged by the decision of General Seregni (who had been promoted on the basis of examination, but had links to Batllism) to resign late in 1968, and later to run for office as the candidate of the Left.[25]

The final military takeover was made possible not only by the creation of new institutions such as ESMACO, and the prestige that came from the defeat of the guerrillas, but also by the emergence of a military interest as such. Partisan differences were effaced, and the new generation of officers actively sought to usurp political power, even over the heads of their commanding officers. After the defeat of the MLN-Tupamaros, the armed forces envisaged a "third phase" of their war against sedition, whose aim − in a classic version of national-security doctrine − was to assume command of national development as a means of removing the "breeding grounds of subversion." With the new confidence gleaned from their experience with counterinsurgency, the military saw civilian politicians as either corrupt or ineffective, and were thus able to justify seizing power from what was, after all, a tough right-wing civilian administration.

Politicians court the military

Though politicians may have tended to downplay their responsibility for the crisis, recall from Table 3.2 that 37% of Colorados and 29% of Blancos ranked "the inadequacies of parties and antagonism between political leaders" among their top two causes of the breakdown. One respected Colorado commented as follows:

Parties were incoherent and fragmented. They had no functioning internal life. Organs were not the real locus of decision-making but places that ratified hidden accords. This got much worse after the constitutional reform. . . . The politics of the party began to revolve around the President.[26]

---

24 Indeed, some accounts hold that the service chiefs actually prevented Pacheco from transforming himself into a dictator by blocking a secret plan to close Congress and suspend the 1971 elections. That version was given to me by a high-ranking retired air-force officer who subsequently participated in the 1973 coup and who obviously had an interest in suggesting that the politicians were as disloyal to democracy as were the military.

25 An old trade-union militant who once had communist sympathies was to tell me during my interviews in October 1984 that the reasons for Seregni's decision remained obscure: "I still do not know why Seregni resigned . . . it was not necessarily to do with the repression of strikes."

26 Personal interview, Montevideo, 10 July 1984.

Table 3.5. *Public belief in the fairness of the 1971 elections*[a]

Degree of fairness	All (%)	Party identification			Age		
		Left (%)	Blanco (%)	Colorado (%)	18–25 (%)	26–50 (%)	51+ (%)
Clean	45	11	38	72	31	48	45
Fraud	38	74	48	14	50	37	35
Don't know	17	15	14	14	19	15	20
Total	100	100	100	100	100	100	100

[a]The question: "Recently there have been a lot of protests about the elections. In your judgment, were these elections as clean as any, or was there fraud?"
Source: Gallup Uruguay, *Informe de Opinión pública*, No. 186–7, February 1972.

The 1971 election produced a consolidation of the majority sectors (*sublemas*) in both traditional parties: *Pachequistas* in the Colorado party and *Wilsonistas* in the National party.[27] However, the Wilsonistas insisted they had been robbed of victory by fraud and refused to cooperate with the new Colorado administration of Juan María Bordaberry (Table 3.5).

Why were Uruguay's parties unable or unwilling to stem the tide of military encroachment into their traditional domain? Tragically, the most important catalyst to the military intervention was the secretive courting of generals by politicians on all sides. What began as maneuvering for advantage became a desperate attempt to survive the inevitable political earthquake. First a rash of retired generals were nominated as presidential candidates (Gestido for the Colorados in 1966; Seregni for the Left and Aguerrondo for the Blancos in 1971). The final complicity of politicians was to abandon Bordaberry when he appealed for help during the military rebellion of February 1973. That even went for the leaders of his own Colorado party: The Batllista senators of the "List 15" had long ceased to support him, but even the senators of the majority Pachequista wing have been alleged to have favored his resignation at a meeting on February 9 in the presidential residence at Suárez. The Left was seduced by the chimera of a progressive Peruvian-style coup. Addressing a rally at La Unión, Broad Front leader General Seregni endorsed the military communiqués of 9 February, in which they made known their demands for

27 As explained in Chapter 2, *sublemas* are intermediate cartels of lists within parties (*lemas*) that pool their votes to minimize "wasted votes." They often share the same Senate and presidential candidates.

reforms.[28] Seregni was to pay dearly for that act of disloyalty to democracy; massive public support in the streets obviously strengthened the resolve of the rebellious colonels and totally undermined the position of the president, who, for all his undemocratic traits, had been elected.

Though the influential independent left magazine *Marcha*, edited by Carlos Quijano, cautioned against belief in the progressive military's strength during the February crisis, the communist daily *El Popular* endorsed the military's demands. So did, albeit "critically," the Christian Democrats' *Ahora*, which had denounced a so-called plan by politicians to "discredit" the military on 15 December 1972.[29] In debates in the Assembly,[30] socialist and communist senators and deputies also supported the idea of a progressive military intervention. According to one of the first scholars to study the military in this period, "the National Party's strategy was to avoid confrontation with the Armed Forces at all times, directing its offensive against President Bordaberry. Wilson Ferreira and National party leaders tried to negotiate privately and separately with Colorado and 'civic' military sectors their own plan for an 'institutional way out' through the calling of elections (with or without military mediation) once Bordaberry had resigned."[31] Supporters of Wilson Ferreira in the Blanco party had no faith in the democratic loyalties of the president; they hoped for new elections that might right what they saw as the unfair result of 1971. In fact, Bordaberry's 1976 proposal to abolish political parties permanently and stay on as president subsequently cast a poor light on his sincerity in the February crisis. It appears that by early 1973, practically all politicians secretly favored his resignation in favor of Vice-President Jorge Sapelli.[32]

---

28 Responding to Colorado attacks more than a decade later in an interview on Radio Sarandí, 16 November 1984, Seregni claimed that he had called on Bordaberry to resign so that there could be a constitutional way out of the crisis, and he argued that the real coup came only on 29 June, when Parliament was dissolved.

29 The eight points of the plan were reprinted (with disingenuous horror) in *Uruguay, Junta de Comandantes en Jefe* (1978, Vol. 2, pp. 65–6). In the main they were perfectly legitimate and certainly loyal to democracy.

30 Speeches by Communist party General Secretary Rodney Arismendi, Senator Jaime Pérez, and a radical socialist deputy, Vivian Trías, referred to "captains, lieutenants, and subalterns who fought in the streets" and who "began to discover the real causes that provoked the emergence of the guerrillas" and a "Uruguay in the hands of a few privileged men who manage the national economy and public life in their interest" (Amarillo 1985, p. 49).

31 Amarillo (1985, p. 51).

32 Bordaberry was not a real Colorado, but a former leader of the right-wing ruralist movement who had run on different parties' lists at different stages. He was also a weak man deliberately chosen as proxy by Pacheco. The most revealing indicator of his lack of support was a Gallup poll of February 1972 (the month before inauguration) in which 25% of Colorados named Pacheco

The dynamics of breakdown: the momentum of
military intervention

By 1972 the guerrillas had been controlled and largely destroyed. The economic crisis had been stanched by a wage-price freeze, though inflation was allowed to rise in the run-up to the 1971 election. Many of the development projects and schemes for export promotion that would be implemented under the military had been drawn up and were about to go ahead. Pacheco's proxy, Bordaberry, won the 1971 presidential race, if not comfortably. Despite (or because of) the "red scare," the Colorados had twice as many votes as the Broad Front and even retained control of the city government in Montevideo, the heartland of the Left.[33]

Authoritarianism was thus not in any sense "necessary" as a result of an uncontainable security threat or an uncontrollable overload of political demands. For example, opinion data suggested that there were consistently critical majorities among the Montevideo public against the trade unions' militancy. Yet public trust in politicians had been severely eroded by accusations of corruption flung by the guerrillas and the security forces, and the politicians' self-serving, inefficient image was the exact opposite of that of the military. Gallup opinion polls in the second half of 1971[34] suggested about 13% of Montevideo's inhabitants thought that Parliament was "acting well," compared with 25% for President Pacheco and 41% for the armed forces.[35]

The politicians' greatest mistakes were to unleash the military against strikers in 1968, to allow them to take over the campaign against terrorists in 1971, and then to turn over to them part of the judicial system for trials of those accused of subversion in 1972. Those moves not only politicized the military but also radicalized the opposition and delegitimated democracy. It is plausible that the military could have been corralled back into subordination, had it not been for the stalemate between President Bordaberry and Wilson Ferreira. Part of the reason for the stalemate lay in the unfortunate arithmetic of the 1971 election results. Because Bordaberry lacked a legislative majority and because not all Colorado factions could even be counted on to support him, he was forced

as their preferred leader for the party; 13% mentioned Jorge Batlle, 6% Amílcar Vasconcellos, and only 5% Bordaberry (Gallup Uruguay, *Informe de Opinión Pública*, No. 186–7, 1972, p. 15).

33 What might have happened had the Blancos won the extra 13,000 votes that would have elected Wilson Ferreira is one of those fascinating historical questions that refuse to go away. If Wilson Ferreira's charismatic leadership had been harnessed to save democracy, rather than oppose Bordaberry, things might have been very different.

34 The military had been called in to defeat the guerrillas, but a temporary truce had been declared by the Tupamaros prior to the elections.

35 Gallup Uruguay, *Informe de Opinión Pública*, (1971, various months).

to seek a deal with the Blancos in 1972. Yet only the Blancos' small conservative factions agreed to join the government; Wilson Ferreira refused.[36]

Politicians had largely managed to ride the storm by a process of crisis management; they had not come up with a new plan for national development. That was what the army and air force demanded during their February 1973 rebellion in a confusingly populist set of communiqués that bore no relation at all to their subsequent policies.[37] President Bordaberry resisted their demands in vain as politicians from all parties (including his own) refused to come to his aid, and even urged him to resign in favor of the vice-president. Finally the president went to the Boisso Lanza air-force base outside Montevideo to negotiate a pact with the military.

Although the truth about Bordaberry's and Ferreira's roles in the February crisis remains unclear, the fact that the president survived was something of a hollow victory.[38] Wilson described him as "the winner of Boisso Lanza." The real winners, however, were the colonels and generals who had rebelled, and the losers were the politicians as a whole. Under the Boisso Lanza pact the president in effect abdicated power to the military by accepting the creation of a military-dominated National Security Council, armed-forces control over promotions to the rank of general, and the firing of certain ambassadors. The minister of the economy was instructed to study the possibility of fully nationalizing the banking system and increasing the state's control over foreign trade.[39]

The victory of the armed forces in the February rebellion was made possible by the refusal of all politicians to come to the president's rescue (and, in some cases, outright plotting with the military).[40] What was clear from my interviews was the high degree of mistrust among all politicians, which implied little possibility for cooperation to save the system.

36 Nevertheless, according to Vice-President Jorge Sapelli, the new Parliament actually proved more amenable to the government's legislative program than had the previous one. The only major rebellions occurred when it voted to lift the security measures in March 1972 and when it refused to lift Senator Erro's immunity from prosecution in May–June 1973.

37 The navy initially supported the president, but he decided that they were not strong enough to save him on their own.

38 A detailed history of the crisis was published shortly before the 1984 elections, when the subject resurfaced. See Washington Beltrán, "Que Significó Febrero de 1973," *El País*, Tuesday, 20 November 1984, p. 8, and "Los Sucesos de Febrero de 1973 y el Frente Amplio," *El País*, Thursday, 22 November 1984, p. 9.

39 Vasconcellos (1973, pp. 56–9).

40 When the Senate conducted a postmortem on the February crisis, the acrimony of the debate underlined how little trust remained between politicians (Uruguay, Camara de Senadores, *Diario de Sesiones*, 15–16 May 1973).

Table 3.6. *Parties' and factions' loyalty to democracy, 1968–73*[a]

Party or faction	Party of respondent				
	Frentistas ($n = 8$)	Blancos ($n = 13$)	Colorados ($n = 19$)	All ($n = 44$)[b]	Rivals only[c]
Party evaluated					
Broad Front	3.1	5.8	6.8	5.8	6.4
Blanco party	4.6	2.2	5.0	3.9	4.6
Colorado party	7.0	3.2	3.5	4.0	4.4
Faction evaluated					
Frente:					
"List 99"	2.4	3.8	5.5	4.2	4.6
Christian Democrats	1.6	4.5	5.6	4.3	4.9
Socialists	2.9	6.0	6.7	5.5	6.1
Communists	3.4	8.2	8.8	7.6	8.5
Blanco:					
Herreristas	7.9	3.8	5.5	5.1	5.5
Por la Patria	3.8	2.7	5.8	4.3	4.9
Movimiento de Rocha	3.9	2.1	4.5	3.5	4.1
Colorado:					
Pachequistas	8.6	6.2	4.7	5.8	6.5
Quincistas	6.9	3.1	3.4	3.8	4.2

[a]The question: "In the crisis of a democracy political parties may be judged by their behavior as loyal to the rules of the democratic game, whether they are in office or in the opposition; semi-loyal when they are only sometimes loyal; or disloyal (anti-system parties). Thinking about parties and their factions from 1968 to 1973, if "1" represents an unimpeachably loyal democratic conduct, and "10" one totally antidemocratic, where would you place the following?"
[b]Includes one Patriotic Union and three Civic Union leaders.
[c]Mean for respondents of parties other than that evaluated (includes Unión Cívica).

When asked to evaluate the behaviors of different parties and factions in terms of their loyalty to the democratic system during the crises of 1968–73, the politicians interviewed were naturally quick to absolve their own sectors, as is clear in Table 3.6. If we take the average of the opinions of all interviewees on the 10-point scale used, however, we get some idea of the perception that politicians had regarding the betrayal of the democratic system on the part of their rivals. If we define any score between 4 and 7 to reflect "semiloyalty" to democracy, then any score above that may be considered to reflect outright disloyalty. On this basis, the Colorado and Blanco parties as a whole were seen as hovering on the fringes of disloyalty during the 1968–73 crises. Two of their major factions were seen as semiloyal: the Colorado majority sector, the Pachequista (5.8), and the Blanco majority, Por la Patria (4.3). So, too, were the Blancos' right-wing minority, the Herreristas (5.1), and, at the opposite end of the ideological spectrum, the Broad Front (5.8) and three of its sectors. The Communist party, however, was seen as frankly disloyal to democracy (7.6), and so were the Pachequistas and Herreristas in the eyes of the left. What these three latter groups had in common was an undisguised attempt to ally with the military.[41]

Greater solidarity among politicians might have been able to hinder the military's rise to power. However, many argue that Uruguayan democracy was already dead by 1973, as a result of Pacheco and Bordaberry's policy of imposing a continuous state of emergency and ruling by decree. The tragic dilemma in which the republic found itself after 1972 was that the elected president was not a loyal democrat. In an interview with a close associate of Bordaberry in 1984, I was informed that he had told the vice-president that: "I want the Parliament to fall like a rotten apple from the branch."[42] In retrospect, Bordaberry was a lesser danger to democracy than were the military, though few understood that at the time.

The political isolation of the president eventually produced a vacuum of power around him that led to his capitulation in the face of the military rebellion. As the crisis wore on, the tacit preference of leaders in all parties was for an alliance with one or another sector of the young colonels or rising generals. That was the great difference compared with the previous political crises during the twentieth century, in which sections of the traditional parties had almost always allied. The politicians' worst miscalculation was to refuse to believe that in Uruguay the military might take power for themselves.

In June 1973 the military accused Senator Erro of links to the guerrillas and demanded that the National Assembly lift his immunity from arrest and prosecution. Too late the politicians decided to make a stand. Their refusal to grant the military's request was in fact the pretext Bordaberry and the armed forces used to close the National Assembly on 27 June.[43] The final blow to democracy had been struck.

41 President Pacheco's preferred tactic during confrontations with Congress was to tour military bases. The Herreristas nominated General Aguerrondo as their candidate in 1971, and he was often linked to pro-coup military factions. The communists strongly supported the military's demands for reform in the February 1973 rebellion, as did much of the Left.

42 The identity of the interviewee is protected by request.

43 Senator Paz Aguirre of the Colorados' "List 15" alleges he met with Senator Ferreira and appealed to him to allow the Blancos a "free vote." In Paz's view, that would have led about two-fifths of the Blanco senators to vote for the lifting of Senator Erro's immunity, and thus the military would have had less pretext for intervention (personal interview, Montevideo, 1984).

4

The failure of military institutionalization and political engineering: the survival of political parties

When a modern military force seizes power in a democracy, the leaders face a number of dilemmas as they seek to institutionalize their rule. As their rule is born of a state of exception, they must early on seek to establish two things: (a) decision-making structures that will clearly distribute authority and (b) succession and promotion mechanisms to designate officeholders. These two goals require the establishment of an internal balance of power as a first priority. Subsequently, military regimes born of a state of exception must seek to regularize their forms of interaction with civil society, restoring the links through which information flows to decision makers and, eventually, by which assent is granted by citizens to state policies. As one Blanco politician who ran for high office put it, echoing Talleyrand: "Bayonets are good for everything except sitting on."[1] This second external dimension, or phase, of institutionalization is necessary if the state is to end its isolation from society, but sooner or later it inevitably must give rise to acute dilemmas regarding liberalization and participation.

The collegial military-technocratic rule that emerged in Uruguay after 1973 ensured complete physical control of the country. The nation's compact size and small population permitted levels of surveillance and social control that reached the upper limits of the authoritarian ideal type. The state penetrated further into the private lives of its citizens than did any neighboring regime, even classifying each citizen as A, B, or C, according to political reliability, and controlling employment on that basis, even in some private-sector activities, such as education. Though largely spared the "death-squad" model of repression, Uruguay had the highest per capita prison population in South America during 1976, according to Amnesty International estimates.[2]

1 Personal interview, Montevideo, 15 March 1984.
2 Twenty-six people "disappeared" inside Uruguay, and five times that many Uruguayans living in Argentina, probably as a result of joint operations between the two countries' security forces. If we include both groups of disappearances, and torture deaths while in detention, the grand total will not exceed 200: a ratio of 1 in 15,000 citizens. The corresponding ratio for Argentina may

The military regime also had the collaboration of an elected president and a few conservative, mainly rural, politicians; yet its attempt at institutionalization was to prove a failure. The traditional forms of Uruguay's polity resisted efforts by the military to "reengineer" the political system from above, and political parties survived, so to speak, in "suspended animation." The mere suspension of the traditional Blanco and Colorado political parties was, however, accompanied by a far more severe repression of trade unions and of the Left. During the initial "reactionary phase"[3] the armed forces consolidated their iron grip over the country, creating the impression of an almost impregnable state and a frozen civil society. The peak of repression occurred in 1976, the year in which elections were canceled.

From about 1976 to 1980, the purely reactionary phase gave way to an attempted refoundation of what they claimed would be a "strengthened" democracy, molded in the image of the military and its national-security ideology. The Constitution was amended to formalize military power by a series of decrees known as "institutional acts," using the Brazilian terminology,[4] and a civilian puppet, Aparicio Méndez, was installed (Table 4.1). However, the chronic lack of links with civil society and the military's peculiar confidence in its support led them to seek a form of belated plebiscitarian legitimation. In 1980, in an extraordinary referendum, Uruguayans decisively rejected the military's proposed repressive new constitution, opening the way to the final phase of the regime. Despite the twists and turns of events, from then on the military gradually recognized the need to seek agreement with moderate civilian politicians on an acceptable set of guarantees for their return to the barracks. The convoluted difficulties of extrication, and their eventual resolution after several false starts, lasted from 1981 until 1984. The unfolding of that process forms the basis of the remainder of this book.

Initial dilemmas of military power consolidation

Despite illusions among many sectors of the Left that the coup might bring to power progressive generals,[5] the immediate response from labor

---

have been five times as high. On the other hand, about 5,000 Uruguayan citizens were jailed during the early years of the regime, a ratio of 1 per 600 citizens. Amnesty International estimates the corresponding ratios as 1 in 1,200 for Argentina, 1 in 1,300 for Cuba, and 1 in 2,000 for Chile.

3 González (1985c, p.104) has described this phase as a commissary dictatorship based on a regime of exception.

4 For a summary of the institutional acts in English, see Latin American Bureau, *Uruguay: Generals Rule* (London: Latin America Bureau, 1979).

5 Great interest was shown in the generals who had seized power in Peru five years previously.

Table 4.1. *Summary of the institutional acts, 1976–80*

Act	Date	Substance
Institutional Act No. 1	12 June 1976	Suspends elections until further notice.
Institutional Act No. 2	12 June 1976	Creates the Council of the Nation, consisting of the Council of State and the junta of generals.
Institutional Act No. 3	1 Sept. 1976	Executive supremacy over judiciary; planning secretariat set up; military local government.
Institutional Act No. 4	1 Sept. 1976	All political activity and voting rights are banned for 15 years for those who ran in 1966–71 for any Marxist or "pro-Marxist" party or those tried (not convicted) of "crimes against the nation." The same provisions apply (except loss of vote) to those of the moderate Left, all candidates for presidency and vice-presidency in 1966 and 1971, and anyone who sat in either the Senate or House.
Institutional Act No. 5	20 Oct. 1976	Human rights are to be respected in accordance with national security and natural law.
Institutional Act No. 6	19 Jan. 1977	Takeover of Electoral Court under three politicians of the traditional parties.
Institutional Act No. 7	27 June 1977	Civil servants lose their job tenure.
Institutional Act No. 8	1 July 1977	The judiciary loses all remaining independence; judges are declared "interim" for four years.
Institutional Act No. 9	23 Oct. 1979	Reorganization of the idependent social-security boards and rationalization of provisions.
Institutional Act No. 10	10 Nov. 1980	Fixes simple majority for approval of the constitution in the 30 November plebiscite.

Source: Actos Institucionales (1 al 17) (Montevideo: Editorial Técnica, 1984).

was the declaration of an indefinite general strike by the CNT.[6] Two weeks of factory occupations, sabotage, and economic paralysis followed that were broken only by a combination of wage increases and mass arrests. Talks were also held with the Left and with students, essentially to buy time, perpetuate the progressive myth, and exhaust the strikers. Soon after the coup, Bordaberry said that the traditional parties remained the "essence of democracy and the backbone of our nationality." Following a

6 The CNT general strike was the only major act of resistance to the military intervention and closure of the National Assembly. From the collapse of that vain effort to the 1 May rally of 1983, unions were almost invisible in Uruguay, and strikes were isolated to a handful of plant stoppages. That labor quiescence, as well as the lack of links between parties and unions, stands in contrast to the situations in Argentina and Chile. On the other hand, the effort, involving the 1973 law, to produce a progovernment labor movement proved a fiasco.

1 December 1973 decree, most of the parties of the Broad Front, as well as the Federation of Students and various other leftist groups, were banned, their presses confiscated and leaders arrested, while the traditional parties remained merely suspended.

On 19 December, the Council of State met for the first time. Consisting of 25 rather obscure nominated civilian politicians, it replaced the closed legislature.[7] A year and two weeks after the closure of the National Assembly, Bordaberry reshuffled his cabinet, appointing Uruguay's leading neoliberal technocrat, Alejandro Végh Villegas, to be minister of economy and finance. The increasingly pronounced rightward shift of what was dubbed the "civil-military process" had become clear to all. In late July, high-ranking officers were appointed to run various major agencies and parastatal enterprises, including the Central Bank, the UTE (electricity utility), ANCAP (oil refining), ANTEL (telecommunications), and the post office.[8] A speech by Foreign Minister Juan Carlos Blanco promised that a new constitution and "Statute of Political Parties" would be drawn up and submitted to the Council of State, before ratification by the people. On 1 September, an open letter signed by 100 politicians was published calling first for a restoration of political activity. This time the response of President Bordaberry was to insist that they give up hope of once more "using their perverted political apparatuses."[9]

The early years of the authoritarian regime were characterized by chronic uncertainty, disagreements, and improvisation as the structure and aims of military domination emerged. As one leading exponent of national-security doctrines in Uruguay lamented, "the *proceso* was not at all like [that of] Brazil. In Brazil the whole thing developed at the Superior War College from 1950 to 1964."[10] Uruguayan officers had had far less practical and intellectual preparation for administration – and the politics to which they had been exposed at the Higher Military Studies Institute in the late 1960s had in many cases been progressive.[11]

---

7 Among the 25 councillors were two former Supreme Court presidents, three former ministers, the public prosecutor, and a director of the conservative Blanco newspaper *El País*.

8 A further setback for the military radicals came at the end of the year, when the leading military progressive and former intelligence chief, Colonel Ramón Trabal, was assassinated in Paris by persons unknown.

9 Lérin and Torres (1978).

10 Personal interview with a retired general, Montevideo, April 1984.

11 Left leader General Líber Seregni had been director of the officer school, Instituto Militar de Estudios Superiores. Unlike Brazil's Escola Superior da Guerra (ESG), Uruguay's National Security and Defense School (ESEDENA) was set up long after the coup in 1978. The philosophy of ESEDENA was influenced by its founder, the retired general Ramagli, who had been military attaché in Brazil, where he had been inspired by the ESG (personal interview, Montevideo, June 1984).

The ouster of Bordaberry

The repeated crises, which involved both economic policy and the future of political institutions, came to a head in 1976 when the military proposed the creation of a "Tribunal de Control Político," allegedly because they suspected Bordaberry was feeding them faked economic data.[12] President Bordaberry circulated a memorandum proposing the permanent abolition of all political parties and his own continuation in office, eventually leading to the creation of a sort of semicorporatist system based on "currents of opinion." What was at stake was a clear choice between two divergent paths, one of which the military rejected as unworkable and undesirable. Whereas Bordaberry wanted an institutionalized authoritarian regime, the military preferred the ambiguity of an authoritarian situation.[13] As it turned out, the generals were reluctant to break with the line that they were cleaning up democracy, rather than killing it. They were also outraged at Bordaberry's suggestion that they should withdraw from administration to concentrate purely on security matters. That unwelcome proposal clashed with national-security doctrine, and it came precisely at a time when senior officers had begun to enjoy running Uruguay's many state agencies and enterprises. Bordaberry was forced to resign.[14]

These rare moments of audibility in the competing internal discourses of the regime coincided with a crucial turning point for its subsequent evolution. One threat to the traditional parties – legal abolition, which might logically have opened the way for an experiment with a nonparty corporatist regime – had been averted. The military remained loyal to the traditional parties as part of their *orientalidad*[15] and believed that such an adventure would be neither successful nor legitimate. In their communiqué of 12 June 1976 (which appeared in the press the next day) they astonished the nation by bluntly denigrating Bordaberry's proposals, insisting that the military did not "want to share historical responsibility for abolishing the parties" and that "sovereignty resides in the nation . . . as expressed . . . in the popular vote."[16] The military promised that no fundamental alterations would be made to the Constitution, but warned

12 Though economic policies were decidedly free-market from 1974, criticisms occasionally were heard from officers who disliked IMF-favored recipes.
13 The distinction was made by Linz (1971).
14 Vice-President Alberto Demicheli was made interim head of state. Bills had been introduced by councillors of state to set up a corporatist constitution, but had repeatedly been blocked by the real power-holders: the generals.
15 "Orientality" has been used in Uruguay to refer to "nationality" since the days when it was the eastern province of the Vice-Royalty of the River Plate.
16 Lérin and Torres (1978).

that it would be made more "flexible" through the enactment of transitory constitutional laws. Possibly they were influenced by the disdain for "corporatism" and the firm liberal belief in the free market favored by Alejandro Végh Villegas, their minister of the economy. Neoliberalism[17] was certainly the prevailing language of the southern-cone military regimes at that time. Under the military, public policy-making became less corporatist: More and more markets (especially the labor market) were "liberalized," and decision-takers were insulated from interest-group pressures. This is, of course, not to deny that the state became far stronger and did not, to the neoliberals' chagrin, decline in size. Corporatism, however, remained a minority discourse within the regime, certainly not a true reflection of the national reality.

The defining characteristics of Uruguay's regime as it stabilized after 1976 were its collegiality (there being no dictator to rival Pinochet in Chile) and the methodical (but rarely radical) influence of technocrats in policy-making. As one of Uruguay's foremost exponents of national-security doctrine stated bitterly, and revealingly,

the commanders changed every two to three years, so lack of continuity was a major problem. There needed to be more intervention in government by the Council of Officers [Junta] and retirees were never consulted. The military have always been politically marginal because they lack experience.[18]

Nonpoliticians, mostly drawn from the world of business, had become common as cabinet ministers during the second half of the 1960s, and their numbers increased under the military regime, as only a few politicians stayed on to work for their new masters. Sizable numbers of colonels and generals had been installed as directors of state enterprises and agencies (each armed service carving out its own fiefdom), but the cabinet itself remained largely civilian; the only exception was the minister of the interior, consistently a general from 1973 onward.

Notwithstanding the foregoing generals' lament, real power lay not with the president but with the Joint Chiefs of Staff (Junta de Comandantes en Jefe),[19] who were in turn kept in line by the 21 top-ranking

---

17 The confusion that often surrounds the use of this term to describe a restored faith in the justice and efficiency of market mechanisms harks back to the Manchester liberalism of the nineteenth century. In the United States, such a persuasion is more often called "neoconservatism," but here European and Latin American usage will be maintained.

18 Personal interview, Montevideo, April 1984.

19 This organ, uniting the commanders of the three services, had been constituted in 1971 in order to coordinate the campaign against the Tupamaros. In 1976 it consisted of the army commander, General Julio César Vadora, the naval chief, Vice Admiral Hugo Márquez, and the head of the air force, Brigadier General Dante Paladino.

generals, who formed the Junta de Oficiales Generales in 1976.[20] They literally became the upper chamber of the Uruguayan legislature, and its joint sessions with the nominated civilian Council of State were called the Council of the Nation. It was the service chiefs who in 1976 ousted Bordaberry and told the interim president, Demicheli, to decree the postponement of elections and some newly devised institutional acts. The Council of the Nation then chose Aparicio Méndez as the next president.[21] Thereafter, the generals not infrequently intervened to give specific orders at every level, with little concern for formalities. Major policies were adopted on the basis of "civil-military conclaves," in which the top brass and technocrats typically retreated to some holiday resort for an intensive seminar on the virtues of tariff reduction or foreign investment.

Economy and politics: the triumph of neoliberalism

From early on, economic policy became an obsession of the regime as economic growth became identified as a surrogate for legitimacy. The military were convinced that it was possible simply to do away with the obstacles that stood in the way of national development. The populist rhetoric of the colonels' demands in February 1973 soon subsided, as the regime came more and more to resemble O'Donnell's model of the bureaucratic authoritarian state. According to O'Donnell, this is designed to achieve the "economic exclusion of the popular sector."[22] Though such actions were in effect the functions of the Uruguayan military regime, it is doubtful that they were perceived as such by the military, with their usually modest social backgrounds and naive belief in archaic codes of honor and national service.[23] O'Donnell argues that the bureaucratic authoritarian regime "endeavors to 'de-politicize' social issues by dealing with them in terms of supposedly neutral and objective criteria of technical rationality."[24] Despite nationalist currents, given inflation, stagnation, indebtedness, chronic trade deficits, and shortages of foreign exchange and government revenues, it is not surprising that most were soon per-

---

20 This figure increased to 26 in 1981.

21 Interestingly, and in line with the erosion of the *proceso*'s civilian content, the regime's third and final president, General Gregorio Alvarez, was chosen in 1981 by the Junta de Oficiales Generales alone.

22 O'Donnell (1979b, p.293).

23 In notable contrast to their Argentine counterparts, Uruguayan military officers were rarely from elite families; they lacked status and sometimes even advanced education. The typical officer came from a struggling rural family that could not find the means to support his higher education. Their socialization was democratic rather that "snobbish." In contrast, many of the Tupamaros were rather well-born.

24 O'Donnell (1979b).

suaded that what was needed was "normalization" of the economy and export promotion.[25]

The only strong economic prejudice held by the military was a severe dislike of strikes, which were seen as damaging to the nation's well-being and growth. The project of economic "liberalization," therefore, was never close to their hearts, but by 1974 it had been sold to them through the qualifications and assurances of the technocrats they hired as advisers and administrators and, it seems, the advice they received from abroad. Technocrats in the authoritarian regimes of the southern cone in the 1970s saw economic policy as a tool for political disarticulation and demobilization of popular movements. The goal was privatization of all but the core institutions of a strengthened state.[26]

The military were torn between nationalist and neoliberal visions of the country's reconstruction, with the latter winning, but often meeting successful resistance and always remaining strongly at variance with the Batllista political values of many Uruguayans and the political economy of the state they had inherited.[27] The state, after all, was the agency for many officers' upward social mobility. In Uruguay, as in Argentina, privatization was blocked by the nationalist sectors of the armed forces, who often saw state industries as geopolitical resources. The government was quite interventionist when it came to large infrastracture projects, such as hydroelectric dams or subsidies to promote nontraditional exports. In sum, the economic model was pragmatic.

From 1974 to 1976 the economy minister and architect of the new policies was Alejandro Végh Villegas.[28] His nomination marked the neoliberal shift in the military *proceso*. It should be added, however, that if Bordaberry was amenable to free-market economic thinking, he disliked

25 At current dollar prices, Uruguay's exports grew 16% per year during the 1970s (Díaz-Alejandro, 1981).

26 Little progress was made with privatization, however, because of military opposition to Végh's. policies.

27 To what extent military regimes exploit ideologies as convenient posthoc rationalizations (or legitimations) for their actions, whether their leaders hold certain ideas or are held by them, is not always clear. The Uruguayan case suggests that the majority of the military used ideology in largely instrumental ways to further personal ambitions and institutional goals. As a retired officer who joined the Left put it, "national-security doctrine (NSD) did not come from the heart of the armed forces, but from outside political power centers . . . the armed forces are very adaptable to any doctrine" (personal interview, Montevideo, 30 April 1985).

28 Végh had trained as an engineer at Harvard and later worked in the Brazilian economic team of Roberto Campos; he was thus a technocrat par excellence. According to a reliably informed Blanco politician who collaborated for a time with the regime, "international banks and industrialists pushed for him hard. President Bordaberry was amenable, but the generals never liked him. He never attended their speeches or parades and was able to block a number of their projects. Végh was very important in blocking the corporatist option" (personal interview, Montevideo, 14 December 1984).

Végh's ideas on politics. For much of the military it was often the reverse.[29] Végh's power as minister of the economy was limited by military interference and bureaucratic resistance. One conservative Colorado who collaborated closely with the military complained that "colonels tried to come to ministers and give them orders. One by one the politicians resigned in frustration at their total dependence."[30] In contrast, a high-ranking retired officer and exponent of national-security doctrine put the blame for the regime's difficulties on bureaucratic inertia:

> The military understand nothing about economics. . . . The major problem of the *proceso* was the lack of an economic project. . . . The huge error of the military was to only intervene at the peaks of state agencies. The Left would have been able to liquidate the bureaucratic resistance that the *proceso* was unable to do.[31]

Having played a major role in saving the traditional parties, Végh Villegas resigned following the appointment of Aparicio Méndez as presidential figurehead. It has been speculated that he did so because of frustration at military interference with his more radical free-market policies, such as privatization.[32] As was unusual for a technocrat, however, his own explanation for his resignation was disquiet at the increasingly wide political void between the state and civil society, which he feared might favor renewed subversion. In his memorandum to the military, skillfully drafted to rebut Bordaberry's opinion, he went as far as to say that "consolidation of a durable regime necessitates a civic consensus far broader than that which a group of technocrats can form."[33] In fact, Végh maintained good relations with Jorge Batlle's Colorado "List 15" and remained close to *Búsqueda*, the neoliberal economics magazine, and the only publication allowed to criticize government policy during the rest of the decade.

The struggle to determine a timetable for the regime

Végh did not propose a rapid return to democracy; postponement of elections was an "evident necessity" while it was necessary for the armed

29 Végh's blend of liberalism and *realpolitik* is illustrated in an article on political forms he published in *Búsqueda* 1 February 1974, cited by Lérin and Torres (1978, p.47). His economic philosophy was set out in *Economía Política: Teoría y Acción* (Végh Villegas, 1977).
30 Personal interview, Montevideo, 28 August 1984.
31 Personal interview, Montevideo, April 1984. Whereas the politician praised Brazil's formal decision-making procedures, the retired general was enthusiastic about the more extreme Chilean policies.
32 Végh became a councillor of state until 1980.
33 Végh's reply to Bordaberry's memorandum was leaked and published by the Argentine magazine *Carta Política*, No. 34, August 1976.

forces to remain "supreme arbiter of the nation."[34] His own view, early on expressed in the magazine *Búsqueda*, was that the preservation of formal political mechanisms had its uses. The resulting legitimacy would mean that the regime would not have to rest on its efficiency alone.[35] Thus, Végh's preferred solution to the problem of institutionalization would have been to copy the Brazilian example of bypassing, but not abolishing, constitutional provisions. Although they disliked Végh, the military mistrusted Bordaberry's ambitions even more, and hence they vetoed the corporatist idea largely in order to ensure their continued influence. How long, however, was a state of exception to continue? If elections and parties could not be abolished, how long could elections be postponed? Some officers, in line with Végh's warnings, began to worry about what might be happening in civil society, from whence they detected an ominous silence. As an old Colorado who collaborated with them put it, "the military wanted to abolish parties in 1973, but by 1976 they realized it was too risky. It would have allowed the Left to take over."[36]

On the day he took office, 1 September 1976, President Méndez signed the Fourth Institutional Act, which banned 15,000 former politicians from engaging in any political activity for 15 years. Here the kind of subtlety that Végh had called for was lacking. The conditions were toughest for the Uruguayan Left; anyone on the left who had stood for office was deprived of his or her vote, in addition to being banned from engaging in politics. Among the Colorados and Blancos, only those who had actually held office were thus banned (*proscrito*), and they were not disfranchised. That leniency had the effect of punishing traditional politicians only if they had been popular! Subsequent institutional acts abolished civil servants' immunity from being fired, subordinated the judiciary to the executive, and intervened in the machinery for the holding of elections.[37] The civil service and the huge state sector, ranging from schools to utilities, were systematically purged of all supporters of the opposition.

The power struggle within the military continued during 1977. Under a new law passed in April, 49 officers were "retired." The number of generals was subsequently increased, and in violation of normal procedure, three of them were given special status in order to remain in the junta of generals. A government communiqué of 9 August 1977 announced that President Méndez had "decided to adopt the proposal put forward by the Commanders-in-Chief of the Armed Forces" and hold elections in 1981. Two weeks later, the timetable (*cronograma*) for a return to de-

34 *Carta Política*, No. 34, August 1976.
35 *Búsqueda*, 1 February 1974.
36 Personal interview, Montevideo, 28 August 1984.
37 Military courts had been trying alleged subversives since 1972, giving rise to serious miscarriages of justice.

Table 4.2. *Party support for the authoritarian regime in the earliest phase*[a]

Group evaluated	Party of respondent			
	Left ($n = 8$)	Blancos ($n = 13$)	Colorados ($n = 17$)	All[b] ($n = 42$)
Broad Front	9.0	8.3	7.8	8.2
National (Blanco) party	6.8	9.3	7.9	8.3
Herreristas	1.9	3.8	3.5	3.5
Movimiento de Rocha	8.8	9.7	9.3	9.3
Por la Patria	8.9	9.9	9.4	9.4
Colorado party	3.3	6.8	7.1	6.6
Pachequistas (UCB)	1.5	2.4	3.9	2.2
Unidad y Reforma (15)	3.9	6.1	8.3	6.8
Vasconcellos/Flores	6.8	8.6	9.1	8.5

[a]The question: "The parties and political groups took differing postures toward the new system [of government]. If we take "1" to stand for total support and "10" total opposition, where would you place the following in the *initial phase?*"
[b]Includes two Civic Union leaders, one Patriotic Union leader, and a political adviser to the regime who was a high-ranking officer in the armed forces.

mocracy was clarified: There would be a new constitution by 1980, and elections, with a single joint candidate of the traditional parties, would be approved by the military in 1981.

Images of support for the regime

Under authoritarian regimes, in the absence of elections and reliable opinion polls, it is often difficult to know which political and social sectors support the government. Given the climate of fear, public statements may be muted or difficult to decipher. One solution is to rely on the perceptions of opposition politicians, though it should be borne in mind that many of them are liable to overestimate opposition to the military. Table 4.2 shows the levels of support that politicians perceived the different parties and factions to have offered the military in the very earliest phase of their rule. The picture of political isolation (except with respect to the dwindling ranks of Colorado Pachequistas and Blanco Herreristas) is strong. But what is also interesting is that the respondents of each *lema* tended to see their own party as being the most opposed to the regime.[38]

38 Colorados tended to refer to leftist behavior in the February 1973 crisis, when the left supported the military's demands and the Blancos remained neutral. Respondents from the Left and the Blanco party, however, tended to refer to the fact that President Bordaberry, who dissolved the Congress on 27 June had been elected on a Colorado ticket.

Table 4.3. *Group support for the authoritarian regime*[a]

Group	Left (*n* = 8)	Blancos (*n* = 13)	Colorados (*n* = 17)	All[b] (*n* = 42)
Big business	1.1	1.7	2.6	2.1
Bankers	1.3	1.9	2.4	2.1
Ranchers and farmers	2.8	4.2	2.8	3.5
Judges	7.1	7.1	6.8	6.8
Civil servants	7.4	6.9	6.2	6.8
Professionals	7.3	6.8	6.9	7.1
Private white-collar	7.6	7.2	6.5	7.1
Blue-collar workers	9.0	8.6	7.7	8.4
Students	9.4	9.2	8.4	8.8

[a] The question: "After the closure of the National Assembly, social groups took different postures toward the government. If "1" is total support and "10" total opposition, where would you locate?"
[b] Includes two Civic Union leaders, one Patriotic Union leader, and a political adviser to the regime who was a high-ranking officer.

Another interesting detail to emerge in Table 4.2 is the comparative disagreement among politicians of different parties regarding the role of the "Unity and Reform" sector of the Colorado party ("List 15"). Whereas leftist politicians saw it as rather close to the regime (assigning an average score of 3.9), Colorados placed it at the opposite end of the spectrum (8.3), and Blancos placed it in the middle, but squarely in the opposition (6.1). It was that faction that during the dictatorship would reemerge as the leading Colorado sector and would elect the first president of the restored democracy in 1984.

The regime's social isolation was only slightly less pronounced, support being limited to business and financial interests and, to a lesser extent, ranchers, in the eyes of almost all politicians interviewed (Table 4.3).' However, Colorados saw rather less class polarization than did other interviewees; they tended to see less social support for the regime among the economic elite (except ranchers), but slightly more support than did other parties among civil servants, blue- and white-collar workers, and students. Another interesting fact was that all parties saw state elites, such as judges, as being strongly opposed to the military regime. Blancos perceived far more opposition among farmers and ranchers (a traditional Blanco constituency) than did other politicians.

Government support from the business elite seems to have peaked in 1978, the year price controls were lifted on meat, to the intense acclamation of the ranchers. Although relations with business associations were intimate throughout the *proceso* (e.g., the president of the Chamber of

Industries was made ambassador to London on retiring), the spokesmen of capital did not go out of their way to make public demonstrations of support for the regime.[39]

Political parties in suspended animation

If the danger of de jure abolition had passed for the traditional parties, two other dangers had not: co-optation by the regime and displacement by a new "officialist" party. In many ways the situation inside the parties was no less confused than that within the regime. Sectors of the Colorado party (principally the Pachequistas)[40] operated within the framework of the new institutions. Somewhat more of the Blancos, however, resisted such overtures, with the exception of some aged Herreristas. In general, the backwardness and lack of fiscal autonomy in rural areas made politicians more cooperative in the interior. Important debates on tactics divided both the traditional parties and those of the Broad Front, between which contact was at that stage nonexistent. The situation was complicated by differences that grew between leaders in exile and those who stayed at home. Yet in the Blanco party, exiled leader Wilson Ferreira made the controversial decision to forge an alliance with the Left, known as Convergencia Democrática en Uruguay.

Given the extremely weak and disorganized position of the traditional political parties, how can we explain their survival? Deprived of their access to state resources, they were unable to operate the patronage networks that had provided many of their sectors with votes. Like American parties, the Colorados and Blancos had no formal membership, no card-carrying or dues-paying affiliates. Since the 1960s, they had benefited from state financing during election campaigns, based on the total number of votes they received. In the most traditional rural areas, patronage may have survived to the extent that it was based on the influence and private resources of *caudillos*, principally in the nongovernmental sphere. However, in cities, electoral machines had ground to a halt, for without a raison d'être they had no money or headquarters. The parties' survival in suspended animation was made possible by the absence of any military project to displace them. And even had such an effort been undertaken, it is hardly conceivable that they would not have one day revived, simply because they were so central to Uruguay's political culture.

Confusion on the Left was severe, given the failure of both the guerrilla strategy and the electoral road. Despite terrible repression, the Mesa Ejecutiva of the Broad Front was very occasionally able to operate in

---

39 That contrasted strongly to the Chilean situation, as González (1985b) has pointed out.
40 One Colorado who did make his opposition to the regime explicit was Batlle.

clandestinity. Some leftist politicians, such as socialist leader José Pedro Cardoso, made political speeches when abroad. The Front's presidential candidate in 1971, General Líber Seregni, continued to smuggle out political pronouncements from jail. Nevertheless, an inevitable tendency for the exiles in Washington, Paris, Mexico, and Stockholm to lose touch with the climate of domestic opinion led to serious doubts about their future levels of support or the extent of their self-criticism.

Perhaps belatedly, much of the Left put political democracy in the forefront of its creed. It might be argued that the rehabilitation of "bourgeois" democracy was merely an instrument of the ideological struggle. However, the communists had always been critical both of the adventurism of the terrorists and of the "petit bourgeois ultraleftism" of the socialists and other neo-Marxists. In fact, Uruguay's Communist party (PCU) to some extent represented a moderating force within the Broad Front.[41] The atomization and confusion of the Left that the authoritarian regime created meant that they were not necessarily in the best position to profit from the renewed mobilization of students and labor as the crisis of the regime accelerated after 1980, and especially before Seregni was released in March 1984.

Political survival strategies

The affairs of the traditional parties were provisionally placed in the hands of two triumvirates.[42] To cast light on the survival mechanisms of the parties, the politicians interviewed were asked how often they had been able to maintain political contacts before the 1980 plebiscite brought limited toleration of political activity. A majority of leaders from all parties reported having had frequent contact with fellow politicians of their own parties, but Frentistas reported fewer contacts than average,. and Blancos more.[43] Conversations with politicians in other parties were reported to have been rare, especially among Blancos and Frentistas. On the other hand, contacts with long-standing political associates had been kept up, though Colorados reported having maintained the least touch.[44]

41 Gillespie (1985).
42 The Blanco executive (*directorio*) chose Carlos Julio Pereyra, Dardo Ortiz, and Mario Heber – all opponents of the military. In the Colorado party, various shades of opponents of the regime appointed themselves without a vote of the national Executive Committee: Jorge Batlle, Amílcar Vasconcellos, and Raumar Judé.
43 As in all the questions that follow regarding contacts and activities, responses were coded 1 for "frequent," 2 for "rare," and 3 for "never." The Blanco average was 1.3, compared with 1.8 for the Frente. (Significance = .17.)
44 Blancos = 1.4, Colorados = 1.7 (p = .10). Frentistas scored 1.5.

Table 4.4. *Contacts and activities of politicians under authoritarianism*[a]

Contacts	Broad Front (n = 8)	Blancos (n = 16)	Colorados (n = 19)	All[b] (n = 47)
Internal party life				
Leaders of same *lema*	50[c]	75	58	60
Longtime supporters	63	69	37	51
Private meetings	75	63	37	50
Leaders of other *lemas*	13	13	37	23
New activists	25	19	17	18
External party life				
Journalists	0	56	53	45
Students	50	27	53	41
Christians	50	27	11	24
Human-rights organizations	38	21	11	18
Trade-unionists	38	7	11	14
Military	11	0	16	11
Exiles	25	7	5	9
Open meetings	0	13	5	7
Business associations	0	7	5	4

[a] The question: "Would you specifically tell me the type and frequency of contacts you had with the following groups between 1976 and 1980?"
[b] Includes three Civic Union leaders and one Patriotic Union leader.
[c] Percentage having "frequent" contacts.

All parties admitted that contacts with new activists had been rare in that period (Table 4.4).

Leaders of the Left and leaders of the Blanco party both claimed to have sometimes attended private gatherings (i.e., those at which strangers were not admitted), whereas Colorados reported such gatherings to have been rare prior to 1980.[45] No party reported having had much contact with human-rights groups, and contacts with exiles had also been infrequent among the traditional parties, including the Blancos, even though their major leader, Wilson Ferreira, had fled the country. One can speculate whether that handicapped the party in its efforts to develop a coherent strategy. Contact with exiles had been more common among the Left, presumably because so many more leftist leaders had been obliged to flee the country.[46] With regard to journalists, the traditional parties had

45 Blancos = 1.5, Colorados = 1.9, Frente = 1.5. The significance of the difference between Blancos and Colorados was .11.
46 Colorados = 2.6, Frente = 2.0 (*p* = .05). With the Blancos' major leader, Wilson Ferreira, in exile in London, one might have expected them to have reported more contact with exiles than did Colorados. In fact, their average (2.4) was not significantly different.

maintained better channels of communication.[47] On the other hand, the Left reported having had closer contacts with members of the Catholic church and lay Christians. It is probably the old anticlerical tradition among Colorados that explains their slightly less frequent contact with church members, as compared with Blancos.[48]

Finally, interviewees were asked about their links with certain key social sectors. Traditional politicians recalled very few contacts with labor leaders, and even leftist leaders reported them to have been rare.[49] There were no strikes in Uruguay during the first decade of military rule, and trade-union activity was extremely dangerous. What is revealing, however, is that the traditional parties also reported having had only infrequent contacts with chambers of commerce and business associations. Such contacts probably had been limited by businessmen's fear of associating with individuals who had been "banned" under the Fourth Institutional Act. All parties reported having had almost no contact with the military (though it is probable that such contacts were underreported).

The picture that emerges is one of retreat into their shells by the traditional parties: Internal party life seems to have dwindled, especially in the Colorado party. In the Blanco party, leaders maintained closer touch with one another. The relative strength of the pro-regime Pachequistas in the Colorado party and the party's less active opposition to the regime probably accounted for their reporting of less contact among the elite of the party. Most interestingly, unlike the politicians in other parties, the Colorados had as much contact with leaders of other parties as with their own longtime supporters. That probably reflected the Colorado's relative lack of militant cadres and perhaps their greater commitment to coordinating with other political groups; they also reported having held far fewer secret meetings than did the other parties. With the exception of their access to the press, the traditional parties remained in relative isolation from social movements. If the Blancos adopted a less passive attitude, it is also notable that they made little effort (or had little' success) when it came to reaching out to formerly organized groups of civil society. Their weak ties to labor were perhaps understandable, given labor's leftist traditions, but the Blancos' lack of contact with students should have concerned those Wilsonistas who sought to mobilize allegedly radicalized youth sectors against the regime.[50]

---

47 Blancos and Colorados = 1.6, Frente = 2.4. (Significance = .01 and .02, respectively.)

48 Blancos = 1.9, Colorados = 2.3, Frente = 1.4. (The significance of the gap between traditional parties and the Left was .09 and .01, respectively).

49 Blancos = 2.5, Colorados = 2.6, Frente = 2.0. (For the Colorado–Frente difference, p = .06.)

50 In the late 1950s, the Movimiento Universitario Nacionalista had been one of the major student organizations.

Despite experiencing much greater repression and internal disruption, the Left cultivated far more links with different components of organized civil society than did the traditional parties, particularly sectors of the Catholic church, students, and (clandestine) trade unions. Although the Left kept up a great deal of clandestine contact with longtime supporters and claimed to have held slightly more private meetings and to have recruited more new activists than did the Blancos, they did not simply retreat into their shells. Rather, they sought to forge links with other social groups, some of which remained legal, in effect, "to metastasize." That pattern accorded not only with the Left's traditional organization and penetration of social movements, such as labor unions, but also with the necessities of political life under authoritarianism. Certain social movements became surrogates for leftist party activity, which was wholly illegal until 1984.

The dilemmas of rule for the military

President Bordaberry's memorandum to the military had warned them that by assuming the tasks of administration they would be equally led to assume public responsibility for success or failure ("as if they were a party"). Not only was this "improper," but it would lead to "frequent clashes and friction with civilians," introduce divisions, and threaten their esprit de corps. One of the few areas of agreement between Végh's and Bordaberry's memos had been that the reality of military power was potentially threatening to the armed forces as an institution. They disagreed on the solution, Végh charging that Bordaberry's corporatist plan would in fact increase the danger of an "internal rupture" of the military.

Despite the militarization of public administration, which tended to jeopardize the attempt to cut spending, the regime made no early attempt to establish its own clientelist support base, either within the traditional parties or by founding a new party (as was loudly favored by Colonel Bolentini) on the Brazilian model. That was somewhat surprising, given the large size of Uruguay's public sector, the number of civil-service jobs to be filled as alleged subversives were fired, and the growth of "perks." The real obstacle was not simply a lack of resources, but the more complex problem that the provision of welfare-state programs could not easily be exchanged for votes when sophisticated Uruguayans had already come to see such programs as their birthright. In structural terms, the possibility of using state patronage to take over an existing party, launch a new party, and/or combine this with some form of corporatist institutionalization was highly circumscribed.

The armed forces were probably influenced by their own rhetoric of "housecleaning" and the common military aversion to "dirty" party politics. As one retired colonel and frequent cabinet minister put it, "the leaders of the *proceso* thought it improper to get involved in politics. . . . Politics was vetoed for everyone for eleven years."[51] They were also hampered by the lack of a clear leader – the same colonel sighed, and stated wanly, "we had the misfortune to lack a De Gaulle." He rejected the view that the absence of any preponderance of historical ties to either traditional party among the officer corps made any difference. In his view, it was simply disdain for politics that stood in the way of creating a pro-regime party. However, another reason seems to have been fear of concentration of power in too few hands. For example, the vast patronage powers of an existing political machine, the Byzantine city government of Montevideo, were left completely intact under the conservative Colorado mayor elected in 1971. As an influential air-force colonel alleged, "they claimed that [Mayor] Rachetti had their confidence, and that they were concerned at potential failure in such an important job, but the real reason was that they were scared of too much power."[52]

Concern that "politicization" of the armed forces might subvert the internal hierarchies and discipline on which they relied led to occasional purges.[53] Ironically, the alternative of avoiding a permanent formalization of military power without building a pro-regime party produced precisely the two problems that both Végh and Bordaberry had identified. The political vacuum was accompanied by a vacillating, subterraneanly divided military. As early as 1976, the seeds of potential military concern for their institutional interests under the authoritarian regime were planted. That pointed to a divergence between the interests of the military as government and their interests as a complex bureaucratic hierarchy committed to survival beyond the ambitions of any particular leaders.[54] Such divergences have the potential to lead to democratic transitions; however, those conflicting roles would only break out into the open much later.

The search for legitimacy and institutionalization

The first cautious attempt to break out of the circularity of the situation of power without accountability fell far short of liberalization, let alone

51 Personal interview, Montevideo, 31 October 1984.
52 Personal interview, Montevideo, 15 April 1985. One wonders if they may not have feared the worst regarding the temptations of corruption as well.
53 On the military purges, see Remmer and Merkx (1982). Although information on events within the hierarchy of this closed bureaucratic institution obviously is scarce, circumstantial, and often suspect, there were reports of differences between figures such as the generals Vadora, Alvarez, and Queirolo, the successive commanders in chief of the army. The alleged disputes in the high command can be traced in the *Latin American Weekly Report*, London (1978–81). Their reliability is difficult to determine.
54 Stepan (1986, pp. 76–8).

redemocratization.[55] In fact, the real transition would not even appear on the horizon until after the attempt at plebiscitary legitimation had failed. Partly as a result of pressure from the Carter administration, the power struggle in the army resulted in a complex victory in 1977 for the proponents of what was called the *cronograma* (timetable) for return to elections in 1981. But first a new constitution would be drafted and submitted to a referendum in 1980, and then the traditional parties would have to agree to a single joint candidate, who would also have to meet the approval of the National Security Council (COSENA).[56] The proposed sequence was to decree a constitution, then write a new party statute and hold elections. As a young military éminence grise of the *proceso* put it, "it was a major mistake to call into being a new constitution before reactivating the parties. It was a huge political error not to allow political activity to produce new leaders: No local elections meant no political leaders. It was like putting everything in the freezer for ten years. I told [the generals] this, but it was like barking at the moon."[57]

The military's motives in risking their continuing position of strength in a more or less clean electoral consultation have never been fully established. Several interviewees suggested that after he retired as army commander in 1979, General Alvarez's personal political ambitions intervened. According to one pro-regime Colorado, "the idea was invented by Alvarez, who thought that with Pacheco and Gallinal they would win."[58] Another conservative (but not promilitary) Colorado stated flatly that "the whole idea of the 1980 plebiscite was that General Alvarez wanted to be president."[59] In fact, as Table 4.5 shows, there is significant disagreement among politicians of different parties as to the military's intentions and reasoning. For instance, in answer to question B, the Colorados were far less willing than were leaders of other parties to believe that vestigial remnants of Uruguay's democratic political culture in the military institution had any influence on regime strategy. This constitutes an interesting first clue to their sober, not to say pessimistic, appreciation of what they were up against.

The Left tended to place great emphasis on the weight of international pressure on the regime, as presumably fitted their greater involvement in exile politics (question C). The leftists were also the most honest in admitting that pressure from social groups, such as the church or unions,

---

55 As reported in Table 4.5, question A, even a majority of those interviewees with military connections agreed that the government saw the proposed new constitution as a means to consolidate their power rather than hand it back to the politicians.

56 Lanzaro (1980). See also Torres (1981).

57 Personal interview, Montevideo, 1984.

58 Personal interview, Montevideo, 22 July 1984.

59 Personal interview, Montevideo, 29 September 1984.

Table 4.5. *Perceptions of military motives in calling the 1980 plebiscite*[a]

Explanation	Broad Front ($n = 8$)	Blancos ($n = 14$)	Colorados ($n = 18$)	Military[b] ($n = 5$)
(A) The government had reached its objectives and sought to consolidate its power	87[c]	79	83	60
(B) The reflections of democratic culture that the armed forces may retain	50	64	17	60
(C) International pressure for civil rights and isolation made legitimation vital	87	64	47	40
(D) Governments since 1973 have been based on force, lacking legitimacy, as liberal traditions are too deep-seated	100	93	72	80
(E) Rising popular pressure and actions by political and social groups made delay impossible	0	50	22	20
(F) Action by the traditional parties (Colorados and Blancos)	0	36	17	0
(G) Fragmentation and conflicts in the civilian coalition which supported the government	0	36	17	20
(H) Questioning of government legitimacy by constitutionalist military sectors	12	7	29	40
(I) Questioning "from inside" by civilians, bureaucrats, technocrats, and experts	12	29	22	0
(J) The example of the Brazilian "opening" (*abertura*)	37	15	18	20
(K) The example set by Pinochet's regime in Chile	37	46	33	0

[a] The question: "The government drew up a Constitution for a new institutional order and eventually submitted its plans to the 1980 plebiscite. Which of the following reasons did they hold?"
[b] Includes two high-ranking officers close to the regime and three in retirement, active in opposition politics.
[c] Percentage agreeing with the explanation.

played no role at all in the military's calculations – a point on which the Blancos were perhaps unduly sanguine (question E). Leftists were also scathing as to the influence of the traditional parties, and military interviewees agreed (question F).[60] The few officers, interestingly enough, were far more likely to see questioning of the regime's legitimacy "from within" as a cause of the decision to hold the plebiscite (question H). None felt that civilians in the regime had provided such pressure (question I).

Crisis and failed institutionalization

The attempt to portray a vote for the proposed new constitution as a vote for democracy failed.[61] "Yes" meant support for the military's past record and for new authoritarian constitutional provisions, such as the permanent executive role of the National Security Council and the proposed "Political Control Commission" under its jurisdiction, which would have had the authority to dismiss any civilian official, including the president. The commission would also have had the power to "sanction national authorities or party leaders for any act seriously affecting the proper exercise of their functions." Most objectionable were the provisions for a single candidate for president in the first transitional election and the new "declaration of a state of emergency" clause to replace the much-abused "prompt security measures" incorporated into the 1967 Constitution. Finally, the proposed constitution would have prohibited all leftist parties and permitted strikes only in the private sector.

The military saturated radio and television broadcast with commercials and controlled almost all of the press, including the Colorado *El Día* and the Blanco *El País*.[62] Given the government propaganda against a "no" vote, it was surprising that only 2% of voters cast blank or spoiled ballots, and even more surprising that the parties were able to organize at all in the very limited time available. The levels of repression and fear remained enormous in the country, and arbitrary arrests of those attempting any kind of political activity did not diminish. In fact, the announcement of the defeat of the proposed constitution led to a new wave of arrests.

In the interior, small towns often were dominated by a military garrison, and deliberate rumors were spread that those who voted "no" would

---

60 An average of 25% of the politicians saw the traditional parties as having exerted pressure, but not one of the five active or high-ranking officers interviewed saw that (significance = .003). Although the representativity of the officers interviewed may be challenged, on this point the evidence was firm.

61 Though a token attempt had been made at consulting conservative sectors of the traditional parties, the military ignored all the politicians' wishes; for instance, the proposed constitution would have abolished both the double simultaneous vote and proportional representation.

62 Reports suggest that the government's campaign cost up to $30 million.

be found out and deprived of their pensions. Yet it was inevitable that the military would not win the support of politicians whom they had banned until 1991.[63] The only major leaders to call for a "yes" vote were Pacheco and Gallinal, so the military's strategy depended upon the electorate ignoring, or being unaware of, the position of the banned politicians. In practice, surrogates sprang up, leaving little ambiguity as to whom they represented, and the traditional parties were allowed to organize a limited last-minute campaign. Opposition Colorados managed to publish two issues of a magazine, *Opinar*,[64] in time for the vote, and both parties were permitted to hold one meeting each in Montevideo cinemas.

The announcement that the *cronograma* had been defeated by 57.2% to 42.8%, on a turnout of 85.2%, stunned the military as much as the opposition (Table 4.6). According to one theory, the government was so convinced that victory would be theirs – as it was Pinochet's in Chile – that they waited too long to falsify the results. Perhaps, too, they had been misled by inaccurate polls due to the reticence of interviewees under the authoritarian regime.[65]

It is plausible that one factor in the defeat was the compression of real wages made possible by abolition of the Consejos de Salarios under Pacheco. That had been followed by the erosion of minimum wage levels because of inflation.[66] Rapid economic growth, the impressive improvement in the trade balance, and the brief balancing of the budget had been achieved at great social cost. It was not true that only the Left-dominated heartland had voted "no" (as investigation of the ecological pattern of voting shows), and, of course, the total "no" vote was over three times higher than the leftist vote had been in 1971. It was also found that young and first-time voters had voted overwhelmingly "no" (they were distinguishable by their higher voter-registration numbers).[67] Nevertheless, the opposition's victory was not overwhelming; more than two-fifths of the voters had voted for the military's plans.

63 Although some conservatives and second-rank leaders had had their political rights restored, there still were about 300 banned politicians.

64 *Opinar* was published by Enrique Tarigo, who was politically liberal but socially conservative. Many of its staff, like Tarigo, had left *El Día*.

65 With circumspection, Gallup pronounced the result "too close to call" in its last published polls before the voting took place. That was based not on the figures for respondents who had made up their minds and were willing to be interviewed but on the large number of "don't know" answers and refusals.

66 Eventually, wages were fully "liberated" – the government no longer announced across-the-board wage increases, although the private sector tended to follow trends in public-sector pay.

67 For further details on the plebiscite and its result, see González (1983a, 1983b). González denies that economics played a part in the opposition victory, arguing that the economy was booming in 1980.

Table 4.6. *Results of the plebiscite by department*

Department	Percentages		Votes			
	Yes	No	Yes	No	Blank	Void[a]
Departments voting "no"						
Montevideo	36.1	63.9	264,696	469,275	4,984	29,791
Interior	47.7	52.4	379,162	416,549	4,950	87,519
Paysandú	33.5	66.4	16,481	32,707	262	6,737
San José	37.2	62.8	16,880	28,484	249	3,628
Salto	38.3	61.7	20,036	32,312	352	7,480
Rio Negro	43.4	56.6	9,913	12,884	133	2,327
Maldonado	43.4	56.6	20,379	26,607	338	2,523
Colonia	44.3	55.7	29,098	36,545	361	5,319
Florida	45.1	54.9	15,899	19,400	205	4,239
Canelones	46.3	53.7	73,064	84,673	1,176	10,106
Durazno	47.0	53.0	12,401	14,000	155	4,090
Cerro Largo	48.8	51.2	18,185	19,105	185	6,194
Departments voting "yes"						
Soriano	50.3	49.7	22,440	22,188	280	4,938
Lavalleja	53.2	46.8	19,157	16,184	207	3,615
Tacuarembó	53.8	46.2	21,241	18,225	245	7,196
Flores	56.1	43.9	8,224	6,457	84	636
Rocha	56.6	43.4	19,176	14,723	227	4,067
Artigas	61.8	38.2	16,012	9,938	130	4,733
Rivera	63.9	36.1	24,990	14,110	238	6,114
Treinta y Tres	67.8	32.2	15,586	7,377	123	3,577
Total for Uruguay	42.0	57.9	643,858	885,824	9,934	117,310

[a] Includes annulled and challenged (*observado*) at first count.
Source: Uruguay, Corte Electoral, Oficina Nacional Electoral, *Plebiscito Constitucional 30 de Noviembre de 1980* (mimeograph).

The important conclusion that Luis González drew from an ecological study of the plebiscite was that opposition to the regime was not confined to what he termed the "modern sector" (*el país moderno*), but was broadly based nationwide.[68]

Postmortem on the plebiscite

Almost all the politicians interviewed agreed that the persistence of democratic values in Uruguayan political culture explained the extraordinary result of the plebiscite. Nearly as much weight was placed on the role of the incipient opposition, particularly the last-minute television debate in

68 González (1983b).

Table 4.7. *Perceived causes of the military's defeat in the 1980 plebiscite*[a]

Explanation	Left ($n = 8$)	Blancos ($n = 14$)	Colorados ($n = 18$)	Military[b] ($n = 5$)
(A) The persistence of democratic values in the culture	100[c]	85	94	80
(B) The role of the incipient opposition and TV debates	75	92	94	80
(C) Discontent at regime policies (other than economic)	75	77	82	80
(D) The influence of political-opinion leaders	87	69	67	100
(E) The survival of political-party apparatuses	50	69	67	60
(F) Discontent at the regime's economic policies	62	62	61	80
(G) The lack of influence of official propaganda	12	31	78	80

[a]The question: "Why did the constitution submitted to plebiscite in 1980 fail to be approved?"
[b]Includes two high-ranking officers close to the regime and three from the opposition.
[c]Percentage agreeing with the explanation.

which a little-known Colorado, Enrique Tarigo, resoundingly denounced the details of the proposed new text.[69] It was more often believed that discontent had been directed at the regime in general rather than at specific economic policies.

One notable finding, as shown in Table 4.7 (albeit on the basis of a small number of cases), concerns the unanimous belief of those military officers interviewed that the influence of politicians, despite their banning from public activity, had contributed to the defeat of the proposed new constitution (question D).[70] Another split opinion concerned the potency of the military's propaganda: The Left and the Blancos seemed inclined to believe that it had had significant influence in the voting, though not enough to bring victory (question G). Otherwise, there was broad agreement that party apparatuses or the influence of opinion leaders mattered little, or not at all.

69 His articles were collected and published (Tarigo 1982).
70 Whereas all military interviewees agreed with this point, 28% of civilian politicians did not (significance = .000).

Repercussions of the defeat in the regime

Defeat for their political plan threw the military into confusion. Hard-line extreme rightists in the regime claimed that the result was a victory for international communism, but the commanders in chief remained silent for a while. Then, on 3 December, they issued a joint communiqué announcing that the government would comply with the people's verdict, pronouncing the political plan of 1977 null and void. They promised that the process of "democratic institutionalization" would continue irreversibly, and a new plan would be sought. In the meantime, however, the *proceso* would continue "on the basis of the current regime."

That decision to mark time did not, however, resolve the immediate question of who should be named president, let alone what new plan to propose. In March of 1981 Uruguayans were amazed to read in the press of financial scandals and corrupt dealings involving various hard-line generals.[71] The ousting of the extreme right was seen as a victory for moderates and liberals, such as General Yamandú Trinidad, who became the new interior minister, and General Abdon Raimúndez (Alvarez's brother-in-law), who was president of the Central Bank. Personalities seem to have counted for a lot, however, and subsequently the moderation of these so-called Alvarezistas was to appear less clear. In terms of the rarefied politics of the military, "moderates" meant those in favor of maintaining the commitment to a gradual return to civilian rule, but no general seems to have favored such a process unconditionally. Politicians would first have to pay a price.

On 28 April, Rear Admiral Rodolfo Invidio became commander in chief of the navy and made a speech at his installation calling for a "government freely elected by the citizens which will guarantee a republican, representative democracy, tailored to reality and the needs of the people." During July, the new head of the Armed Forces Commission on Political Affairs (COMASPO) summoned Colorados, anti-Wilsonista Blancos, and representatives from the small Civic Union for talks on the political future. Those groups were invited to propose new members for the Council of State. Though the anti-Wilsonista Blancos reportedly were amenable, the Colorados insisted that freedom of speech and association must first be restored, and the proscription of nearly 300 traditional politicians, still banned under the Fourth Institutional Act, had to be lifted. At the end of July, the commission set up under the 1976 insti-

---

71 The minister of the interior, General Manuel Núñez, was forced to resign, and so were the Montevideo police chief, Colonel Walter Arregui, the head of the Arms and Services School, General Alberto Ballestrino, and General Julio César Vadora, former army commander and ambassador to Paraguay.

tutional acts began to lift the bans on about 100 moderate conservatives. It was also announced that indoor political meetings of up to 40 people would be allowed. The boycott of the Council of State by the majority, however, continued.

The military continually tried to justify every action as necessary for the promotion of democracy and the elimination of threats to its restoration, thereby in many ways revealing the inhospitable climate for authoritarian ideologies. Whether reluctantly or willingly, the armed forces remained trapped in the discourse of democracy.

The military regime's crisis of legitimacy

A fundamental approach to explaining regime stability revolves around legitimacy, or its absence. The weight of tradition or of law, so often emphasized by Weber, was almost entirely lacking in Uruguay's military regime. Somewhat as Dworkin has defined rights as entitlements that "trump" utilitarian calculus, we may define legitimacy as a quality that trumps regime performance. Thus, regimes that are performing quite poorly may survive for relatively long periods precisely because they are legitimate. One can also imagine the opposite circumstance: a regime that performs well (i.e., makes effective decisions vis-à-vis challenges), but nevertheless becomes unstable because it is viewed as illegitimate. One interpretation of the defeat of the proposed 1980 constitution at a time of relative peace and prosperity centers precisely on the military's lack of legitimacy.[72]

The Achilles' heel of Latin American authoritarian regimes – more so than for authoritarian regimes in the rest of the Third World – has been precisely their lack of legitimacy in the eyes of the majority of their populations. This is particularly apparent if we compare them to prewar fascist or populist rule. Much of the time they are forced, more or less lamely, to claim to be defending democracy from "subversion" or from "totalitarianism." A pretended transitory nature almost by definition rules out institutionalized legitimacy. However much national-security doctrines may have influenced elites and been inculcated in the armed forces, nowhere have they achieved mass popularity. So long as the military retain power, therefore, a *state of exception* effectively exists.[73] Their search for

72 The heart of legitimacy is a willingness among citizens to abide by legal norms and rules regardless of their substantive content or implications. Such loyalty to a political system is most apparent when to some eyes it may appear to run counter to immediate self-interest.

73 This does not imply that authoritarian regimes inaugurated by military intervention can nowhere achieve institutionalization and legitimacy. It does, however, mean that they cannot forever remain as "stratocracies," a term coined by Finer (1985) to mean rule by the military as such, rather than civilian dictators merely installed and maintained by military force.

legitimacy is thus fundamentally *apologetic*. An attempt at legitimization and institutionalization that "gets out of hand" is in fact a common means by which transitions from authoritarian regimes begin.

Luis Eduardo González has argued that the crisis of the Uruguayan authoritarian regime began as an unintended consequence of its own failed project to found a plebiscitary dictatorship.[74] Unlike the new Chilean Constitution, also submitted to plebiscite in 1980, the blueprint was rejected by Uruguayan voters. However, as an explanation for a democratic transition, analysis of legitimacy is incomplete. The regime was clearly shown to be illegitimate by 1980, and almost certainly well before that, but power was not handed over to civilians for almost another five years. One could say that a legitimacy crisis was a necessary background condition for the transition, but had little bearing on either its subsequent timing or characteristic path. Though unstable, illegitimate regimes can always use coercion to survive, which is essentially what the Uruguayan military did. A focus on legitimacy problems thus offers an explanation of why a transition occurs, but says almost nothing about how or when. The latter questions are taken up in Chapters 6 and 7, but first we turn to the revival of political parties in the wake of the military's defeat in the plebiscite.

74 González (1985c).

PART II

From authoritarian crisis to transition

5

Attempts at party renewal: from above and below

Military regimes may attempt to co-opt or displace political parties; in Uruguay, little success was achieved in either direction. Continuing reliance was therefore placed on repression, and in the case of the Left the military's aim was permanent destruction. Yet the effect of attempted elimination by an authoritarian regime can be to force a party's leaders into exile and to force its cadres underground, without totally disarticulating its organization, as happened, for example, to the Communist party in Uruguay. One result can be the breakup of parties into rival factions disputing a common heritage, as happened to the Christian Democratic party and the pro-Tupamaro "26th of March" movement. These factions may survive or they may wither, possibly even to the point of exhausting the lineage. Other policies pursued by authoritarian regimes may have unintended consequences, particularly where they achieve socioeconomic modernization, or simply change. In Uruguay, it was the unintended effects of the military's political strategy that had the most impact on parties, causing them to revive.[1] In 1976, the military stipulated by means of the Fourth Institutional Act that only the most cooperative leaders would be allowed to engage in political activity. Over the next four years an obscure commission slowly began to "deproscribe" the military's allies.

Following the disaster of defeat in the plebiscite, the military's long-term plan – to strengthen and purge the traditional parties – was not abandoned. Rather, emphasis shifted from revising the Constitution to first restoring a limited degree of party activity in order to fill the void between rulers and ruled. It was admitted that more "deproscriptions" were necessary (300 traditional politicians were still deprived of their rights at the beginning of 1981). Political parties would, however, have to be more firmly structured and less subject to factionalism in order to make them bulwarks against the Left.

1 The unintended effects of their economic strategy (a slump) affected the parties, too, by rousing popular discontent.

The ideas and aims of those who sought to renovate the Colorados' and Blancos' decayed apparatuses were wholly different from those of the military. Rather than reforms "from above" based on legal regulation and interference, the opposition renovators sought reform "from below" to expand participation in their parties – from campaigning against the authoritarian regime to candidate selection and programmatic renewal. Among the most significant renovator groups in the Colorado party were Enrique Tarigo's Libertad y Cambio (Freedom and Change) and Manuel Flores Silva's Corriente Batllista Independiente (CBI), which had a younger and more progressive following. In the Blanco party the renovators were to be found in both major Wilsonista factions – Por la Patria and Movimiento de Rocha – and in the so-called *coordinadoras* (neighborhood committees) that developed into a radical faction with the name of Corriente Popular Nacionalista (CPN), loyal to Wilson's son, Juan Raúl.

The convocation of "valid interlocutors"

Within the military, the 1980 defeat of the proposed constitution led to a power struggle between those who argued that redemocratization must continue, with more input from the "valid interlocutors" of the traditional parties, and those who thought that democracy should be taken off the agenda. Out of that bitter conflict the retired general Gregorio Alvarez achieved his goal of becoming the regime's first noncivilian president, by ruthlessly exposing the corrupt dealings of his opponents, in particular the extreme rightist General Ballestrino. That betrayal of esprit de corps likely earned him further enemies.[2] Alvarez often was mistakenly seen as a soft-liner regarding a return of power to civilians. In fact, he did not favor a return to an apolitical and professional military. On the contrary, political ambitions led him to harbor a form of military populism.

Defeat of the proposed authoritarian constitution logically suggested the need for a dialogue with the opposition. The military, however, were still wedded to their list of demands regarding the "strengthening" of democracy. Eventually, COMASPO (the Armed Forces Commission on Political Affairs) began talks with the traditional parties. Following President Alvarez's inauguration in September 1981, it was announced that new machinery for primary elections would be set up so that the traditional parties might choose fresh leaders. In that same month the Wilsonista magazine *La Democracia* was temporarily closed down for publishing a

---

2 According to a businessman who maintained social relations with prominent interests backing Alvarez, he was able to swing the junta behind him only by threatening even larger exposés of corruption (personal interview, Montevideo, August 1981). According to a pro-regime Colorado, Alvarez's former ally and subsequent rival, General Raimúndez, missed becoming president by one vote (personal interview, Montevideo, 28 August 1984).

Table 5.1. *The double simultaneous vote*[a]

Answer	Left (%) ($n = 17$)	Blancos (%) ($n = 23$)	Colorados (%) ($n = 25$)	All[b] (%) ($n = 70$)
Yes	0.0	34.8	64.0	34.3
No	100.0	60.9	20.0	58.6
Other[c]	.0	4.3	16.0	7.1
Total	100.0	100.0	100.0	100.0

[a] The question: "Uruguayan electoral law incorporates the double simultaneous vote. Should it be maintained?"
[b] Includes one Patriotic Union and three Civic Union leaders and a political adviser to the regime.
[c] Includes those wishing to see the double simultaneous vote retained for legislative or presidential elections only, or as a temporary arrangement.

letter from a banned Christian Democrat. When the Christian Democrats' magazine protested, it, too, was closed. Thus had begun the clear pattern of stick and carrot: Certain things could be said by certain people, but there was no question of freedom of expression and association for all.

At the end of 1981, talks were held between moderate leaders of the traditional parties and the generals, but this time at the headquarters of the Joint Chiefs of Staff (ESMACO) rather than at COMASPO. That shift seems to have represented an effort to make a fresh start in relations between military and politicians.[3] The draft for a "statute on parties" that emerged from those talks maintained the exclusion of the Left and the bans on many leading Colorado and Blanco politicians, but restored the double simultaneous vote and attempted to dictate the internal functioning of the parties through a complex set of rules regarding electoral lists, the party conventions, the executive bodies, and their programs. As Table 5.1 shows, the Left unanimously condemned the double simultaneous vote, as did three-fifths of Blancos. Sensing on which side their bread was buttered, almost two-thirds of Colorados supported its retention. Quite simply, the party had done well under the existing electoral arrangements, losing control of the executive branch only twice during this century (1959–67). Nevertheless, the realization that factionalism might have globally damaging consequences for democracy (and therefore for politicians) seems to have been gaining ground. As a leader

3 Allegedly, the proposed statute on parties that emerged from those talks was heavily influenced by three Colorados (Barbagelata, Rodríguez, and Sanguinetti) and General Raimúndez (personal interview with a Colorado editor, Montevideo, December 1984).

associated with Libertad y Cambio put it, "parties should have no more than two internal currents – for this reason we have stayed with Batllism."[4]

The double simultaneous vote has been repeatedly linked to a variety of characteristics of Uruguayan politics (or their absence), such as adaptability, dogmatism, personalism, indiscipline, stability, traditionalism, and transformism. Quite apart from the alleged directions of such effects, politicians and commentators have also disputed the *desirability* of particular phenomena. Thus, it was unsurprising that rejection of the system should turn out to be bound up with differing views as to its precise impact, as Table 5.2 shows. Majorities of interviewees in each party agreed that the double simultaneous vote was a barrier to dogmatism, but whereas the Colorados saw it as a source of flexibility, the Left saw it as a great obstacle to change and party adaptation. Blancos were less likely to agree that the double simultaneous vote accentuated personality disputes, and they were also far more likely to disagree that it had been a cause of party survival over the years (especially for the traditional parties, as the Left believed). As a party frequently in power and widely agreed to be favored by the system, the Colorados were reluctant to admit (unlike the other parties) that the double simultaneous vote might favor parliamentary indiscipline. Finally, whereas Blancos were the most likely to believe that the double simultaneous vote tended to favor interparty alliances, a majority did not think that was a good thing, unlike the Colorados. Here we see the subtle, transformist Colorado synthesis: Strong executive authority should be combined with flexible, consensual, and undogmatic government.

The draft of the new statute, known as the "Second Organic Law," was submitted to the Council of State in January 1982. It banned parties "with foreign links" and those "advocating violence," while stipulating that in order to register for elections, parties had to be internally democratic. The intellectual justification for intervening in the internal processes of political parties, which had never before been subject to legal regulation in Uruguay, was based on the theme of protecting the nation from aggressive "foreign" ideas. Society was also to be guaranteed access to the leadership of political parties, which were to be made accountable through internal party democracy. A deliberate attempt was made to portray the banned parties of the Left as not only opposed to liberal democracy but also internally undemocratic. The latter accusation was, however, implictly directed against the Colorados and Blancos as well.

Revealingly, the Council of State fought to have a number of provisions

---

4 Personal interview, Montevideo, 12 July 1984. For a defense of the electoral system by a Colorado, see Jorge Luis Elizalde, "Doble voto: un sistema aún útil," *Opinar*, Thursday, 24 March 1983, p. 8.

Table 5.2. The effect of the double simultaneous vote[a]

View	Party	Agree strongly (%)	Agree (%)	Neither + nor − (%)	Disagree (%)	Disagree strongly (%)	Total
(a) Allows parties to adapt to change	Blancos:	9.1	54.5	0.0	27.3	4.5	100[b]
	Colorados:	29.2	50.0	8.3	8.3	4.2	100[b]
	Left:	0.0	29.4	17.6	33.3	33.3	100[b]
	All:	13.4	43.3	10.4	20.9	11.9	100[b]
(b) Stops parties taking dogmatic positions	Blancos:	9.5	52.4	9.5	19.0	9.5	100
	Colorados:	12.5	45.8	8.3	29.2	4.2	100
	Left:	11.8	41.2	11.8	23.5	11.8	100
	All:	12.1	45.5	10.6	24.2	7.6	100
(c) Accentuates personality conflicts and rivalries	Blancos:	18.2	27.3	9.1	18.2	27.3	100
	Colorados:	17.4	39.1	13.0	21.7	8.7	100
	Left:	22.2	44.4	5.6	16.7	11.1	100
	All:	19.4	38.8	9.0	17.9	14.9	100
(d) Promotes parliamentary indiscipline	Blancos:	23.8	38.1	4.8	9.5	23.8	100
	Colorados:	8.3	25.0	29.2	33.3	4.2	100
	Left:	25.0	37.5	6.3	31.3	0.0	100
	All:	21.2	33.3	13.6	22.7	9.1	100
(e) Permitted the survival of parties for a long time	Blancos:	28.6	23.8	0.0	28.6	19.0	100
	Colorados:	41.7	29.2	8.3	8.3	12.5	100
	Left:	47.1	35.3	5.9	5.9	5.9	100
	All:	40.3	26.9	4.5	14.9	13.4	100

Table 5.2. (cont.)

View	Party	Agree strongly (%)	Agree (%)	Neither + nor – (%)	Disagree (%)	Disagree strongly (%)	Total
(f) Permitted the predomination of the traditional parties	Blancos:	19.0	14.3	4.8	38.1	23.8	100
	Colorados:	20.8	20.8	20.8	16.7	20.8	100
	Left:	64.7	23.5	0.0	5.9	5.9	100
	All:	34.8	19.7	9.1	19.7	16.7	100
(g) Makes cross-party alliances easier, blurring parliamentary cleavages	Blancos:	22.7	50.0	9.1	18.2	0.0	100
	Colorados:	4.2	50.0	4.2	16.7	25.0	100
	Left:	27.8	27.8	1.5	22.2	16.7	100
	All:	16.2	42.6	7.4	19.1	14.7	100
For those agreeing or agreeing strongly: Is this positive? (% saying "yes")	Blancos:		29.4				
	Colorados:		71.4				
	Left:		22.2				
	All:		40.5				

Blancos, $n = 22$; Colorados, $n = 24$; left, $n = 18$; total, $n = 68$[a].

[a] The question: "Regardless of whether or not you favor retention of the double simultaneous vote, with which of the following points of view about the double simultaneous vote do you agree?"

[b] Includes one Patriotic Union and three Civic Union leaders.

of the statute altered (such as the stiff requirements for party-convention support in order to be candidates). Presumably they regarded their futures – as obscure politicians who had collaborated with the regime – as bleak.[5] In this way it was probably intended to disrupt the ability of leaders to form cohesive blocs, to reduce the clarity and public impact of the whole process, and, as a result, to increase the power of the smaller, local bosses. An antimilitary Colorado argued that "the military did not want to renew the leadership but for Pacheco to win."[6] According to a more pro-regime Colorado, "Pacheco and Gallinal were the keys to the armed forces' strategy of taking over the traditional parties."[7]

The renewal of internal life in the traditional parties

The weakness of the political parties meant that they were not immediately able to capitalize on their unexpected victory in the 1980 plebiscite. Yet, day by day, politicians became more active, and their followers more daring. The major development of the ensuing months was the growth of the opposition press, including the advent in July 1981 of *La Democracia*, clearly aligned with Wilson Ferreira, who was still banned and in exile.[8] All magazines were subject to sanctions if it was deemed that they had overstepped the arbitrary (and inconsistent) limits of license. The sanctions included closure for a number of issues if they mentioned the names of banned politicians.

In order to probe deeper into the survival mechanisms of the parties, politicians were asked how frequently they had engaged in certain kinds of political contacts before and after the 1980 plebiscite. Political activity clearly grew markedly after 1980, presumably in response to the halting

5 In order to blunt the opposition's impact, direct election of the permitted parties' leaders was dropped in favor of nomination by the 500 delegates to the national convention of each party. Candidates for the convention could appear on an electoral list in one *departamento* only; the lists. could not use the old numbers by which the voters knew the lists of each party; and the pooling of votes among lists (*sublemas*) was banned. The final version of the statute appeared in Uruguay's *Diario Oficial* for 10 June 1982, and subsequent rulings by the Electoral Court were published in *El Día*, 3 October 1983.

6 Personal interview, Montevideo, 29 September 1984.

7 The same politician went on: "Pacheco might have even won a fair election in 1976, but they tried to jail him in 1973, and he was only saved by President Bordaberry" (personal interview, Montevideo, 28 August 1984). Pacheco's abject support for the regime lost him a lot of moderate support in the Colorado electorate, and he allegedly became "bored" with politics.

8 In order to stress the point, the regime publicly reissued a military arrest warrant for the Blanco leader. At about that time, the neoliberal mouthpiece *Búsqueda* transformed itself into a weekly magazine with a greater politics-and-news orientation and became more critical of the delay in returning to democracy. Running to catch up, the more traditional Batllistas brought out *Correo de los Viernes* to compete with *Opinar*, and anti-Wilsonista Blancos eventually relaunched the old Herrerista organ *El Debate*.

Table 5.3. *The changing contacts and activities of politicians*[a]

Contacts	Broad Front (n = 8)	Blancos (n = 16)	Colorados (n = 19)	All[b] (n = 47)
Internal party life				
Leaders of the same *lema*				
1976–80	50[c]	75	58	60
1980–84	88	100	100	98
Longtime supporters				
1976–80	63	69	37	51
1980–84	88	100	95	96
New activists				
1976–80	25	19	17	18
1980–84	88	88	83	84
Leaders of other *lemas*				
1976–80	13	13	37	23
1980–84	100	69	69	77
Private meetings				
1976–80	75	63	37	50
1980–84	75	63	74	68
External party life				
Journalists				
1976–80	0	56	53	45
1980–84	88	94	95	94
Students				
1976–80	50	27	53	41
1980–84	100	60	68	72
Open meetings				
1976–80	0	13	5	7
1980–84	13	87	74	64
Trade-unionists				
1976–80	38	7	11	14
1980–84	63	47	47	50
Human-rights organizations				
1976–80	38	21	11	18
1980–84	75	43	47	48
Christians				
1976–80	50	27	11	24
1980–84	63	33	21	35
Others				
Exiles				
1976–80	25	7	5	9
1980–84	75	20	26	31
Military				
1976–80	11	0	16	11
1980–84	0	19	16	17
Business associations				
1976–80	0	7	5	4
1980–84	0	7	16	11

process of liberalization. The picture that emerges in Table 5.3 is one of a selective rebuilding by the traditional parties of their contacts with *political society*, represented by activists, other parties, and the communications media. The lack of contact with the economic elite was a striking feature of the Uruguayan situation and would tend to confirm what many have seen as the high degree of "relative autonomy" of Uruguay's "political class."[9] The Left, on the other hand, cultivated its links with *civil society*, particularly relations with sectors of the church, students, and trade-unionists.

Renovation at the grass roots?

The military were to give an ironic boost to their opponents by calling primary elections in the traditional parties. Yet the opposition also made a sustained effort to renovate the Blancos' and Colorados' decayed structures. Most leaders were willing to admit that more young people were needed, as well as better organization and more attention to a party program. But how successful was the renovation effort? Politicians interviewed in 1984 and 1985 were asked what proportions of their activists and fellow leaders had been involved in politics prior to the advent of the authoritarian regime in 1973. All parties reported that less than half of their militants had previously been active, and on average over a third of their leaders were also newcomers (Table 5.4). Blancos reported a particularly large influx of new activists, but the Left surprisingly claimed the least new leadership blood. This finding probably reflects the impact of efforts by Wilsonistas in the Blanco party to recruit young militants into the neighborhood committees known as *coordinadoras*. It may also reflect

9 Cocchi and Klaczko (1985).

Notes to Table 5.3.

*The question: "It is often said that the failure of the "yes" vote in the plebiscite led to a decisive change for political parties and that political life since 1980 has been quite different compared to the period 1976–80. Would you specifically tell me the type and frequency of contacts you had with the following groups in the two periods?"
*Includes three Civic Union leaders and one Patriotic Union leader.
*Percentage having "frequent" contacts.

Table 5.4. *Proportions of new activists and leaders reported by parties*[a]

Party	Activists (%)	Leaders (%)
Left (*n* = 7)	48.6	74.3
Blancos (*n* = 11)	39.6	65.0
Colorados (*n* = 18)	46.6	60.4
All parties[b] (*n* = 39)	46.0	63.2

[a]The question: "In your *sublema*, what proportions of activists and leaders were involved in politics prior to 1973?"
[b]Includes three Civic Union leaders.

difficulties experienced on the Left as a result of the greater repression leftists continued to experience.

Successful renovation required not only generational change among leaders and activists but also an effort to conquer the hearts of the electorate. Another question that revealed Blanco optimism regarding the process of renovation asked whether there had been an increase in identification with the traditional parties among citizens. As Table 5.5 brings out, the Colorados tended to have a sober appreciation of the impact of over a decade of authoritarianism. The Blancos, on the other hand, were the least likely to say that loyalty to the traditional parties had decreased. Leaders of the Broad Front were the most inclined to argue that the impact of social and generational changes had reduced voter identification with the two major parties.

Table 5.5. *Voter identification with the traditional parties*[a]

Party	Traditional identification			Total (%)
	Decreased (%)	Stable (%)	Increased (%)	
Broad Front (*n* = 7)	57.1	28.6	14.3	100
Blancos (*n* = 13)	30.8	38.5	30.8	100
Colorados (*n* = 18)	38.9	44.4	16.7	100
Respondents[b] (*n* = 43)	46.5	34.9	18.6	100

[a]The question: "Given the (1973) change of political regime, the advent of new generations, and the changes in Uruguayan society, would you say the majority of Uruguayans still identify with the traditional parties? In other words, has those parties' support declined, increased, or stayed the same?"
[b]Includes all parties, plus one nonparty military officer.

Table 5.6. *The modern relevance of Battlism and nationalism*[a]

Response	Left (%) (n = 8)	Blancos (%) (n = 13)	Colorados (%) (n = 17)	All[b] (%) (n = 43)
Distinct traditions of Battlism and nationalism still survive and retain their relevance.	12.1	15.4	47.1	27.9
The diverse changes in national politics mean that although the two traditions still exist, they are less and less relevant.	37.5	30.8	23.5	34.9
The transformation of political society produced major redefinitions of what it means to be a Colorado or Blanco, making them relevant to contemporary problems.	50.0	53.8	29.4	37.2
Total	100.0	100.0	100.0	100.0

[a] The question: "The traditional parties have existed in one form or another for one and a half centuries of Uruguayan history. Nevertheless, there are those who say that their survival is more a matter of purely formal appearances – that is to say, their nature is constantly changing, and, in reality, the inheritance of traditions does not mean much. Thinking back only over the past half century, which of the following statements best fits your views?"
[b] Includes all parties and a high-ranking officer close to the regime.

Blancos were likewise more liable to perceive programmatic and ideological renewal in the traditional parties, as Table 5.6 shows. If we assume that Colorados and Blancos were mainly referring to their own parties in their responses, we can see dramatic evidence of the impact of Wilson Ferreira's ideas in redefining the National party's traditional oppositionism in more libertarian and radical ways. We can also detect in the Colorados' response a far greater fundamental confidence in the continuity in Batllist thought, with its paternalist concern for the masses, emphasis on strong and responsible government, and belief in assuring citizens opportunities for advancement. Though the leaders of the Left were more inclined (at 37.5%) than Colorados or Blancos to argue that

Table 5.7. *The impact of the dictatorship on youth*[a]

Response	Broad Front (%) (n = 16)	Blancos (%) (n = 24)	Colorados (%) (n = 23)	All[b] (%) (n = 68)
Much more radical	18.8	41.7	26.1	29.4
Rather more radical	25.0	33.3	21.7	27.9
Slightly more radical	25.0	8.3	34.8	23.5
Same as before	6.3	4.2	13.0	7.4
Less radical	25.0	12.5	4.3	11.8
Total	100.0	100.0	100.0	100.0

[a]The question: "Has the impact of the regime since 1973 produced a radicalization of youth?"
[b]Includes all parties and a highranking officer in the regime.

the traditional parties were becoming less and less relevant to modern political problems, far more of them (50%) saw a process of ideological renewal. This was not significantly less than the proportion of Blancos saying the same.

Blancos were also the most inclined to believe that the military dictatorship had had a radicalizing impact on youth (Table 5.7), with 41.7% believing that the regime had made youth "much more radical." In light of the extreme radicalism of young people at the time of the 1973 coup, and the subsequent course of events, such a view was perhaps not realistic, although it was surely revealing as to the Blancos' belief that popular protest might one day force the military to leave power. The Colorados showed their usual phlegmatic and less euphoric outlook: 47.8% thought that young people were either the "same as before" or only "slightly more radical." Oddly enough, by comparison with the Blancos' 12.5% and the Colorados' 4.3%, one-quarter of the leftist leaders interviewed thought that the regime had had a *deradicalizing* effect on the younger generation. This can be interpreted as a sign of both moderation and pessimism in the Broad Front regarding the possibilities for a radical transformation in Uruguayan politics. That pessimism may well have been at the root of the moderate tactics that the Broad Front was later to adopt in the transition.

The renovation of the parties was reflected in the remarkably high estimates politicians gave of the proportions of activists under 20 years of age. What also emerges in Table 5.8 is the Colorados' perception of relatively fewer young activists in their ranks. This was especially marked in the teenage group[10] (i.e., those who had never voted in any election),

10 In the youngest cohort, using a standard t test, the significance of the Blanco–Colorado difference was .048. For the Front–Colorado difference, it was .006.

Table 5.8. *Reported age structures for party activists and leaders*[a]

	Activists				Leaders			
Age (years)	Front (%) (n = 17)	Blancos (%) (n = 12)	Colorados (%) (n = 17)	All[b] (%) (n = 40)	Front (%) (n = 7)	Blancos (%) (n = 12)	Colorados (%) (n = 17)	All[b] (%) (n = 40)
20 or less	21.4	21.4	12.2	18.2	6.4	4.0	2.5	4.3
21–30	27.1	30.0	25.7	26.7	20.0	18.0	22.5	20.6
31–40	22.1	26.8	30.6	26.7	32.9	35.0	33.5	33.3
40+	29.3	21.8	31.5	28.5	40.7	43.0	41.4	41.8
Total	100.0	100.0	100.0	100.0	100.0	100.0	100.0	100.0

[a] The question: "What would be the percentages of activists and leaders in your *sublema* in each of the following age categories?"
[b] Includes one Patriotic Union and three Civic Union leaders.

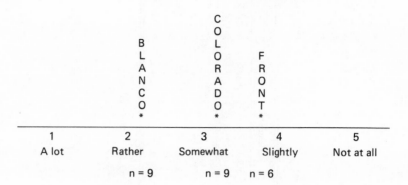

Figure 5.1. The impact of the *proceso* on parties' social composition. The question: "How far has the social composition of your sublema or list changed with respect to the pre-1973 period?"

but also to some extent in the next cohort 21–30 years of age). The latter group included those who might have voted in the 1980 plebiscite or the 1982 primaries, but could not have done so in 1971.[11] The Colorados reported more activists in the 31–40-year cohort than did the other parties.[12]

Not surprisingly, Table 5.8 also shows that the average age of leaders was much higher. More interesting is the fact that the Blancos did not report a much younger leadership profile than did the Colorados.[13] In other words, the process of renewal had not had as much apparent impact on the upper party echelons as at the grass roots. Figure 5.1 shows how far the politicians estimated that the social compositions of their *sublemas* had changed under the military. Again the Blancos claimed to have undergone the greatest renewal. It was not clear just how the social background of the Blancos had changed, apart from the influx of youth, but some liked to claim that the party had become more urban and more working-class.

Looking at all the foregoing questions on party renovation as a whole, we find a consistent pattern of the Blancos reporting the most change and renewal. This may, of course, reflect wishes as well as reality. Yet this in itself would also be revealing of the Blancos' great ambitions to revive and transform their party as an agent of political change and future government. The responses of the Colorados and the Left, however, do not seem to reflect an attitude of complacency so much as one of realism

11 Those who had been just eligible to vote in 1971, having turned age 18, would by 1984 have been 31 years old.

12 Although the Blanco–Colorado difference was not significant, the probability for the Frente–Colorado gap was .025.

13 The only cohort to produce a barely significant difference between any of the three parties was the youngest: The probability of the difference observed between the Colorados and the Left was .101.

Table 5.9. *The military's motives in calling primaries*[a]

| | Percentage agreeing | | | |
| | Left (n = 11) | Blanco (n = 17) | Colorado (n = 20) | All[b] (n = 52)[c] |
Motive				
(A) Marginalize banned parties	100	65	90	83
(B) Promote officialist politicians	100	71	90	79
(C) Diminish the power of old leaders	91	81	75	78
(D) Mitigate opposition to dialogue	90	88	75	76
(E) Renovation of political parties	50	57	55	58
(F) Postpone real elections	50	29	40	35
(G) Strengthen political leadership	18	18	10	15
(H) Deepen democracy in Uruguay	0	18	11	14

[a] The question: "The government imposed a new system of primaries for the party conventions. What were its aims and motives?"
[b] Includes one Patriotic Union and three Civic Union leaders.
[c] Number of cases may vary.

in the face of their limited ability to operate under conditions of repression and the apparent tide of support for Wilson Ferreira.

Politicians' attitudes toward the military

If the Blancos, or at least the followers of Wilson Ferreira, were firmly committed to the renovation of their party, how did they view the military's ambitions to guide the process of democratic reconstruction? One aim of the primaries that was suggested in interviews was the "renovation of political parties"; respondents from all three parties divided more or less evenly over whether or not that had been the military's aim, with a tiny majority agreeing in the traditional parties (Table 5.9). Four-fifths. also agreed that the military had intended to "reduce the power of former leaders," and three-quarters agreed that they were "trying to mitigate opposition prior to the dialogue" they had proposed. Significant differences did, however, emerge regarding the hypothesis that the primaries were intended to "promote officialist politicians." Whereas 29% of Blanco leaders disagreed, no Frentista did.[14] The most controversial suggestion concerned whether or not the armed forces had also planned to "marginalize banned parties" with the primaries; 35% of Blancos rejected that argument, but only 10% of Colorados, and no Frentistas at all.[15]

14 The significance of the difference between Blancos and Frentistas was .05.
15 The significance of the difference between Blancos and Colorados was .08, and between Blancos and Frentistas .03.

Eighty-three percent of those interviewed refused to believe the claim that the primaries were intended to "strengthen political leadership." Exactly the same proportions of politicians from the traditional parties rejected the hypothesis that the military had sought to "deepen Uruguayan democracy," but the Frentistas were unanimous in discounting such an assertion, perhaps because of their greater repression by the military and a different conception of what democracy entails.[16] The pattern that emerges in all the foregoing is that whenever statistically significant divergences occurred in appreciations of the military's aims, *the greatest differences were consistently between Blancos and Frentistas*, the latter more often imputing antidemocratic aims to the generals. The Colorados tended to exhibit an intermediate position.[17] Why, given their later inflexibility regarding negotiations, did the Blancos seem to distrust the military less than did the Colorados? In part, that may have reflected their general attitude of confidence and, in some cases, a certain naive good faith and tendency to underestimate their military opponents. Hard-line opponents of the regime were bitter about the statute on parties, the Second Organic Law. One Wilsonista alleged that it "was an attempt to co-opt and transform the parties into an appendage of the dictatorship, making them reflect its anticommunist ideology. What they wanted was barracks politics."[18] The Left, needless to say, was incensed at being excluded. Nevertheless, the traditional parties decided that they had no choice but to accept the manipulation of the terms they were being offered: The government's supporters would in any case do badly.

Gallup opinion polls detected a major swing toward hard-line opponents of the regime during the last two weeks of the campaign.[19] The government presumably realized the danger: They began studiedly to downplay the significance of the vote, which, unlike the plebiscite, was not com-

16 The significance of the difference between Blancos (82% "no") and Frentistas (100%) was a marginal .15.

17 On longer-term issues, the pattern was quite distinct. For example, leaders were asked whether (in the abstract) they favored "open" or "closed" primaries (i.e., those based on prior voter registration as supporters of a particular party). Whereas 73% of the Left favored closed primaries, only 41% of Blancos and just 29% of Colorados did so. On an issue that picked up the degree to which leaders saw their parties as committed to a cohesive line, rather than a circumstantial responsiveness to voters typical of the nonideological "catchall" party, the Blancos had the more intermediate views.

18 Personal interview, Montevideo, 14 July 1984. According to a leftist leader, incensed at the exclusion of the Frente from the primaries, "we were more damaged by the Second Organic Law than the National party by the Naval Club pact" (personal interview, Montevideo, 5 November 1984).

19 I am grateful to Luis Alberto Ferreira for letting me browse through Gallup's extensive reports of public opinion stretching back two decades. See also "Los nuevos resultados solo aportan más dudas," *Búsqueda*, Wednesday, 10 November 1982, p. 6; "Gallup: significativo avance de Pivel Devoto y Sanguinetti," *Búsqueda*, 24–30 November 1982, p. 1.

pulsory, and to step up harassment of the opposition press. At the eleventh hour they arrested five candidates, four Blancos and one Colorado, on charges of attacking the honor of the military (they had criticized the government with too little circumspection).

The results of the primaries: a triumph for the Wilsonistas

In the event, the turnout of 60.5% was not as low as it might have been, given the silence of the news media, the confusion surrounding the new lists' names, the abolition of absentee voting, and the recent high level of emigration. Nor can there be any doubt that economic conditions played an important role in the regime's defeat – just 48 hours before voters went to the polls, the government was forced to announce the floating of the Uruguayan peso, undoing at a stroke the centerpiece of their antiinflation policy since 1978. The Left entered the poll in some disarray, with the communists committed to their alliance with Wilson Ferreira in the Convergencia Democrática (headquartered in Mexico City and Washington), and the imprisoned general Líber Seregni convincing the Mesa Ejecutiva of the Frente Amplio in Montevideo to call for a blank ballot. Almost at once the Christian Democratic magazine *Opción* was permanently closed for calling for a blank vote.

In practice, the Convergencia's call for endorsement of whoever within either party were the most ardent opponents of the regime would largely have meant voting for the Wilsonista Blancos. Some former leftists probably did opt for the latter strategy, and the communists' support for the blank ballot was halfhearted at best. The other leftist parties, however, were determined to protest their exclusion from the primaries and to avoid the charge that they were attempting to take over the traditional parties, by voting. Nevertheless, in Montevideo the Wilsonista "ACF" list won in every district,[20] whereas nationally the blank vote was 6.8%, well down from the 18.2% of the Frente Amplio in 1971 (Table 5.10). Furthermore, in all but four departments of Uruguay's interior the Blancos outpolled the Colorados, nationally attaining 49.2% to 41.9%.

The clear message of the primaries was an even greater rejection of the regime than in the plebiscite held two years previously. However, the patchwork of competing lists made the job of determining the exact support for the major pro- and anti-regime tendencies in the traditional

20 The polls greatly underestimated the support for Wilson, probably because of methodological problems as well as last-minute swings; see the article by Diego Veiga, "Los Eternos Perdedores," in the Por la Patria (PLP) journal *Propuesta*, December 1982/January 1983, pp. 22–35.

Table 5.10. *Results of the 1982 primaries*

Party/major list	Montevideo		Interior		Uruguay	
	Votes	%/(%)[a]	Votes[b]	%/(%)[a]	Votes[b]	%/(%)[a]
Colorados	221,002	40.1	306,560	43.2	527,562	41.9
Tarigo "85"	49,181	(22.3)	[c]	[c]	[c]	[c]
Sanguinetti "15"	85,868	(38.9)	169,225	(59.3)	300,804	(60.1)
Pachequistas	60,545	(27.4)	80,546	(28.3)	139,557	(27.9)
Blancos	250,450	45.4	369,495	52.1	619,945	49.2
Wilsonistas	191,229	(76.4)	214,431	(63.0)[d]	405,595	(69.4)
Lacalle	11,730	(4.7)	28,409	(8.4)	40,139	(6.8)
Gallinal	20,728	(8.3)	34,112	(10.0)	54,840	(9.3)
Civic Union	5,512	1.0	9,474	1.3	14,986	1.2
Blank	69,102	12.5	16,271	2.3	85,373	6.8
Invalid	5,094	0.9	7,546	1.1	12,640	1.0
Total votes	551,160		709,346		1,260,506	100.0

[a]Percentage in parentheses refers to votes for a faction divided by the total votes for its party; all other percentages are proportions of total votes, including invalid and blank ballots.

[b]Votes and percentages for Colorado and Blanco factions in the interior and nationwide are based on calculations made by the magazine *La Razón* using results from the first count. Votes and percentages for parties, blank, and invalid votes are based on the slightly higher figures at the definitive count. So are the figures for the factions in Montevideo.

[c]Because Colorado lists in the interior often were allied to both major wings of Batllismo – Unidad y Reforma (15), led by Sanguinetti, at the national level, and Libertad y Cambio (85), led by Tarigo –it was impossible to specify the breakdown between them outside Montevideo.

[d]The total vote for Wilsonistas in the interior includes lists allied either to Por la Patria or to Movimiento de Rocha, or both, and also Lacalle's Consejo Nacional Herrerista, where it joined with them.

Sources: All data based on the definitive results as published in Corte Electoral, *Elección de autoridades de los partidos políticos Folleto No. 1* (Montvideo, 1983, Alfredo Albornoz, author), except the breakdown by factions for the interior, which are based on press reports of the first count, supplied by Prof. Juan Rial.

parties complex.[21] Using reasonable assumptions, however, the opposition candidates may be held to have won just under three-quarters of the votes, if we include the 7% of blank (i.e., leftist) ballots.[22] In the Colorado party, the pro-regime followers of the former president Pacheco obtained a disappointing 27.8% (more or less evenly distributed between the capital

21 I should like to thank Juan Rial for the detailed figures he compiled from the press, including *El Día*, 28 November 1982.
22 76.2% within the National party, based on the figures compiled by the magazine of the Herreristas, *El Debate*.

and the interior). In the Blanco party, the pro-regime vote was somewhere between 13.7% and 18.9% – according to whether one believes the Wilsonista magazine *La Razón* or the Herrerista *El Debate*.[23]

In a postelection poll that inquired how interviewees had voted, Gallup found that support for the united Wilsonista list (ACF) headed by Pivel was multiclass, slightly feminine, but above all young and urban rather than suburban. Supporters of the Batllistas' old "List 15" slate, led by Sanguinetti, were an odd mixture: below-average support among those under 26 years of age, the lower classes, and those with university education, but strong support in the 46–50 age cohort. This latter finding may reflect the allegiance of the postwar generation to what was once the reformist sector of the Colorado party. Table 5.11 gives the percentages of the relevant social groups, not factions, and must be read horizontally. If we sum the votes for the ACF and the blank ballots, we obtain a picture of the radical opposition to the regime: young, urban, intellectual, and slightly upper-class.

The ecology of resistance

Survey data are available only for the capital and thus tell us nothing about how over half the Uruguayans voted. One method for delving into the nationwide significance of the primary results is to undertake ecological regression analysis using aggregate data for the 19 *departamentos* into which Uruguay's territory is divided.[24] The same model that Gonzáles has used to "predict" the leftist vote in 1971 performs surprisingly well when applied to the pattern of blank voting in 1982, despite a decade of

23 To this may be added the 0.8% won by Pons Echeverry in Montevideo, a leader who urged a "no" vote in the plebiscite, but who apparently later flirted with being the candidate of the pro-regime camp before drawing back. The 1.2% achieved by the Unión Cívica, the tiny third party, allowed to register (consisting of Christian Democrats who refused to join the Broad Front in 1971), was sometimes considered a pro-regime vote, though the party has since distanced itself more from the government. Humberto Ciganda, a popular leader from San José, had always been openly critical of the *proceso*.

24 The technique was first adapted to Uruguay by Luis González (1983b), to whom I should like to acknowledge my debt. I also thank him for discussing the methodology of ecological regression as he first applied it to Uruguay's 1980 plebiscite. Two important limitations on the validity of such an approach must, nevertheless, be emphasized. First, the fact that almost half the population of Uruguay lives in the department of Montevideo means that the technique is necessarily crude. Second, if abused, the technique of ecological regression can be misleading. The well-known "ecological fallacy" prevents us from inferring the behavior of *individuals* from evidence of correlation between district vote totals. Social-structure data are from the following sources: Filgueira (1976) for the 1963 census and the figures for rural unemployment that refer to 1966; the 1975 Census (I should like to thank César Aguiar for providing me with this); and the 1982 household survey.

Table 5.11. *Reported votes of sociodemographic groups, Montevideo, retrospective survey, December 1982*

Group	Sanguinetti (%)	Tarigo (%)	Pacheco (%)	Pivel/ACF (%)	Blank (%)	Other (%)	Total (%)
All interviewees	12	5	9	24	4	46[a]	100
Men	13	4	7	23	6	47	100
Women	11	6	10	26	1	46	100
Upper class	20	5	5	25	5	40	100
Middle class	13	5	8	23	4	47	100
Lower class	6	3	16	25	—[b]	51	100
Primary education	13	4	12	20	—	52	100
Secondary education	14	6	6	27	4	43	100
University	7	4	7	22	15	45	100
Age 18–25	3	3	7	38	7	41	100
Age 26–35	11	5	5	30	5	43	100
Age 36–45	10	—	13	19	—	57	100
Age 46–50	23	8	4	19	4	43	100
Age 51+	13	5	11	19	3	49	100
Urban Montevideo	14	4	8	29	5	41	100
Periphery	10	6	9	18	2	54	100
First-time voters	3	3	3	20	3	69	100
Previous voters	14	5	10	24	4	44	100

[a]Consists of disfranchised (8%), other Colorados (1%), Gallinal (2%), other Blancos (2%), Civic Union (1%), abstentions (14%), no reply (18%).
[b]Zero votes.

Source: Gallup Uruguay, *Informe de Opinión Pública*, No. 331, Table 13.

repression.[25] Using more recent census data than those available to González (1975 as against 1963), we obtain only marginally better results. Unfortunately, however, the elimination of Montevideo from the equation leads to a dramatic deterioration in the fit of the model.[26] Finally, the strong correlation between the blank vote in 1982 and the leftist vote in 1971 comes as little surprise; it remains rather high even if Montevideo is excluded.[27]

The attempt to apply the first social-structure model used to predict leftist and blank voting to a narrow measure of Wilsonista support fails: Wilson's core support simply does not appear to be significantly associated with the attributes of "modern" departments: urbanization, salaried employees, and industrial workers.[28] If we take a broader measure of Wilsonista support, including pro-Wilsonista Herreristas, only one "modern" variable proves significant: the proportion of the labor force in industry.

The most interesting findings are obtained when we regress the two

25 With some danger of measurement error, given that the census was seven years old:

$$\text{BLANK } 82 = -6.07 + 0.21(\text{INDLAB } 75) + 0.30(\text{M/U EMP } 75)$$
$$t = 4.4 \qquad t = 3.8$$
$$\text{adj. } R^2 = .88 \qquad \text{beta} = .54 \qquad \text{beta} = .47$$

The variables, as before, are the proportion of the labor force classified as industrial workers (INDLAB) by the census and the proportion of middle and upper salaried employees (M/U EMP).

26 The equation, excluding Montevideo, is,

$$\text{BLANK } 82 = 2.91 + 0.15(\text{INDLAB } 75) - 0.09(\text{M/U EMP } 75)$$
$$t = 4.56 \qquad t = -0.965$$
$$\text{adj. } R^2 = .53 \qquad \text{Not signif.}$$

(Notice that "upper and middle employees" now has the "wrong" sign.)

Montevideo is the department with the most industrial workers and salaried professionals. Because the model rests on this extreme value, it ought to be treated with a pinch of salt until the votes for the capital become available in broken-down form. The only consoling feature is the continued strong influence of the industrial labor force, although the possibility of measurement error is, likely to be highest with this term, given the "deindustrializing" impact of certain recent economic policies. Substantively, we conclude that the structure of leftist support may be rather different in rural areas. We shall not abandon the general equation, because the fact that Montevideo represents half the nation's population might in fact constitute grounds for weighting its effect more heavily.

27
$$\text{BLANK } 82 = -2.353 + 0.484(\text{LEFT } 71)$$
$$\text{adj. } R^2 = .950 \qquad t = 18.553$$

28 We are faced with a choice: Either (a) take the combined PLP and Movimiento Nacional de Rocha (MNR) vote, plus the Consejo Nacional Herrerista (CNH) whenever they presented joint lists, or (b) take the total for all three, including CNH lists to maintain comparability, even where they were separate, as in Herrerista strongholds Rivera and Cerro Largo. The advantage of the latter broader measure is that it gives a truer picture of the support Ferreira could have expected in a hypothetical presidential contest, given the double simultaneous vote. Although the factions have not always seen eye-to-eye in the Blanco convention, a narrower measure has the disadvantage of introducing severe fluctuations (and missing values) into the Wilsonista vote.

measures of Wilsonista support in the 1982 primaries on Ferreira's votes in the 1971 election, at which he narrowly missed becoming president. Even the narrow measure (unsurprisingly most associated with the 1971 vote) does not give strong results.[29] Put simply, Wilson Ferreira's support apparently had undergone a massive shift during the decade of authoritarian rule. Of particular interest is the 11.5-percentage-point jump in his vote in Montevideo, and the even higher 16.6 points in Canelones.[30]

When we regress the vote for the Colorado Pachequista lists in the primaries on the referendum vote for allowing Pacheco a second term in 1971, we find almost no association at all. On the other hand, if we use the "yes" vote in the 1980 plebiscite, the association is relatively strong, implying that the shift in the strength of what we may call the "authoritarian Colorado" vote had already occurred by the end of the decade.[31] In the two most populous departments, Montevideo and Canelones, his vote fell 21.1 and 19.1 points, respectively, from 1971 to 1982. Though the modern sector had been abandoning him, his support had not yet become skewed enough for social-structure indicators to account for the variation across departments.[32]

If we look at the result obtained by Pacheco's bitter rival and enemy, Jorge Batlle and the "List 15," we find a rather different picture. The list was headed by Julio María Sanguinetti in Montevideo, because Jorge Batlle had not yet been allowed to participate in politics. Historically, Batllismo was seen as being associated with the middle-class urban and industrial population. There is no doubt, however, that Batlle's leadership

---

29 The 1971 vote predicted an almost negligible amount of the variation in Ferreira's 1982 support (corrected $R^2 = .046$) and was not conventionally significant ($t = 1.37$).

30 Canelones is an area of small farms and dormitory towns around Montevideo in which "ruralism" was once strong, support for Wilson and his allies possibly being due to the severe crisis of agriculture there.

31 Pacheco's 1982 vote has changed dramatically in distribution:

$$PACH\ 82 = 17.653 - 0.133(PACH\ 71)$$
$$adj.\ R^2 = -.044 \qquad t = -0.490$$
$$PACH\ 82 = 3.951 + 0.205(YES\ 80)$$
$$adj.\ R^2 = .101 \qquad t = 1.739$$

Examining the regional pattern of Pacheco's loss in support, we find that only in four rather small and underdeveloped departments was he able to hold the decline to less than 10 percentage points (Artigas, Rivera, Treinta y Tres, and Lavalleja), and there the impact of strategic development plans by the military may have helped.

32 Although he obtained just 11.0% in Montevideo, that was a sizable bloc of his national electorate, because the bastions of his strength (20% of the vote or more), where his vote loss was minimal, consisted of underpopulated areas of the periphery.

of the once-progressive "List 15" transformed it into an essentially conservative faction. He maintained good relations with Ramón Díaz, editor of the neoliberal magazine *Búsqueda*, and Végh Villegas, twice minister of the economy. The more social-democratic-leaning Sanguinetti only partially made up the ground lost to the Wilsonistas. We obtain a rather poor fit when regressing Batlle's 1982 vote on his 1971 result; his support, however, had been more stable than that of Pacheco.[33] The advent of new factions such as Enrique Tarigo's Libertad y Cambio list may have eaten into Batlle's votes in the capital, but the collapse of support for Pacheco significantly offset that elsewhere.

Although the overall increase in anti-Pacheco forces was great, it apparently had not much changed the social-structure roots of Batllism. In the aftermath of the primaries, the disputatious inheritors of that legacy were able to agree on a joint list in the 500-delegate Colorado party convention. Thus, they prevented Pachequistas from obtaining any representation in the talks with the armed forces on the form and limits of the transition.[34]

The political impasse of authoritarianism

As they acquired a taste for power, many in the Uruguayan military began to wish they could create a new party in the manner of their Brazilian counterparts.[35] As late as 1983 that was still President Alvarez's ambition, and other generals apparently used that possibility as a threat to bring the traditional parties into line. Yet the setback for the military's few civilian allies in the 1982 primaries that had prompted a renewal of the threat also undermined its credibility.

Under pressure from the traditional parties, the military had agreed to restore the double simultaneous vote, which they had deliberately dropped from the ill-fated text defeated in the 1980 plebiscite. The double simultaneous vote rendered any attempt to found a new party virtually·

33   BATT 82 = 15.477 + 0.795(BATT 71)
          adj. R^2 = .274 t = 2.789
          BATT 71 = −80.04 + 0.972(LO ED)   + 0.585(URBAN)
                                 t = 2.546 t = 2.567
          adj. R^2 = .222   beta = .956   beta = .963

     For the 18 interior departments alone, education is not significant.

34   To an even greater extent, the anti-regime Wilsonistas were able to dominate the Blanco leadership. Significantly, however, two conventioneers who were closely associated with Wilson and his radical son failed to get into the executive body, which was elected by secret ballot. The subtle possibilities for dividing the Blancos were there, if only the military could see them.

35   In June of 1982, retired Colonel Néstor Bolentini, a member of the nominated legislature, had announced that he would form a new political party, subsequently named the Patriotic Union.

doomed to failure, by making it far more difficult to divide the opposition. The only advantage for the military was that it allowed the regime's conservative allies (most of them rural bosses reliant on national resources to maintain their popularity) to maintain a toehold in the Colorado and Blanco parties.

The military and their civilian allies favored strict control over the transition toward democracy by means of reform "from above," but they were severely divided over strategy. Most of them agreed that the Left should never be allowed to operate again, but they continued to disagree whether or not a new party should be founded, or even one of the existing parties commandeered. When the new leaders adopted a hard-line tone, the military faced the decision whether to negotiate as promised or stage some form of punitive involution. The latter, however, would have been costly, given the trouble they had taken to call valid interlocutors into being. The decision to hold the primaries had transformed the opposition. Once elected leaders are in place, they cannot easily be ignored, nor can it be pretended that they are unrepresentative.

Under the statute on parties, candidates for the presidency had to have 25% of the delegates to the 500-strong national conventions. That was significantly lower than the 35% originally suggested, but it still turned out to be more than all the anti-Wilson forces in the Blanco party combined. The right-wing former president Jorge Pacheco subsequently obtained, at most, 28% of the Colorados' votes in the primaries, putting him at the mercy of the particularist (and fickle) local bosses in his coalition if he were to be nominated. When the conventions met, they debated a methodical list of issues, such as respect for law, trade-union rights, treatment of political prisoners, and the banning of parties and politicians. Never had they been forced to define positions so concretely.[36] With the strong cooperation that emerged between Tarigo and Sanguinetti, Pacheco's hopes of becoming president were finished. In effect running to catch up, he later called for his allies to withdraw from the nominated Consejo del Estado, but too late to prevent the defection of minor provincial bosses in an unseemly *sauve qui peut*. In any case, Pacheco's hopes would have rested on a repeat of the outcome of the 1971 elections. That is to say, the Colorados as a whole would have had to win more votes than the Blancos, and he would have had to be their leading candidate, which clearly had become unfeasible, given the rise of Sanguinetti and Tarigo. Furthermore, the Blancos had pulled ahead in the primaries (which were open to all comers, and thus gave an indication of the relative standing of each party).

Those new faces that had emerged from the primary elections – such

36 "Las Convenciones se ponen en marcha," *Opinar*, 20 January 1983, p. 24.

as Dr. Enrique Tarigo in the Colorado party and Professor Juan Pivel Devoto in the Blanco party – were strongly committed to restoring a fully democratic system, free from military tutelage. The Blanco party convention overwhelmingly endorsed the same presidential formula as in 1971: Wilson Ferreira, with Carlos Julio Pereyra as running mate. Wilson, however, remained in exile, banned and under warrant for arrest on charges of "attacking the armed forces' morale," "exposing the republic to foreign reprisals" (for campaigning for the end of U.S. military aid), and alleged links with subversives. The Colorados chose Julio María Sanguinetti and Enrique Tarigo as their candidates, the moderation of their mood contrasting with that of the Blancos.

The militant pole of opposition to the regime after 1980 had become the Blanco party, its ranks swelled by an influx of young, militant Wilsonistas. Though a number of Por la Patria leaders were former Herreristas, Wilson deliberately added large numbers of young names to the ACF list in Montevideo. These were taken from among the militants of the Blanco *coordinadoras* (coordinating committees). According to one young Wilsonista active in these committees, "Wilson liked the participatory style and nonpersonalism of the *coordinadoras*." Their vision of the correct strategy for ousting the military and radically reforming Uruguay's economy and society was drastically different from that of the traditional Blancos, and in the primaries the Wilsonistas managed to consolidate effective control over the party. For the regime, it seemed as though a nightmare was coming true.

6

Party and military strategies in the "dialogue": from partial opening to confrontation after the Parque Hotel talks

Almost a decade after the 1973 coup, Uruguay remained something of a paradox in terms of the abstract conditions favoring a transition to democracy. The regime was the most illegitimate of the southern-cone dictatorships, but it had experienced nothing like the opposition mobilization seen in Chile or the internal fragmentation that dogged Argentina. Nor had it given birth to a strong liberalizing coalition, as in Brazil. For the military, therefore, a great deal of uncertainty continued to surround the calculus of costs of toleration versus costs of repression.[1] Only with hindsight is it easy to see that top generals were coming to feel that power was becoming a liability. So much depended on the strategy of the opposition. Nevertheless, the public pronouncements of the military remained sternly intransigent. The only solution to Uruguay's political stalemate was a negotiated "extrication," but the military continued to demand repressive constitutional changes inspired by national-security doctrines. For that reason many commentators were pessimistic regarding the chances for any agreement.

The performance of the authoritarian regime in terms of the economy was becoming a serious concern for both the military and the business elite. On the eve of the primaries, the peso had collapsed in value, and the country was entering a slump that would cause negative growth of more than 17% over the next three years.

This chapter first outlines the growing economic crisis of the early 1980s as a symptom of seriously declining regime performance. It then examines the internal evolution of the balance of forces in the military during 1981–2 and traces the structural deadlock that arose in 1983 between them and the opposition parties. It is argued that it was the military's continued insistence on the impossible conditions of a restricted

---

1 Dahl's simple dictum (1971) states that the probability of regime democratization increases the more the costs of repression exceed the costs of toleration.

Table 6.1. *The return of external disequilibrium, 1978–84*

Parameter	1978	1980	1981	1982	1983	1984
Real effective exchange rate	100.0	81.4	77.9	90.2	113.1	n.a.
Exports ($ million)	686	1,059	1,215	1,023	1,045	925
Imports ($ million)	710	1,651	1,599	1,110	788	776
Trade deficit ($ million)	− 24	− 592	− 384	− 87	258	149
Current account ($ million)	− 127	− 692	− 478	− 468	− 171	n.a.
External debt ($ million)	1,240	2,161	3,129	4,255	4,589	n.a.
Debt interest/exports	10.4%	14.6%	13.2%	26.4%	26.9%	n.a.

Sources: U.N. Economic Commission for Latin America (1986). Noya (1986). Inter-American Development Bank (1986). *Búsqueda*, No. 364, 31 December 1986/7 January 1987. Macadar (1982).

democradura[2] that drove the traditional parties into a radical alliance with the illegal Left. Only after much soul-searching were the military as an institution to become committed to a full extrication from government, as discussed in later chapters. First they were thoroughly to explore the dead end to which the authoritarian regime had led.

By the early 1980s, the challenge for those who had sought to explain the advent of military rule in the advanced nations of Latin America in terms of political economy was to adapt their theories to explain the crisis of authoritarian regimes. Bureaucratic authoritarianism was a failure in terms of the goals of those who brought it into being. That was clearly the case in Uruguay, if we consider, for example, the opinion data cited by Stepan, which suggested that more of the upper classes thought that a democratic transition would accelerate economic recovery than thought the opposite.[3]

The decline in regime performance: the political economy of crisis

Between 1974 and 1980, Uruguay's gross national product (GNP) had grown at the historically high rate of 5% per annum; despite the oil shock, trade surpluses were achieved (Table 6.1). Export diversification was encouraged by tax rebates and subsidies, as envisaged in the National Development Plan drawn up prior to the military takeover.[4] The social

2 The *democradura* concept was coined by Philippe Schmitter and refers to a pseudodemocracy without full democratic freedoms (O'Donnell and Schmitter 1986).
3 Stepan (1985b, p. 327).
4 So-called nontraditional exports (including clothing, leather goods, rice, and fish) grew from 26.2% of total exports in 1973 to 57.0% in 1977 (World Bank 1979).

cost, however, was enormous, as measured in terms of emigration, falling real earnings, income concentration, and physical repression of all trade-unionists. Financial liberalization brought not an influx of foreign investment into productive areas of the economy but an expansion of the financial sector.[5]

With the announcement of a preestablished *tablita cambiaria* below the domestic rate of inflation from 1978 to 1982, there was a definite shift in economic policy away from the adjustment of relative prices and the pursuit of export-led growth (broadly speaking, the Brazilian model) toward an attempt at reducing inflation to single digits (as in Chile). However, attempted application of international monetarist theories, rather than the "orthodox monetarism" of Milton Friedman, proved very damaging to the real economy. Far from wiping out inflation, the overvaluation of the currency began to wipe out domestic producers of tradeable goods and produce massive trade deficits. By an unfortunate coincidence, due to conditions in the world economy, access to foreign private bank loans allowed this experiment to continue for a dangerously long time. Because peso overvaluation led to an import boom, the earlier hopes of drastically reducing protectionist tariffs had to be given up. When the peso finally collapsed in November 1982, firms with dollar-denominated debts were quite unable to pay, causing banks to fail.[6]

Despite the military and the technocrats' unfettered commitment to development and pro-business policies, one business sector after another had become alienated by 1982. Manufacturers for the domestic market were severely hit by tariff cuts after 1975, exporters by overvalued exchange rates from 1978, petty commerce by the massive contraction of real earnings that returned in 1982, and construction by the refusal to mitigate the slump that began in 1981 with countercyclical public investment. As the slump deepened, practically everyone was hurt by the high-real-interest-rate policy and resistance to helping firms that had taken on heavy debt in order to invest. Even support from financial sectors for the government can be overstated.[7]

Undoubtedly, many of Uruguay's problems were external to its small economy: the second massive rise in oil prices at the end of the 1970s; new trade barriers to nontraditional exports, such as shoes; and the collapse of the Argentine peso in 1981 and 1982, which ruined the crucial tourist trade and sent it briefly into reverse. But those shocks were amplified by

5 By 1984, 20 of Uruguay's 22 banks were in foreign hands.
6 The Central Bank then adopted a policy of buying up bad-loan portfolios in order to act as midwife in the acquisition of those banks by foreign banking groups.
7 My interviews with bankers in 1981 showed clear signs of irritation at the policies pursued by General Raimúndez as president of the *Banco de la República* (the state commercial bank, not to be confused with the Central Bank).

Table 6.2. *The massive contraction of the real economy and the return of fiscal and monetary disequilibrium, 1978–84*

Parameter	1978 (%)	1980 (%)	1981 (%)	1982 (%)	1983 (%)	1984 (%)
Growth of GDP	6.2	4.5	1.9	−9.4	−5.9	−2.4
Inflation"	44.5	42.8	29.4	20.5	51.5	66.1
Fiscal deficit/GDP	−0.9	−0.3	−1.5	−9.0	−4.0	−4.7

"Rise in consumer price index (CPI).
Sources: See Table 6.1.

trade liberalization and currency overvaluation. Until 1980, the regime could derive a surrogate for legitimacy from the revival of economic growth for the first time in two decades. Thereafter, they lost even that (Table 6.2).

The estrangement of the economic elite from the military government

The ranchers were highly critical of both the government's early policies and the later exchange-rate overvaluation.[8] There may have been an important noneconomic reason for this, however: Sheep and cattle raisers represented the traditional elite who had survived by adopting capitalist techniques and by intermarriage with urban and professional families. To them, the military were a caste of ill-bred and uncouth upstarts who had "muscled in." Efforts to mollify the heavily indebted ranchers, announced by the new Alvarez administration in late 1981, proved inadequate.[9]

Industry had been so scared by labor militancy, strikes, and factory occupations, and had since benefited from such total labor peace and massive wage compression, that businessmen were, on the whole, quite pro-regime until the slump became really serious. However, the Chamber of Commerce clearly was more committed to the neoliberal ideas of dis-

---

8 Finch (1985). Although Bordaberry was a rancher and former head of the defunct Ruralist League, early regime policy had been erratic regarding landed interests, with the military making a vain attempt to favor medium and small producers in 1975.

9 Personal interview with Walter Pagés, former president of the Rural Federation, Montevideo, August 1981. The Rural Federation held its 65th Congress at the end of May 1982, and there the agriculture minister received extremely rough handling. The final resolution openly attacked the government. See *Desde Uruguay*, 1982, No. 12 (an exile newsletter published in Mexico).

mantling tariff protection.[10] By contrast, industrialists had an increasingly jaundiced view of the war on inflation by means of currency overvaluation and ultrahigh real interest rates in a country that was also attempting to lower its tariffs.[11] By February 1982 there was a state of open confrontation between government and industry.[12]

Why were policy decisions taken by bureaucratic authoritarian regimes not altered rapidly when they turned out to be suicidal? The answer seems to lie less in the structural constraints of the international economy than in the inflexibility and compartmentalization of military-technocratic decision-making structures. The complex interaction of the military's mentality of national sacrifice with the technocrat's ideology of neoliberalism led to the retention of policies that subsequently produced massive business discontent. Under an authoritarian regime, opposition to policies or to ministers is much more liable to snowball into opposition to the manner of decision making than under democracy. Support from the economic elite for the continuation of the *proceso* thus gave way to neutrality by 1980 (in marked contrast to the situation in Chile), and tight-lipped hostility by 1982. Yet the precipitous decline in the regime's economic performance in no way determined the path of the subsequent transition. Like the crisis of legitimacy, it helps explain why the military became anxious to hand back power to the politicians, and it may have accelerated their decision, but it did not prescribe how they would do so.

Military ambitions and dilemmas

The weakness of politicians in the wake of the 1980 plebiscite should not cause one to lose sight of the military's own dilemmas: If they retained power collectively, their hierarchies of command might be disrupted by internal politicization and "bureaucratic capture." If they allowed a strongman to emerge, they could become chained to his mistakes, alienated by his ambitions, and ultimately tempted to sacrifice him. Yet the alternative of allowing elections, as repeatedly promised, left the question of how to

10 Interviews with the Chamber of Commerce president, Nelson Sapelli, showed that he was enthusiastic about the new model: "It was evident that the only way out for Uruguay after a long period of stagnation, and in the face of the oil crisis, was to change the paternalistic pattern of ultraprotectionism. . . . Sadly, in certain sectors this *apertura* was not much of an opening . . . it was not total. Today we are paying dearly for this" (personal interview, Montevideo, 11 August 1981).

11 Interview with the chief economist at the Chamber of Industries, Carlos Folle, Montevideo, August 1981.

12 The interior minister, General Trinidad, refused to receive a delegation from the Chamber of Industries following the angry denunciations of government policies at their congress. See *El País*, Saturday, 13 February 1981, p. 1.

Table 6.3. *Major institutional acts, fundamental laws, and decrees, 1981–3*

Act or decree	Date	Substance
Institutional Act No. 11	28 July 1981	Enlarged the Council of State; new president to hold office September 1981 to March 1985.
Institutional Act No. 12	10 Nov. 1981	Modified Institutional Act No. 8, which had placed the judiciary under executive control.
Statute on parties	7 July 1982	Calls primaries in the Colorado, Blanco, and Civic Union parties, but declares Left illegal.
Institutional Act No. 13	12 Oct. 1982	Superseded Institutional Act No. 9, creating a Dirección General de la Seguridad Social.
Executive decree	2 Aug. 1983	Suspended public activity by parties except for talks with the military on a new constitution.
Institutional Act No. 14	2 Aug. 1983	Permitted the banning of more politicians.

Source: *Actos Institucionales (1 al 17)* (Montevideo: Editorial Técnica, 1984).

prevent Wilson Ferreira, their most feared opponent, from winning (Table 6.3).

The reasons for the military's hatred of Wilson were several and seemed to stretch back to the murky power struggle prior to the 1973 coup. Particularly important had been his testimony before the Koch committee in the U.S. House of Representatives in 1975, when his accusations of torture were instrumental in imposing the ban on further military aid to Uruguay. After escaping assassination in Buenos Aires in 1976, Wilson had moved to London and actively worked in the international campaign for human rights in Uruguay. He was the only politician from the traditional parties to do so, and his scorn for the military was continually reiterated. No less important, he insisted on a complete restoration of democracy and trials of military leaders and torturers.[13]

Within the military, a number of tendencies could be discerned. The navy had become largely disillusioned with the *proceso* (it had opposed the coup coalition in 1973), and the air force was split, even though it had sustained particularly heavy purges, and despite containing some of the most antidemocratic elements in the military. Yet it was the army that constituted the backbone of the regime: Its generals had an overall majority in the Junta de Oficiales Generales, and that had been slightly increased

13 When I asked him early in 1983 if his position was not overly intransigent, Ferreira bluntly replied no (personal interview, Washington, DC, January 1983). By contrast, when asked what might happen if Wilson were to become president, a retired general argued that the result would be "vendetta, vendetta, and more vendetta!" (personal interview, Montevideo, April 1984).

in 1981 when Alvarez was made president (partly, perhaps, to sidestep rivalries that were becoming intense). One group within the army was allied to the president, and may be termed "Alvarezistas" for convenience. The exact composition of the group seemed to vary over time, and what they stood for even more so.[14] What they shared was a conjunctural allegiance to the ambitious president. President Alvarez did not, however, have the total support of the Junta de Oficiales Generales.

Presumably in order to strengthen his support from the military institution, Alvarez began his presidency by naming more retired military officers to cabinet portfolios, and he appointed a number of high-ranking officers to be local governors (*intendentes*) in the interior. Among the generals in active service, Yamandú Trinidad, in particular, was seen as an Alvarezista, and he became interior minister. Military retirements and promotions in February of 1982 had an important effect in completing the departure of the original leaders of the military regime. Hard-liner General Queirolo retired as army commander and was succeeded by General Hontou, who was seen as more flexible in his views.[15] Also retiring was General Raimúndez, who as chief of the Fourth Army region and president of the Armed Forces Commission on Political Affairs had tried to push the political opening. He was replaced by General Rapela, who was seen as more of a hard-liner, but not one who was anti-Alvarez.[16] The overall effect was to strengthen support for the president among the junta of generals. Some even linked that to the possibility that he might launch an official regime party with himself as leader.

By 1982, most of the generals were men who had been colonels or lieutenant colonels at the time of the 1973 coup. They were all men of the *proceso*; anyone who had not been had long been purged or languished without promotion. In their mass, the members of the junta formed a group loyal to the military institution rather than to the president. Some of them were more opposed to returning to democracy than others.[17] None was willing to accept investigations of human-rights abuses (*revisiónismo*), and all were anxious to exclude Wilson Ferreira, as well as the Left, from

---

14 In this sense the Alvarezistas were a "faction" rather than a "tendency," as defined by Richard Rose, that is, a group of individuals who can be traced over time by their (loose) loyalty to one another, rather than by their principles.

15 "Cambios militares en Uruguay," *Clarín* (Buenos Aires), 20 January 1982, p. 17.

16 The net effect of the promotions was ambiguous regarding the weight of the soft-liners, who had been weakened by the forced resignation of Brigadier Borad the previous year. The air-force chiefs maintained a line of siding with the winning army faction, whereas the navy was unambiguously favorable to a rapid return to democracy.

17 Reissig, Barrios, and Berois were sometimes mentioned as the most in favor of a transition, and Siqueira as opposed. Generals Hontou, Rapela, Aranco, Trinidad, and Medina were all committed to handing power back to the politicians, with varying degrees of strictness regarding the conditions they felt must be extracted as "guarantees."

elections. Where there may have been more disagreement was over the continued proscription of other traditional politicians, such as Jorge Batlle, and over the minimum provisions for strengthening the Constitution that would be acceptable. Disagreements, however, can only be surmised from the twists in the regime's strategy. Unlike Argentina, Uruguay saw no open disagreement among its generals.

President Alvarez

General Gregorio Alvarez had been associated with the progressive faction of the officer corps in the military rebellion of February 1973.[18] In 1971 he was put in charge of coordinating the war against the Tupamaros, and he set up the Joint Chiefs of Staff, or Estado Mayor Conjunto (ESMACO), becoming its first head. Tragically, he lost his brother in a terrorist assassination. After the February 1973 rebellion led to the creation of the National Security Council (COSENA) to oversee the president, Alvarez was made its secretary. Also in February he had a hand in drafting the communiqué that called for land reform, and he supported the attempt to favor small ranchers in state meat purchases, leading to a conflict with President Bordaberry in 1975. However, accounts of Alvarez's allegedly progressive views turned out to be exaggerated.[19]

In his speech before the Council of the Nation, while taking office as president on 1 September 1981, General Alvarez spoke at length regarding the future of the regime:

The Armed Forces have accepted the result of the popular vote [in 1980] and without equivocating have publicly expressed their proposal to elaborate the bases of a new institutional order, in consultation with the members of the traditional parties. . . .

I feel it necessary, [nevertheless,] to make it clear that the full re-establishment of citizens' rights and the exercise of representative democracy will not imply in any circumstance the accommodation of the actions of those who would destroy it. This means the firmest rejection of the aims, maneuvers and subterfuges of Marxism-Leninism and all types of extremism.[20]

As the Alvarez presidency took shape, the naive view, repeated in the press in 1981, that "normalization" would lead to democratic transition

---

18 Vasconcellos (1973). His father had been an artillery colonel and had made a brilliant career during the 1950s and 1960s, ascending in 1971 to the rank of general by competitive examination (*concurso*) rather than by seniority or political connections.

19 As Sanguinetti noted as early as May 1973, "if any line dominates the Uruguayan Army it is the conservative and authoritarian. They attempt, of course, to attract the people, and this presupposes demagogy, certain concessions to the masses, but no more" (Kaufman 1979, pp. 59–60).

20 Uruguay, Consejo de la Nación (1981, pp. 2–4). The president also promised that labor-union activity would be allowed once more (p. 13).

began to wear off. Rather than favoring a professionalization of the military as a preliminary to a return to the barracks, the president apparently favored an attempt to inject some *popularity* into the regime. Despite promises to the contrary, he engaged in a spending spree in a vain attempt to cushion the effects of the economic slump that hit the country in 1982, pushing the fiscal deficit up to 9% of GDP (six times higher than the year before).[21] At the end of 1983 he appointed Juan Carlos Paysée, a renegade former associate of Blanco leader Wilson Ferreira, as mayor of Montevideo, and a further bout of public largesse began.[22]

If Alvarez was increasingly ambitious politically, he inadvertently helped in two ways to bolster those sectors that favored professionalization of the armed forces. First, he destroyed the most reactionary and anti-democratic clique, including the generals Ballestrino and Vadora, as well as the Montevideo police chief, Colonel Walter Arregui, by unleashing the corruption revelations in 1981.[23] Apart from undermining the ultra-reactionary sectors, however, President Alvarez's personal ambitions also caused a slow reaction in favor of military professionalization to build up, even among those who were not naturally in a hurry to return power to the politicians.

Politicians' dissatisfaction at the pace of change

By February 1982, the parties were becoming openly dissatisfied with the new government and the statute on parties as it was taking shape. However, they were especially disappointed that no more political bans had been lifted: Leading Colorados and Blancos remained proscribed. Interior Minister Yamandú Trinidad stated bluntly that it was "a subject which for the moment must not be raised."[24] At the end of the year, the army chief, General Queirolo, denounced "attempts to infiltrate the parties from abroad."[25] The reason for that warning was an attempt by Wilsonistas and leftists to hold a lightning antigovernment demonstration in Montevideo. The incident caused party leaders to be summoned to the Armed Forces Commission on Political Affairs (COMASPO) and threatened that

---

21 That stood in stark contrast to the guidelines laid down by the governmental conclave at Piriapolis in November 1981.

22 That was despite the fact that, to the president's chagrin, Végh Villegas had been forced back into the office of minister of the economy by pressure from the international financial community.

23 General Ballestrino was the former chief of a paramilitary antidemonstration squad within the police force, and later head of the School of Arms and Services; General Vadora was a former army commander and, since his retirement, ambassador to Paraguay.

24 "No se estudia levantar nuevas proscripciones, dijo Trinidad," *El País*, Thursday, 4 February 1982, p. 1. During 1982, however, most middle-level Blancos and Colorados had their rights "restored."

25 *El País*, Wednesday, 9 December 1981.

such things "would not be allowed to happen again" and that "never will we go back to the old political times."

The politicians' trust in the new president was low from the start, not least because of his leading role in the entire *proceso*. A retired general, Dante Paladini, meeting with Alvarez shortly after he had been designated the future president, commented to the newspapers that "in the difficult years [he] was the driving force of all this process which Uruguay has been living through."[26] Another factor that bred politicians' suspicions of the new president was the widely held view that he had favored himself as the future joint presidential candidate of the Colorado and Blanco parties had the military's proposed constitution been adopted in 1980. The fact that there had been a flurry of hope when top generals had called in leading politicians in September of 1981 and promised that the proposal for the statute on parties would be thoroughly revised after consultations made subsequent disappointments more acute.[27]

Brigadier Borad's hints that more bans might be lifted were repudiated. A low point was reached with opposition parties on 19 March, when their permitted leaders were summoned to COMASPO to be lectured by General Rapela, its head. The main factors that had irritated the generals were the calls for further lifting of political bans, and even an amnesty, but they also warned against criticism of economic policy and institutional acts and implied that the new opposition weekly magazines were skating on thin ice. Rapela bluntly stated that "we must not go back to a demagogic system nor a political pluralism or liberalism akin to that which existed in 1973" and went on to warn politicians to "abandon these demagogic practices because this is inevitably going to lead to government measures that might to some extent slow down the development of the political timetable."[28] The Colorados decided not to respond formally to that warning, but the Wilsonista sector of the Blanco party promised that "the party will put forward its opinion on political, social, and economic problems each time it considers it necessary with the manner' and responsibility which have always been its norm."

The threat of founding an official party

Uruguay's military were committed to retaining the traditional parties. Yet the failure of the 1980 plebiscite had dashed hopes that Colorados and Blancos might be persuaded to adopt a single presidential candidate

26 *La Mañana*, Friday, 21 August 1981, p. 3.
27 Those early talks had been held in the office of Brigadier Jorge Borad, director of the state oil corporation ANCAP; especially important was the fact that some of those invited were still proscribed.
28 "COMASPO advirtió a partidos sobre el futuro del proceso," *El País*, 20 March 1982, p. 1.

from within the *proceso* (such as General Alvarez). After the inauguration of the new president by the Council of State, rumors continued to circulate regarding his ambitions to found an official party.[29] Yet nothing ever came of it. The minister of the interior, General Trinidad, steered a fine course when he announced in mid-February 1982 that "the Armed Forces do not have political interests or aspirations," but added that "any *citizen* may aspire to join a party or start a new one."[30] The implication was that retired military personnel might have the right to start a party, but that it would have to remain quite separate from the armed forces as an institution. There could be no clearer statement of the differences in interests between the armed forces as an institution, under the generals in active service, and a government led by a general who had retired.[31]

In August, the retired colonel Néstor Bolentini (who was also a councillor of state) announced the creation of a new party to be known as the Patriotic Union.[32] But almost at once General Rapela (the president of COMASPO) publicly promised that the creation of a *partido del proceso* was totally alien to the armed forces' aims.[33] There the matter lay until after the triumph of the opposition in the November primaries. Then, on 8 February 1983, the president made a speech in which he decried the behavior of opposition politicians, their lack of respect, and the return of extremism, demagogy, and Marxist takeover tactics in unions and student meetings. Two months before the talks with political leaders on a new constitution were due to begin at the Parque Hotel, President Alvarez finally came out and called for the creation of an official party, grouping together conservative politicians from all sides. In a speech at Aceguá, a tiny town on the Brazilian border famous for being the site of a historic treaty between Colorados and Blancos, the president reiterated his dissatisfaction with the leaders elected in the primaries:

[W]e find ourselves with elevated leaders who will transform themselves inevitably into the seeds of destruction of their own parties.[34]

---

29 See "Cambios militares en Uruguay," *Clarín*, 20 January 1982, p. 17.
30 "Trinidad Concurre Mañana al Consejo; Reunida la COMASPO," *Ultimas Noticias*, 17 February 1982 (emphasis added).
31 This important distinction between the military's professional and political interests, and the predominance of the former, is the major reason that the concept of the military as a "substitute political party" is misleading.
32 "Bolentini anunció la creación de una nueva corriente política luego del 31 de agosto," *El Día*, 24 August 1982. At the end of 1983, Alvarez was to name him minister of labor and social security, but the party was a total failure.
33 "Creación de Partido del Proceso es Ajena a las Fuerzas Armadas," *El Día*, 27 August 1982.
34 Uruguay, Presidencia de la República (1983).

The response to such a tardy venture was a deafening silence among those who might have been tempted to sympathize, as well as a wave of caustic comment in the opposition magazines.[35] Yet concrete steps to build the movement were never taken, and the idea vanished without a trace following the conspicuous absence of public or elite enthusiasm. Any conceivable bases on which a pro-regime party might have won a free election had all been eroded, clientelistic politics was becoming marginalized (to the good of the country), the credibility of the national-security ideology was nonexistent, and almost every major economic interest, from business to labor, was angry at the slump.

Ferreira's radical line and the posturing by parties and military

COMASPO continued to insist that prior constitutional revisions to guard against subversion were the price for holding elections. Most leaders of the traditional parties, naturally enough, remained highly resistant to those demands. They feared that any pseudotransition that would allow the military to remain the power behind the throne might turn them into hostages of the generals and prove disastrously unpopular among voters. Above all, the major obstacle to agreement between the parties and the military was the continued climate of repression. Uruguay experienced nothing like "relaxation" that began in Brazil in 1974. For instance, the Christian Democrats' magazine, *La Plaza*, was permanently closed down for calling for a political amnesty.[36]

Given such circumstances, it is not surprising that even moderate leaders of the traditional parties publicly questioned the sincerity of the regime's commitment to a return to democracy by means of elections in November 1984.[37] In the long run, the armed forces' actions (or the actions of some of its sectors) hampered the political renovation that a realistic policy might have sought to promote. In the short run they also harmed the position of moderates in the traditional parties.

By constant effort, Wilson Ferreira was able to maintain his position of leadership in the Blanco party, even though banned, in exile, and

35 Reactions to the president's speech are to be found in *El Día*, 27 March 1983, p. 5, *Correo de los Viernes*, 8 April 1983, and Enrique Tarigo, "El pronunciamiento de Aceguá," *Opinar*, 7 April 1983, p. 24.

36 A dozen other newspapers and magazines continued to be temporarily or permanently closed for such actions as mentioning banned politicians or reporting their statements, criticizing government policies, or asking questions about the country's "disappeared" and political prisoners.

37 As self-censorship declined, the government was quite willing to arrest and try editors and journalists of the old daily newspapers that had largely supported them in the plebiscite, but that began to move toward the opposition.

wanted for arrest by the military. Again and again in speeches in various world forums he denounced human-rights abuses in Uruguay and called for an unconditional withdrawal of the military. In an interview shortly after the triumph of his allies in the 1982 primaries, I asked him if his strategy of insisting on unconditional military surrender of power was not excessively inflexible. His reply was simply that "I think that this is definitely the best way to accelerate democratization. The military's time-table is dead, and is no longer any use even to them. The problem now is guarantees. Their mistake was to try and choose their interlocutors."[38] When I asked him if some sort of compromise would be possible if the military agreed to lift the bannings, he said it would not: "The National Security Council and the bannings cannot be accepted, whatever the State Department may wish. I prefer an open dictatorship to a disguised one."[39]

In the last days of January 1983, each party's convention elected a working group of Colorados and Blancos[40] to formulate a joint position for the talks that were due to begin in May with COMASPO under the chairmanship of General Julio Rapela. The Blancos passed motions calling for a return to the 1967 constitution, immediate elections, changes in economic policy, and contacts with other political and social organiza-tions.[41] The following day the Colorado party convention also passed a motion calling for the complete restoration of the constitution and der-ogation of the institutional acts.[42]

Despite forewarnings of the divisions that would recurrently handicap the Blancos' strategy, the nine Wilsonistas in the *directorio* were able to pursue a hegemonic pattern of leadership in the party.[43] Though there were tensions in the Colorado party, it was far more united by comparison. On 9 April the Colorado convention met for the second time in its decaying headquarters.[44] It immediately approved the bases for the dialogue with the military: full public freedoms and a return to the 1967 constitution.[45]

---

38 Personal interview, Washington, DC, 4 January 1983.
39 Ibid. Ferreira then went on to make a prediction that was to come sadly true: "Either there will be a change of government in eight months or in two years, not in between." It was to be the latter.
40 The Civic Union also did the same.
41 "La sesión inaugural de las Convenciones," *Búsqueda*, 2 March 1983.
42 Symptomatic of the Colorados' greater unity and organization was the fact that on the last day of the month five internal commissions had already begun to function: (a) elections, (b) rules, (c) powers, (d) membership, and (e) administration.
43 Of the six non-Wilsonista members of the *directorio*, Lacalle, García Pintos, and Lorenzo Ríos increasingly sided with the Wilsonistas. The remaining three often did not attend meetings for fear of being booed.
44 The convention hall of the building in Calle Andrés Martínez Trueba had been turned into a

The Blanco *directorio* designated Dr. Gonzalo Aguirre, Fernándo Oliú, and Father Juan Martín Posadas (all committed radical Wilsonistas) to represent the party in the talks with the military. To begin with, the Colorado party sent only Dr. Julio María Sanguinetti and Dr. Enrique Tarigo.[46] At the first meeting, the Blancos read a statement from their *directorio* outlining the conditions under which they would take part; the Colorados and Cívicos called for political, press, and trade-union freedoms.

The military were represented by the army generals Rapela and Medina, Brigadier Fernando Arbe and Colonel Jorge Martínez (both air force), and Rear Admiral Jorge Fernández. They at once handed over a 10-page document outlining their agenda for talks. Their demands were enumerated in a list of 24 points entitled "Events Having Occurred in the Republic Which Justify a New Constitutional Text."[47] The document provided a classic statement of the danger of subversion and the need to "protect" democracy with a range of tough measures, such as preserving the authority of the National Security Council, giving the security forces the right to search homes at night (a traditional taboo in Uruguay), and giving the president the right to declare a so-called state of subversion, permitting the holding of suspects for 15 days without trial.

The collapse of the Parque Hotel talks

In May, talks began, but according to most politicians the military had hardly shifted from their 1980 demands, which the electorate had rejected, and were not really committed to handing over power. The generals argued that their proposals – retaining the National Security Council, allowing the president to declare a state of subversion, the holding of suspects for 15 days, and incorporation of military judges into the judiciary – would be placed in the hands of a democratically elected president. They also complained that inflammatory speeches were being made outside the talks in order to provoke them into overreacting. The military evidently had difficulties with the political negotiating style, accustomed as they were to giving orders.

basketball gymnasium and youth club. See "El deplorable estado de nuestra casa," *Opinar*, 3 February 1983, p. 6.

45 General Rapela, chief of COMASPO, described the Colorados' points as "worthy of the best style of communists," on radio and TV, 11 April 1983. On the 15th of the same month, and again on 11 May, Interior Minister Trinidad threatened that the tone the parties had adopted might mean the dialogue would not begin. On the 25th, all major parties called for support for the May Day rally being organized by the new PIT (interunion workers' plenary) labor federation.

46 Both were Batllistas. The Civic Union sent Dr. Juan Vicente Chiarino, Humberto Ciganda, and Julio Daverede.

47 Published in *El Día*, 14 May 1983.

In May, the Wilsonista magazine *La Democracia* was again closed. When the Blancos announced that they would not attend further meetings at the Parque Hotel so long as their magazine was shut down, General Rapela responded that there would be a pause.[48] On that day the three parties met and decided to struggle on, despite internal wrangling within the Blancos' executive body. However, Por la Patria leaders Dr. Fernándo Oliú and Father Juan Martín Posadas resigned as Blanco delegates to the talks on 6 June and were replaced by Dr. Walter Santoro, an independent. A Por la Patria convention subsequently backed their decision.[49] At the second session, held 9 June, General Rapela announced to the dismay of the politicians that the transition to democracy would begin only in 1985 and that the problem of proscriptions would be dealt with only by the next government.[50] With typical moderation, the Colorados parried the military's opening demands by suggesting that their 24 points be grouped under seven headings, and that was agreed.[51] At the fifth meeting (20 June), progress was reported, but a week later talks were less successful.[52] On the tenth anniversary of the closure of the National Assembly, 27 June, a major peaceful demonstration occurred in downtown Montevideo that the police did not attempt to disperse. At that moment of extreme delicacy, when the parties were discussing the legislative percentages that would be necessary for declaration of the proposed emergency powers and the period they might last, a member of the Blanco executive, Carminillo Mederos, was arrested by the military and charged with "attack against Armed Forces morale" (30 June).[53]

Gonzalo Aguirre felt obliged to pull out of the talks in protest at that arrest of a fellow member of the Movimiento de Rocha, and on 5 July the last meeting was held, following the decision of the Blanco party as a whole to pull out, and the decision of the Colorados and

---

48 *El Día*, 29 May 1983, p. 8: "Rapela: se postergó dialogueo y cronograma." *Búsqueda*, 1–7 June 1983: "Por la Patria se considera marginada de la negociación" and "Entre protestas y temores de ausencias llegó la suspensión de la negociación."

49 "Amplia mayoría aprobo el retiro del dialogo," *Búsqueda*, 15–21 June 1983. On the other hand, the latter article also reported that the Por la Patria convention rejected a motion calling on Pivel Devoto to resign for continuing to favor talks.

50 See "Transición empieza en 1985," *El Día*, Friday, 10 June 1983, pp. 1 and 5.

51 The third meeting the following Monday (13 June) was interrupted by the announcement that the interior minister, General Trinidad, had died suddenly. He was replaced by General Linares Brum, *El Día*, Thursday, 16 June 1983, p. 1.

52 "Sanguinetti: Persisten Diferencias Respecto al 'Estado de Emergencia'," *El Día*, 28 June 1983, p. 5.

53 "Movimiento de Rocha: El ambiente es de ruptura," *Mundo Color*, 1 July 1983, p. 1. "Piden liberación de Mederos Galván, MNR decidió el retiro del diálogo," *Mundo Color*, 2 July 1983, p. 2.

Cívicos to follow suit.[54] General Rapela's declarations to the press were measured: "The Armed Forces are open to conversation and dialogue at any time. We have not shut off the dialogue, politicians have not put it that way."[55] Sanguinetti disagreed: "We used the words interruption and suspension in the meeting. The meaning is clear." He added that the parties "could not come out in favor of a caricature of democracy." For the Blancos, Gonzalo Aguirre stated that "citizens can be quite certain that in the course of the negotiations the parties never abdicated the principles we put forward in the campaign prior to the primaries."[56]

When asked why a Blanco leader had been arrested at such a delicate juncture, a colonel who was an important figure in the COMASPO responded gloomily and rather lamely:

Carminillo Mederos tried to sabotage the dialogue by saying things that he knew would get him arrested. It was inevitable the military would fall into the trap. The military are not politicians, they cannot bear criticism. Here the opening was military not political, unlike Brazil. Remember that there was no single man in charge.[57]

Yet the parties had simply been unable to detect any willingness to compromise on the military's part.[58] The representatives of the three permitted parties listed five major points of disagreement, in a special interview with the COMASPO head, General Rapela, immediately after the arrest of Mederos:[59]

1   the length of time that subversive suspects can be held without seeing a judge,
2   the problem of the jurisdiction of military courts,
3   the declaration of a state of emergency,
4   the concept of military command (*mando*), and
5   the definition of "national security."[60]

54   "Hubo consenso en el directorio para abandonar la negociación," *Mundo Color*, Tuesday, 5 July 1983.
55   Gallup Uruguay, *Informe de Opinión Pública*, No. 335, p. 3.
56   Ibid.
57   Personal interview, Montevideo, 14 December 1984. Mederos was a strong supporter of Wilson Ferreira, although he was in the Movimiento de Rocha.
58   The full proceedings of the dialogue in the Parque Hotel were published by the government as a supplement to all newspapers on 6 August 1983. It was a typically civic (some would say naive) gesture on their part.
59   The three representatives were Sanguinetti for the Colorados, Pivel Devoto for the Blancos, and Ciganda for the Civic Union.
60   Gallup Uruguay, *Informe de Opinión Pública*, No. 335, p. 2.

The natural leaders of both parties were still banned, and they could not be mentioned or quoted in the news media, let alone participate directly in the negotiations.[61] That was merely one of the ways in which the lack of any liberalization caused the transition to remain stuck.[62] The combination of inflexible demands, provocative arrests, and censorship meant that opinion in the moderate sectors of the traditional parties was utterly alienated. Thus, whereas in June the 15-man *directorio* of the Blanco party had voted 12 to 3 against pulling out of the talks, subsequent outrage at military obduracy and harassment was such that late on 4 July it voted 14 to 1 in favor.[63]

The military's failure to divide the opposition

The military were incensed by the politicians' decision to walk out of the talks. When I put it to an influential colonel who had worked at COM-ASPO that the list of military demands at the Parque Hotel had been basically the same as in the proposed 1980 constitution, he strongly denied that:

We maintained about a third of the [previous] points and were willing to go as low as a quarter. In the first place, parliamentary approval would have been necessary for a declaration of a state of emergency. Second, the National Security Council was to be advisory. Third, the system of military courts would have been placed under the Supreme Court. Fourth, the problem of military promotions would have been solved by the "rule of three" [allowing the president to choose among three names selected by the services themselves]. Fifth, night searches would have required a judge's warrant.[64]

Whether or not such changes in details represented a fundamental move toward the opposition position, the military ignored the primary tenet of authoritarian political tactics: divide and rule. Some progress had been reported on the proposed state-of-subversion power to be given the presidency.[65] The criticisms of Wilson Ferreira's alliance with the Left in exile that were being heard offered a crucial opportunity for the regime to

---

61 Resistance on both sides had been heightened by the first important labor demonstration since the coup, on 1 May. As many as 150,000 demonstrators had been permitted to rally at the National Assembly.

62 The case for prior liberalization was expressed in the editorial "Liberalizar para democratizar," *Opinar*, 2 June 1983, p. 3.

63 "Politicians Walk Out on Dialogue," *Latin American Weekly Report*, London, 15 July 1983. It was two years to the day since contacts had begun with the military at a 4 July reception at the U.S. Embassy.

64 Personal interview, Montevideo, 14 December 1984.

65 "Poderes de Emergencia: Existen Algunos Puntos de Acercamiento," *El Día*, Tuesday, 21 June 1983, p. 1.

weaken its most serious opponent,[66] an opportunity that was lost. The heated debate over negotiating posture between Wilson's faction, Por la Patria (PLP), and his allies, Movimiento Nacional de Rocha (MNR), was another such lost opportunity. Wilson was against negotiations without prior liberalization, and he came close to accusing his associates of betrayal for even attending the talks.

Yet for the first nine months of 1983 the military spoiled their chances of manipulating the traditional parties by using "all stick and no carrot." It is difficult to identify the causes of the military's mistakes, and it would be too easy to conclude that they did not really want to see democracy restored except as a façade. Rather, we must assume that their flawed strategy was the product of internal divisions. Apart from generals who really never wanted a return to democracy were others with their own visions of how democracy should be guided, leading to hopeless contradictions.

Negotiations, as promised by Alvarez when he took office, seemed the only way out. But what would be the price for the military? Full-scale amnesty for terrorists and the legalization of all leftist parties would not have been required at or before the Parque Hotel talks to convince the traditional parties to participate in a compromise over the conditions for elections. What was, however, almost certainly indispensable was a clear commitment to restoring habeas corpus and freedom of expression and association. In the absence of those guarantees, the traditional parties constantly felt coerced. President Alvarez's intentions remained ambiguous, while all the military remained inflexibly wedded to their demands for "strengthening" democracy, even though that maximalist model had been rejected in the plebiscite.

The failure of negotiations in 1983: an interpretation

What lessons were to be drawn from the frustrating experiences of both sides at the Parque Hotel talks?

1 Negotiations without prior liberalization were fundamentally precarious because of the perceived inequality between the two sides and the weaker party's fundamental distrust of the stronger.
2 The dynamics of negotiation were hampered by the publicity of the deliberations: Both sides made frequent declarations to the press between negotiating bouts.
3 The attitudes of extremists in both camps opposed to the negotiations eventually weakened those at the bargaining table when talks dragged on without early results.
4 Rather than focusing on the interests of both sides, the military's 24 initially announced

---

66 Because it included the communists, the Convergencia alliance was widely criticized within the Blanco party, and it did not in fact exert much influence inside the country.

points constituted a textbook case of positional bargaining. So did the tough initial declaration of the Blanco delegates, in which they emphasized that they were bound by the mandate of those who had elected them.

5   Positional bargaining, in which each side begins by making an extreme first offer and then tries to haggle over a compromise, has at least three disadvantages: (a) Parties may become chained to particular positions merely in order to avoid losing face, but thereby lose sight of their underlying interests. (b) Foot-dragging and stalling are promoted, as each side attempts to hold out longer. (c) The long-term consequences are bad for relations between the two sides, even if agreement is reached.[67]

The attempt by the Colorados to put aside the military's irreducible starting position and discuss seven problem areas was, in effect, an attempt to move toward a different style of negotiation focusing on basic interests and mutually satisfying options. However, the other negotiators (both the military and the Blancos) did not appreciate the full significance of that shift in negotiating strategy. Finally, the talks stagnated because all parties felt that they had more attractive options than the sort of negotiated agreement that looked feasible. It should be remembered that it was the political parties who broke off the talks by walking out.

Public opinion seems to have strengthened the politicians' resistance to the military's demands. An overwhelming 87% of those interviewed by Gallup in Montevideo during July favored elections even if no new constitution could be agreed upon by 1984.[68] Fifty-seven percent favored the rehabilitation of all political parties (Table 6.4), according to polling undertaken during the talks in May and June.[69]

Public opinion in July overwhelmingly blamed the military for the failure of the dialogue, as Table 6.5 shows. Much the same picture of the radicalized sectors of the population emerges as previously: males, youth, and the educated. Interestingly, however, it was the upper classes that most blamed the military, not the middle or lower classes. That finding suggested that the regime had lost its supposed base of support among the bourgeoisie. Regarding party identification, it was the supporters of the Left (coyly referred to by Gallup as "other parties") who were most inclined to absolve the politicians for the breakdown of the talks. The question of which side should make concessions produced practically identical results.

67 Cf. the discussion of "sham bargaining" by Iklé and Leites (1962).
68 Gallup Uruguay, *Informe de Opinión Pública*, No. 337, Table 12A.
69 Gallup Uruguay, *Informe de Opinión Pública*, No. 334, Table 22.

Table 6.4. *Should all parties be legalized?*[a]

Group	Agree (%)	Disagree (%)	No reply (%)	Total (%)
All respondents	57	36	8	101
Sex				
Male	63	32	5	100
Female	52	39	9	100
Age (years)				
18–25	75	9	16	100
26–35	62	38	—[c]	100
36–50	66	28	6	100
51+	45	46	9	100
Class				
Upper	58	35	7	100
Middle	60	32	8	100
Lower	49	44	7	100
Education				
Through primary	44	48	7	99
Secondary/university	69	23	8	100
Party				
Blanco	63	29	8	100
Colorado	50	44	6	100
Other[b]	59	32	9	100

[a]The question: "Some think it would be useful to legalize all parties whose activity has not been allowed until now. Do you agree or disagree with this?"
[b]Includes no reply, the Left, no party, and minor parties.
[c]Zero votes.
Source: Gallup Uruguay, *Informe de Opinión Pública*, No. 334, Table 22.

Reactions to the collapse of the dialogue: opposition radicalization and unity versus growing military divisions

General Rapela's response to the breakdown of the Parque Hotel talks was to state that the transition to democracy had not begun and would not begin until the inauguration of the new president in March 1985. The government also announced that because the parties had walked out, it reserved the right to implement new constitutional provisions without further consultation. In protest at that, the parties called a demonstration that was promptly banned.[70] On 2 August, following a lengthy secret conclave by the Junta de Oficiales Generales, came the announcement of a harsh new package of measures: All public political activity and its

70 *Opinar*, 4 August 1983, p. 24.

Table 6.5. *Who was more to blame for the collapse of the Parque Hotel talks?*[a]

Group	Politicians (%)	Military (%)	Both (%)	No reply (%)	Total (%)
All respondents	8	40	23	29	100
Sex					
Male	7	48	21	23	99
Female	9	33	25	34	100
Age (years)					
18–25	4	57	21	18	100
26–35	10	45	20	25	100
36–50	4	35	33	28	100
51+	12	35	18	35	100
Class					
Upper	6	52	34	8	100
Middle	8	39	20	33	100
Lower	10	31	18	41	100
Education					
Through primary	12	36	20	33	101
Secondary/university	5	43	26	26	100
Party					
Blanco	5	50	29	17	101
Colorado	9	45	25	21	100
Left	—	75	25	—[b]	100
No party	9	32	20	39	100

[a]The question: "Who showed themselves to be the most intransigent in the disagreements that rose in the dialogue between politicians and the military that led to the suspension of the negotiations?"
[b]Zero votes.
Source: Gallup Uruguay, *Informe de Opinión Pública*, No. 337, Table 9.

reporting in the press were "temporarily suspended," and the regime gave itself the right to ban new politicians "who by their conduct, actions, or omissions disturb the peace and public order."

According to some, because the promise of elections was not formally abandoned, the 2 August decrees represented a victory for the moderates, such as the new interior minister, General Linares Brum, and the army commander, General Boscan Hontou.[71] President Alvarez was reported to have favored their cancellation and the imposition of an official party. In effect, the military had the worst of both worlds: Negotiations had collapsed, but they could not agree on any alternatives. Looking on from exile, Wilson Ferreira must have been well satisfied at the vindication of

71 "Uruguay bans all political activities and censors press," *The Times*, London, 4 August 1983.

tactics that many had considered too inflexible and hard-line. Nothing gave the opposition radicals such hope as the massive pot-banging and blackouts of 25 August (copied from those in Chile) that greeted the new wave of repression.

The vacillations (themselves the probable symptoms of the power struggle) continued.[72] During September the government ordered a crackdown, arresting a leading Blanco from San Jóse, Eladio Fernández Menéndez, and later 60 striking construction workers.[73] Yet the chief of the COMASPO, General Rapela, continued secret discussions with banned politicians other than the still-exiled Wilson Ferreira. Though the discussions failed,[74] by late September the armed forces belatedly began a strategy of "divide and conquer," lifting the remaining bans on Colorados and Blancos, except for Wilson.[75]

The deproscriptions came too late to split the opposition and overcome their insistence that all bannings (including those on the Left) be lifted. In fact, the traditional parties for the first time established formal links inside Uruguay with the still-illegal Left. That led to the extremely important authorized rally organized by the newly formed Intersectorial on 27 November, at Montevideo's obelisk. All political parties (banned and legal), plus the unions and popular movements, took part, drawing a crowd reportedly as high as 400,000 (in reality, even half that would have been enormous). For almost the first time in Uruguay's history, politicians from both the traditional parties shared a platform with the Left.

There were worrisome signs of a strategy of increasing tensions in some sectors of the regime: beatings of students by military cadets, clashes in the carnival celebrations, and a series of small bombs at stores that had advertised in the left-wing press. Optimists argued that such events were symptomatic of the impotence of those who opposed the transition. Others were uneasy. Reports that cannot be documented, but that were repeated by many interviewees, suggested that President Alvarez encouraged Labor Minister Bolentini to allow the industrial-relations climate to deteriorate. Unions staged an illegal march

---

72 Surprisingly, the student organization ASCEEP was allowed to hold a week of celebrations on the 25th anniversary of the law of 1958 granting autonomy to the university. (The military had suspended it.) On the negative side, the Supreme Court pronounced itself not competent to consider legalizing the Christian Democratic party (PDC), as it had been asked to do in a private suit.

73 The magazines *Opinar* and *Aquí* were also closed for four issues. See "60 strikers arrested in Uruguay," *The Times*, London, 19 September 1983; "Uruguay Arrests Top Political Leader," *International Herald Tribune*, 27 September 1983.

74 *Latin American Weekly Report*, London, 83–43, 4 November 1983, p. 12.

75 Unlike Ferreira, Movimiento de Rocha leader Carlos Julio Pereyra had his rights restored. See *El Día*, 12 November 1983.

on 9 November 1983 (which was brutally dispersed), and by December striking workers had started a factory occupation at the ILDU textile firm, the first since the coup. On 18 January 1984, Montevideo and parts of the interior were paralyzed by the first general strike in over a decade.[76] The president was ready with a secret plan, dubbed the "octopus plan," to retaliate for the general strike by ordering mass arrests of politicians, but it seems that the commanders refused to comply without written orders.[77] The traditional politicians, particularly the Colorados, went out of their way to dissociate themselves from the strike in order to avoid playing into the hard-liners' hands.

Shortly after the restoration of his political rights by the conclave of the Junta de Oficiales Generales, on 11 November, the former Colorado senator Jorge Batlle made a clever appeal to the military in a magazine article claiming that the obstacles Alvarez was placing in the way of the transition ran counter to their interests. Batlle went on to warn the armed forces against identifying with an official party that could only be a sham or a failure, insisting that Alvarez should have the right to stand in the 1984 presidential election, but only on a ticket that was distinct from the military as an institution.

The size of the rally of 27 November evidently strengthened the hand of the moderates in the Junta de Oficiales and further cast doubt on Alvarez's ability to press *continuismo*.[78] The parties' strategy of calling the military's bluff ran the risk of provoking an involution of the authoritarian situation.[79] Yet all dangerous moments, such as the 27 November rally, passed without the feared military action.

For the military, the need to defeat Wilson raised the dilemma that the surest way to prevent a radical Blanco victory was to legalize at least some of the leftist parties. A deal with the Colorados made sense, but many generals were utterly opposed to legalization of the Left, whom

76 According to a young leftist militant, "the level of spontaneity was very high, and the military were scared of initiating a bloody repression" (personal interview, Montevideo, April 1985).
77 This information is taken from an interview with a moderate Colorado editor who was consistently a reliable source of evidence. It must be regarded as a secondhand account, but it was corroborated by a leading Blanco, who stated that "Alvarez deliberately provoked the strike in cahoots with Bolentini by allowing factory occupations. The entire Council of Ministers objected to [Interior Minister] Linares Brum's *plan pulpo* and refused to accept that politicians should be arrested when they had never supported the strike" (personal interview, 15 March 1984). General Rapela himself took over as interior minister on 8 February 1984.
78 "Time is Running Out for Alvarez," *Latin American Weekly Report*, London, 9 December 1983; "La multitudinaria concentración en Montevideo evidencia el creciente aislamiento del regimen militar uruguayo," *El País*, Madrid, 29 November 1983, p. 2; "Poll Pressure on Uruguay's Junta," *The Financial Times*, London, 6 December 1983; "Riot troops seize 100 in Uruguay," *The Times*, London, 31 December 1983.
79 This is what O'Donnell and Schmitter (1986, pp. 24–5) call "playing coup poker."

they had consistently portrayed as subversive enemies of the republic. By 1984 the military had to consider removing Alvarez, yet they were loath to clash publicly among themselves.[80] Many argued that the inauguration of a democratically elected government in Buenos Aires and the generals' fear of disorders would eventually clinch their determination to ensure that the promised elections would be held in 1984. Yet the arrest of former military presidents across the River Plate only increased the dilemma of the Uruguayan armed forces.

80 A further point in Alvarez's disfavor was the rumor that he had held talks with the British on allowing their planes to refuel en route to the Falkland Islands.

7

From mobilization to negotiation: the exhaustion of alternatives

In early January 1984 the minister of the interior, General Linares Brum, was asked point-blank by journalists whether or not the government would be handed back to politicians in 1985. His reply was somber:

That is a rather difficult question to answer. . . . People are full of fervor, and those who perhaps do not know what happened in 1973, or what happened before 1973, go to demonstrations. [It] is possible that there will be [violent] confrontations with those who do not agree with these demonstrations. . . . I would say that if this situation gets worse the consequences are unpredictable.[1]

On 18 January, Montevideo was paralyzed by the first general strike since 1973, leading to the banning of the Plenario Intersindical de Trabajadores (PIT) and hurried legislation to regulate the right to strike. During an official visit to Brazil at the end of February, President Alvarez made a point of guaranteeing that a liberal type of democracy would not return.[2]

Uruguay's political future hung in the balance. There were no real prospects for *continuismo* (continuation of the authoritarian regime in its current form), nor any immediate prospects for its overthrow (*ruptura*). However, the Wilsonistas still hoped for the possibility of "democratic rupture" without negotiations. There were also still some sectors of the military who thought it possible to reform the system, if necessary without the agreement of the politicians elected in the primaries. These were the options that were to be exhausted during the first six months of 1984.

The limits to opposition mobilization

The dream of all opponents of tyranny is that civil society will mobilize enough popular resistance to force a complete democratic rupture. For

1 "Gral. Linares Brum," *La Semana de El Día*, 7–13 January 1984.
2 "Alvarez Habría Rechazado Volver al Liberalismo," *El Día*, 29 February 1984.

authoritarian regimes that have not managed to mobilize political support, strikes, demonstration, and protests pose a grave threat. The modern exclusionary authoritarian regime in Latin America is determinedly atomizing in its impact on political society. Nevertheless, under authoritarian regimes, *some* autonomous institutions survive (such as professional bodies, church groups, academic faculties, rural organizations, and even labor unions), and new ones may be nurtured into life. Few authoritarian regimes were as successful as the Uruguayan regime in totally disarticulating the institutions of opposition, in effect crushing or flattening civil society and "privatizing" politics: The academy was purged, unions repressed, and professional bodies silenced. The church had never been influential during this century, and rural workers continued unorganized.[3]

Even short-lived authoritarian regimes have been accompanied by quite important changes in social structures, notably an increase in female participation in the labor force, and growth of the informal sector caused by deindustrialization. In many cases the responses of opposition groups have been to attempt to promote *new social movements*.[4] If the industrial proletariat is under physical assault, and in any case has never reached the proportion of the population attained in core capitalist economies, there seems to be little sense in pinning hope for social transformation on it alone. The general aim has been the strengthening of civil society vis-à-vis the state, as well as mobilization of new political subjects "from below." The prototypical new movements include women's groups, shantytown dwellers, ecclesiastical base communities, and so on. In Uruguay, shanty dwellers were politically apathetic or even reactionary, but some new popular movements did begin to emerge, probing tolerated spaces and exploiting them. From 1981 the "rebirth of civil society" (to use Fernando Henrique Cardoso's phrase) became quite marked.

Established interest associations assumed an attitude of passivity under the first decade of the authoritarian regime. The only major exception was the Rural Federation.[5] But how important were the *new* social movements in affecting politicians' perceptions of the balance of power between state and society? Only two of the major social movements to emerge by

3 The only exception to the lack of rural unions in Uruguay's history had been the cane workers in the 1960s, organized by Tupamaros leader Raúl Sendic.

4 I use the term loosely to refer to any movement that had not previously existed. Others emphasize non-class-based "postmodern" movements.

5 To take one example, the lawyers' association, Colegio de Abogados, reached an accommodation with the regime, despite wholesale undermining of legal procedures under the institutional act that set up the Ministry of Justice. Only in 1984 did the Colegio become a little more active in calling for the reestablishment of the rule of law and denouncing the charges against Wilson Ferreira. In the same year the Uruguayan authors' association began to call for a political amnesty, and the psychologists' association expelled members who had been accused of collaborating with military torture.

1983 were really new: the cooperative housing association, FUCVAM, and the human-rights movement, including the watchdog modeled on the Argentine organization of the same name, Servicio de Paz y Justicia (SERPAJ).[6] The Peace and Justice Service, which worked on behalf of political prisoners and the "disappeared," was allied to a more "underground" constellation of groups, such as Familiares de Presos Políticos (Relatives of Political Prisoners).[7] The most impressive achievement of the latter groups was to organize a march of over a hundred thousand people in total silence in the middle of 1984 to protest Uruguay's disappeared. The self-discipline of the crowd was extraordinary. That march had been preceded by a poster campaign in which simple life-size human outlines had been spray-painted on public buildings, and the names of missing persons written in by hand. Both events constituted a chilling propaganda coup, but the influence of human-rights groups was not nearly as great as in Argentina or Chile.

The other wholly new social movement that reached major proportions was the cooperative housing association. Under a law of the early 1970s, individuals could form housing cooperatives, which would then be eligible for reduced-rate loans from the state mortgage bank for the construction of new housing. The people who formed such co-ops usually needed to have some prior organizational experience. Thus, many of the cooperatives were formed by trade-unionists, often from the same industry. Once installed in the new housing projects, physically side by side, this mass of leftist militants could not be broken up, even though union activity was suppressed.[8] If the head of household was in jail, the spouse and teenage children remained behind. When pot-banging protests began in 1983,[9] the noise was particularly loud in the cooperative apartment complexes. FUCVAM became a surrogate focus for opposition to the regime.[10]

The two most important social movements were new in name only:

---

6 Although a variety of women's groups emerged, they suffered from the usual divisions between those who saw women's issues as transcending issues of class and those who saw them as subordinate to class.

7 Much of the Catholic church hierarchy was on good terms with the military, but some priests had become radicalized. One of the best known was a SERPAJ leader and Jesuit, Father Luis Pérez Aguirre. Another important radical church group was the monastic group known as "Conventuales," with whom the Tupamaros guerrillas lived following their release. However, such groups were not particularly prominent.

8 Interview with Amalia Alonso, Montevideo, 3 July 1984.

9 Copied from Chile, the first *caceroleo* began rather spontaneously in reaction to the decree of 2 August 1983 "suspending political activity."

10 During the early part of 1984 it made a heroic effort to collect half a million signatures to force a referendum on government housing policies. Though the referendum attempt failed, it led to a great spurt of organizational activity. Critics of the attempt, however, sometimes emphasized the waste of effort it entailed, and the resulting disillusion.

Associación Social y Cultural de Estudiantes de la Enseñanza Pública (ASCEEP), the student association that replaced the old Federación de Estudiantes Universitarios del Uruguay (FEUU), and the Plenario Intersindical de Trabajadores (PIT), which replaced the old CNT union federation. They were by far the largest organizations in terms of militants: the PIT's 1 May rally in 1983 dwarfed the officially supported rival gathering. A call for peace (a code word for amnesty) and freedom was read out to over 100,000 demonstrators.[11] In September 1983 ASCEEP held a week-long conference to commemorate the statute that had granted the university autonomy 25 years earlier, even though that autonomy had been abolished by the military. Both of them played leading roles in the committee of parties and social movements known as the Intersectorial, which organized the rally of 25 November 1983 at the obelisk. The PIT was able to paralyze the capital on 18 January 1984 by calling a general strike, somewhat to the dismay of its older leaders and the traditional political parties. That same night the decree that banned the PIT (in name only, for it continued to function) was greeted by another pot-banging protest.

As protests grew, hopes began to rise among radical sectors that the country might become "ungovernable." In fact, the disturbances never approached the level seen, for example, in Chile. Nevertheless, Gallup asked interviewees for their reactions (Table 7.1). First they asked whether surprise demonstrations were beneficial or prejudicial to public peace and tranquillity.[12] They then asked whether or not interviewees approved of the blackouts and pot-banging of 25 August. Not surprisingly, few interviewees (except about half the leftists) went so far as to assert that protests "benefited peace," yet what was striking was the high level of support for opposition demonstrations all the same. The typical profile of the radical sectors of the population emerged, though it is interesting that those under age 25 were the most in favor of demonstrations, and those between 26 and 35 the most approving of pot-banging.

Ultimately, the rhetoric of popular movements is in tension with the practical fact that few authoritarian regimes are susceptible to overthrow by *frontal* assault. There exists, however, a nonrevolutionary path mapped out by Stepan as "society-led regime termination."[13] This essentially consists of a violent paroxysm of social protest, such as the Argentine Cordobazo of 1969, or the strikes in Peru in 1977. This galvanizes the

11 See "Masiva presencia popular," *Correo de los Viernes*, Friday, 6 May 1983.
12 The wording of the question was not ideal; many respondents may have answered that such demonstrations were prejudicial to peace, but still favored them either for that reason or, more likely, as a necessary evil.
13 Stepan (1986).

Table 7.1. *Public attitudes toward demonstrations and protests*

Group	"Do demonstrations benefit peace & tranquillity?" (% "yes")	"Do you approve of the pot-banging protest?" (% "yes")
All respondents	16	55
Sex		
Male	17	58
Female	14	53
Age (years)		
18–25	21	62
26–35	15	74
36–50	15	60
51+	14	45
Class		
Upper	12	53
Middle	17	56
Lower	16	55
Education		
Through primary	15	55
Secondary/university	16	56
Party		
Blanco	10	n.a.
Colorado	17	n.a.
Left	50	n.a.
No party	16	n.a.

Source: Gallup Uruguay, *Informe de Opinión Pública*, No. 337, Tables 8A and 32.

authoritarian regime's decision to extricate itself and initiate a transition.[14] Yet, despite widespread approval of protests, Uruguayans appeared not to believe that they could shake the military's will; a growing climate of pessimism also gripped the country. Public order was maintained throughout.[15] After the failure of the Parque Hotel talks in August 1983, public opinion was evenly split as to whether the timetable for elections would be postponed, and whether the dialogue would start again soon.[16] Particularly pessimistic were youth and the lower classes.

To what extent were politicians' perceptions of the prospects for a

14 The subsequent evolution of the regime may involve other "paths" and mechanisms, such as reform pacts.
15 The only exceptions to the overall peace of 1984 apparently were isolated and anomic outbreaks of vandalism during the Mardi Gras carnival. The press made much of those incidents, and they probably mobilized conservative opinion, but in a sense their minor scale serves to remind us of the largely peaceful nature of Uruguayan society.
16 Thirty-seven percent were optimistic on both counts, and 38% pessimistic. Gallup Uruguay, *Informe de Opinión Pública*, No. 336, Tables 2 and 4.

Table 7.2. *Politicians' perceptions of the importance of social movements*[a]

| | Relative importance | | | | | |
Party	Highly (%)	Rather (%)	Somewhat (%)	Little (%)	Not political (%)	Total (%)
Frente	39	44	11	0	6	100 (n = 18)
Blancos	24	32	28	16	0	100 (n = 25)
Colorados	20	16	36	28	0	100 (n = 25)

[a]The question: "Do you think organizations, groups, and people not affiliated to parties, such as civic neighborhood associations, activist groups, especially those related to housing, Christian base communities, women's movements, etc., have played an important role in the opposition to the present government?"

democratic transition influenced by their attitudes toward the social movements? Opinions were divided as to the precise influence of these nonparty organizations in pressuring for the regime transition (Table 7.2).[17] Colorados answered, on average, that such movements had some importance, but Frentistas believed that they were very important (partly, perhaps, because they were far more involved in such arenas, because of their need for surrogate organizations while their parties remained banned).[18]

There are two fundamentally different outlooks regarding transitions: One emphasizes the role of mass organizations in civil society; the other stresses elite consensus, particularly among politicians. Table 7.3 shows the strong connection between the view that elites were the key to ensuring a successful transition to democracy and the view that little importance could be assigned to the new social movements. That stands to reason: For those anxious to nurture the formal procedures of conflict resolution and democracy, direct mobilization of the masses was a potential threat.

Just how great a threat from the new forms of mass praetorian mobilization might have frightened the elite into renewing their support for authoritarianism? Interviewees were asked if they thought that the new social movements would eventually lead to the formation of new parties, or if such militants would be absorbed by existing parties, or if neither would occur, but the organizations would survive as independent pressure groups. Table 7.4 shows that those on the Left clearly perceived the new

17 There may have been a tendency to discount the importance of organizations that were potential rivals to parties, and so one should compare responses across parties rather than emphasize absolute levels. On the other hand, most politicians did see social movements as having played a major role.

18 The mean Colorado response was 2.7 (nearer to "somewhat" influential than to "rather" influential), and the mean Frentista response was 1.9 ("rather"). The difference in means yields a significance score of $p = .02$.

Table 7.3. *The perceived importance of social movements × politicians'*
attitudes toward elite versus mass transition strategies

| "What do you think is more important for a transition to democracy and its consolidation?" | "Do you think organizations, groups, and people not affiliated to parties... have played an important role in the opposition to the present government?" Relative importance (%) | | | | |
	Highly ($n = 17$)	Rather ($n = 17$)	Somewhat ($n = 19$)	Little ($n = 8$)	Number
(a) The capacity of party leaders to act with some consensus, create institutions, respect minorities, be loyal...	35	59	79	88	($n = 38$)
(b) Acceptance by different social sectors, interests, organizations, trade unions, business groups, military, foreign interests...	65	41	21	12	($n = 23$)
Total	100	100	100	100	($n = 61$)

movements as temporary substitutes for parties that would be reabsorbed.
Majorities of Colorados and Blancos agreed, although almost as many
thought that the movements would develop into permanent pressure
groups. For those who were concerned that the political opening might
produce an explosion of non-party-channeled political participation, the
politicians' predictions, if they held, were good news.

The new social movements were in fact dominated by the Left, primarily
by the Broad Front parties. The cooperative housing association
(FUCVAM) had an influential Trotskyist among its leaders. The student
union (ASCEEP) had an occasional Wilsonista Blanco in its executive

Table 7.4. *What will happen to the new social movements in the future?*

Option	Frente (%) ($n = 11$)	Blancos (%) ($n = 15$)	Colorados (%) ($n = 17$)
(a) "They will lead to the formation of new parties."	9	0	0
(b) "Their militants will join existing parties."	82	60	59
(c) "They won't be absorbed, but will continue as pressure groups"	9	40	41

body. Those were, however, exceptions to the rule. Phenomena such as the *ollas populares* (community kitchens) were organized by the Left.

In February, Sanguinetti proposed reorganizing the existing Intersectorial into two halves: One, consisting of just the parties, with the participation of the union federation as the most important social movement, would be named the Multipartidaria; the other would group the various smaller social movements under the banner Intersocial.[19] The Blancos immediately opposed the idea and elevated the caliber of their delegation to the forum. Crucially, however, the representatives of the PIT labor federation, Richard Read and Andrés Toriani, both of whom were close to the parties of the Broad Front, agreed with Sanguinetti's proposal, and it was adopted. That was a revealing early sign of the Blancos' desire to mobilize social movements against the military regime, as well as the Broad Front's increasing preference for a negotiated transition, arrived at by concerted action among political leaders.

The role of popular movements in the transition became one of close subordination to the Left by the time of the "civic stoppage" of 27 June 1984. The latter was really a general strike, but at Colorado urging the parties chose not to call it one. The pressure of mobilization was used largely as *potential power*, as, for example, in such symbolic one-day strikes, rather than in permanent disorder, which might have been counterproductive.[20] Negotiation with the military was the only solution, as even a fully united and militant opposition almost certainly would not have toppled the regime. With their limited links to social movements, the Blancos had even less leverage to force the military to capitulate.

Politicians' perceptions of the military's interest in extrication: the balance of external and internal pressures

What assessments did the politicians have to offer regarding the military's calculations in the critical first months of 1984, once the alternatives to negotiation seemed finally to have been exhausted? Although most politicians agreed that the generals' motives had not been the same in promising elections as they had been in calling the plebiscite on the tough new constitution proposed in 1980, a significant minority of Blancos (29%) disagreed. In other words, they still saw the military as pursuing an undemocratic prolongation of their influence. Only 10% of Frentistas

---

19 "Se está negociando," *Jaque*, 24 February 1984, p. 3.
20 There were some long and bitter strikes during 1984, particularly in fishing and textiles. Nevertheless, the fact that the conditions for mobilization were closely related to economic crisis may have made social movements fundamentally more defensive. Furthermore, the communists insisted on a strategy of caution and fought hard to gain control of the PIT.

were as cynical, and 6% of Colorados.[21] In other words, politicians from the latter parties thought they detected a change of heart.

Perceptions, even if erroneous, can have a real impact on events by influencing calculations. Broadly speaking, when questioned as to the military's motives in seeking to negotiate a transition, the politicians emphasized the external *challenges* to the regime, such as the pressures from parties, popular movements, the economic crisis, and so on. They saw those pressures as having an *exhaustion effect*, far more important than internal splits among elite supporters, technocrats, or military factions. The overwhelming picture that emerges from Table 7.5 is that politicians saw the military as being exhausted by the problems of government, aware of their own illegitimacy, dispirited by the economic crisis, beleaguered by popular pressures, and anxious to hand over power.[22]

Almost all leaders interviewed rejected the view that significant pressures for change emanated from within the regime, especially not from its military sectors, and few believed that the military felt a sense of having accomplished their mission. This question tells us much about the differences in the parties' perceptions. Whereas the Colorados in almost every case were *less* likely to mention extraregime pressures than were the other parties, they were *more* likely to mention internal factors. That general perception would eventually have profound consequences in committing the Colorados to a strategy of trying to strengthen the forces favoring democratization within the regime, rather than escalating the pressure of opposition.

Two questionnaire-based interviews with military figures in the regime[23] differed substantially regarding the armed forces' motives.[24] Though the military officers confirmed the politicians' view that there was no internal crisis in the regime, they saw the pressure for transition

---

21 The significance of the difference between Colorados and Blancos was .12.

22 The 12 factors mentioned are listed in descending order of frequency for all interviewees, including those of minor parties not in the table.

23 One respondent was a minister, the other an officer posted to the COMASPO. Open-ended interviews with other active and retired officers close to the regime confirmed their responses.

24 According to these sources, though the economic slump and the need for unpopular austerity had had the effect of accelerating the urgency of the transition, the main factor was the military's constant commitment from 1977 onward to a negotiated restoration of democracy. Popular pressures did not count; international pressures, on the other hand, did. The same officers confirmed that the regime's legitimacy was not questioned from inside, but stressed (as did the politicians) that its isolation was fundamentally a product of the deep-seated traditions of liberal democracy in Uruguayan political society. Unlike the politicians, they even saw redemocratization as favored by the political culture of the military themselves. They rejected the view that fear of conflicts in the military hierarchy played any role, but agreed that the public actions of the traditional parties were offering a political solution for transition.

Table 7.5. *Motives imputed to the military for continuing the transition*[a]

Motive	Broad Front (%) (n = 17)	Blancos (%) (n = 20)	Colorados (%) (n = 24)[b]
External factors			
(A) The military government is exhausted and feels incapable of solving problems, trying to pass them to politicians.	94	86	92
(B) Since 1973, governments have been based on force and have not achieved legitimacy, as democratic traditions are too deep.	94	90	83
(C) The economic crisis, foreign debt, and the need for more and more severe austerity.	100	69	80
(D) Growing popular pressures and the actions of different social and political forces (e.g., church, unions) make delay impossible.	94	90	75
(E) The public action of the traditional parties is offering a democrtic alternative for the future.	65	75	87
(F) International pressure, pressure for civil rights, and Uruguay's isolation.	88	75	62
Internal motives			
(G) Fear of conflicts in the military.	47	42	50
(H) The reflections of democratic political culture that the armed forces managed to conserve as a corporation.	40	44	53
(I) Fragmentation of the civil coalition that backed the government; interest conflict.	44	25	54
(J) Questioning of the legitimacy of government by military constitutionalists.	20	19	35
(K) Questioning of governmental legitimacy "from within" by civilian sectors.	30	0	20
(L) The government has reached its objectives and wants to return to democracy.	6	25	8

[a] The question: "The government has insisted that there will be free elections in 1984 and a new elected president in 1985. What motives do they now have?"
[b] *n* may vary.

more in terms of Uruguayan traditions than as due to social mobilization.[25] To an outsider, their account would have been plausible except for one detail: the crucial question of *timing* (seven years was a long time to maintain an inflexible agenda for constitutional changes while claiming a commitment to democracy). It would seem that their accumulating economic difficulties and foreign pressure hastened their search for an acceptable set of politicians to whom they might entrust the ship of state. To sum up, the foregoing data suggest the paradoxical nature of the military's position and how it was perceived by politicians. The armed forces were strongly committed to handing over power to elected civilians according to the promised timetable, and they were aware of their lack of legitimacy, but they remained remarkably united and in control of the situation.

The evolution of the balance of power in the high command: President Alvarez's struggle to hold on to power

The commitment to elections was broadly held among all generals, but there was far less agreement on the terms they should extract, and which politicians they should allow. Given their desire to hand over power to responsible leaders, the military were determined that they would not simply abdicate. For that reason, the annual February promotions were of great importance. The alliance between the traditional parties and the Left enraged the military, though it did not necessarily strengthen the hard-liners in the long run. A climate of pessimism in the military parallel to that in the population seems to have arisen regarding the possibility for negotiating acceptable terms for the transition.

February 1984 saw the final round of military promotions under Alvarez's presidency, and leading generals used the occasion to reaffirm their commitment to handing over power. Given the relative unity of the army, outgoing generals remained influential. For example, on the occasion of a retirement ceremony, General Hontou had announced that "we can say that the *proceso* has entered its final phase."[26] He went on to insist, however, that the opposition must not see the military's decision to restore democracy "of their own accord" as a sign of weak-

---

25 Responses by four retired high-ranking military officers who were interviewed in their capacity as politicians (two Colorados and two Frentistas) showed a hybrid pattern: both the importance of popular pressure and residual democratic values in the military were emphasized.

26 "Podemos Decir Que el Proceso ha Llegado a su Etapa Culminante," *El Día*, Friday, 10 February, 1984, p. 7. The translation is mine. Occasionally, translation of the military's speeches is rendered difficult by their convoluted style. I have tried to strike a balance between ensuring the intelligibility of their sentiments and conveying a sense of their awkwardness.

ness. The themes laid out by General Hontou clearly held out the prospect of a negotiated transition: a commitment to a return to democracy, a desire to work with the moderate sectors of the opposition, and a warning to politicians not to play into the hands of military hard-liners. Speeches by the generals continually tried to portray the unity of the armed forces and suggest that the military institution was behind the commitment to extract the best possible guarantees as the price for returning to democracy.

When attempts were made to shunt them aside in February, soft-liners fought back.[27] As a leading Blanco politician commented, with characteristic faith in the impending demise of the *proceso*, "eleven Generals have been promoted in the past two years, but they know they will have to complete their command under a democratic regime. Alvarez is more and more isolated."[28] Just before he left office, the interior minister, General Linares Brum, told the press that "renewal of the dialogue must be immediate."[29] Two days later, his successor, General Rapela, predicted that 1984 would be a year of conflict and difficulties, but he also described censorship as "not . . . positive."[30] By the end of the month, secret contacts between politicians and the military had been reestablished.[31] Meanwhile, public military declarations fluctuated from harsh to encouraging. In an interview with the press early in March, the head of the navy, Rodólfo Invidio, expressed optimism that a deal was near.[32] Regarding the problem of political bans, such as that on Wilson Ferreira, Invidio referred to "positions which can be understood a little, which may be delicate . . . but we have to look at the goal, what the country wants. What does the country want? Democracy? We have to put aside certain problems, certain personalities, a few names, because the greater objective is the democratic transition of the country."

27 "Nomina Completa de la Junta . . . ," *El País*, Saturday, 18 February 1984. In particular, General German de la Fuente refused to go to Washington, but finally accepted the directorship of the military school. "Mañana asumira el ministerio del interior el General Rapela," *El País*, 9 February 1984.
28 Personal interview, Montevideo, 15 March 1984.
29 "La Reanudación del Diálogo Debe Ser Inmediata," *El País*, 9 February 1984.
30 The Interior Ministry is perhaps the most crucial political portfolio in the cabinet, having control over the prisons and police. "Rapela definió a este año como conflictivo y difícil," *El País*, 11 February 1984, p. 1.
31 "Politicos y militares harán entre hoy y mañana sondeos para el diálogo," *La Mañana*, Monday, 6 February 1984, pp. 2 and 8; "Se está negociando," *Jacque*, 24 February 1984, p. 3. *Jaque* revealed that the parties insisted that they would at first negotiate only an easing in the climate of tensions and securing the necessary liberties for the elections, while the military renewed the theme of constitutional revisions. The commanders were also adamant regarding their refusal to countenance lifting the political ban on Wilson Ferreira.
32 "Invidio Opinó Que se Está Muy Cerca de Alcanzar un Acuerdo," *El Día*, 8 March 1984.

Asked if divergences existed in the armed forces, he denied that such was the case. However, when the reporter asked him if elections might be postponed if no agreement was reached with the parties, the naval chief refused to answer the question.

On the occasion of the 71st anniversary of the founding of the air force, its commander, Lieutenant General Manuel Buadas, dedicated the new Aviation Plaza in Montevideo. His remarks were calculated to be stern and yet not to shut the door for further talks,[33] and he spoke as if he assumed that the opposition parties had the same goals as the military. Speaking to the parties, he called for dialogue, while urging them to put aside hubris and personal ambition (an appeal presumably directed at Wilson Ferreira in particular). Meanwhile, for hard-liners in the military, he renewed the armed forces' commitment to the transition and offered reassurance that politics would not degenerate once more to the pre-1973 situation. The commitment to elections was repeated by the army commander, General Pedro Aranco, on the day commemorating those who had died during the subversion.[34] It was surely significant that he chose that day, one on which it might have been tempting to continue the rhetoric of military self-justification.[35] The outcome of the complex struggle inside the armed forces had decreased the authority of President Alvarez and led to the triumph of those who, though not actually soft-liners in their hearts, were committed to preserving the unity of their institution.

In April 1984 the hard-liners apparently made a major miscalculation. In the notorious Roszlik case, a small-town doctor of Russian descent was arrested and tortured to death, and it was the first such case that was widely reported and condemned inside Uruguay. Machiavellian speculation had it that the incident was a ploy designed to discredit General Medina, commander of the Third Military Region, where the event took place. Medina was alleged to have a commitment to military professionalism and to favor sticking to the timetable for withdrawal. According to this theory, the more pro-Alvarez General Siqueira would ascend to the key post of commander in chief. If that was in fact the plan, the maneuver backfired. In May it was announced that the leader of the brigade in charge of the operation, and the major involved in the torture, would be court-martialed – the first such trial ever.

33 "Guerra Fría Bloqueó el Diálogo y Amenaza con una Guerra Caliente," *Ultimas Noticias*, Saturday, 17 March 1984, p. 3.
34 "Sostienen Que 'Decisión de Retornar a la Normalidad Institucional es Irreversible'," *El Día*, Saturday, 14 April 1984.
35 However, Rapela made it clear that there could be no compromise regarding the system for promotion to general that the military had created.

Sanguinetti, Seregni, Medina: the emergence of a trilateral alliance

On 18 March 1984 the military finally released the former general, Líber Seregni, leader of the Broad Front.[36] The decision was made by the entire junta of generals. However, Seregni remained banned; he could neither vote nor run for office. Seregni's acceptance of those terms immediately posed a great problem for the Blancos, who had insisted on the restoration of political rights to all politicians, so as once more to be led by Wilson Ferreira. Significantly, Seregni's massively attended (and reported) first speech from the balcony of his house was highly conciliatory. Above all, he called for pacification of the country and claimed that such was the Broad Front's mission.[37] The importance of that appeal for "peace" was that it both justified a call for the release of political prisoners (including the Tupamaros) and held out the prospect of moderation by the still-illegal Left.

Years of detention apparently had not left him eager for revenge against his former captors.[38] Any remaining doubts that the Left might back the Blancos' radical position were dispelled when the plenum of the Broad Front voted, with Seregni's strong backing, that all supporters must cease their activities in the Convergencia Democrática.[39] When I asked General Seregni if that was always inevitable, he replied "no, it was not inevitable given the existence of the *ley de lemas* [double simultaneous vote]. There were some talks, but they could not get anywhere. The National party has different economic interests."[40]

A number of clues suggest that much was known to the Colorados and generals in advance regarding the moderate line that Seregni would take. In the first place, at the end of February, the Colorado magazine *Jaque* had hinted in a story on secret talks with the military that certain parties *other* than those that were legal (i.e., the Left) were preoccupied by the possibility that violence might return. When the news came that the general would be freed, Sanguinetti immediately granted an interview to

36 "Uruguai liberta mais importante preso politico," *Jornal do Brasil*, 20 March 1984, p. 13. News of his impending release had been sent out by United Press International almost a fortnight earlier and had appeared in Uruguay: "Aseguran Que es Iminente la Liberación de Seregni," *El Día*, 8 March 1984.

37 Addressing the crowd (and hinting that they should disperse), he stated that "before you leave, I want to tell you the great preoccupation right now, in order effectively to go down the path to democratic restoration, is the pacification of spirits; we feel national pacification is a necessity; there can be no democracy without peace." *Aquí*, No. 45 (special supplement).

38 See the interviews in *Le Monde Diplomatique*, March 1985, p. 21, and *Cinco Días*, 20 March 1984, p. 1, a left-wing newspaper later closed down by the government.

39 This occurred on 8 April 1984.

40 Personal interview, Montevideo, 30 April 1984.

a friendly magazine in which he predicted that Seregni would be "a very important factor in the pacification of the country" and praised his qualities of intelligence and democratic convictions.[41] It is highly unlikely that he would have done that without foreknowledge of the political line that Seregni planned to adopt.

Sanguinetti was anxious to emphasize the reincorporation of the Left as a loyal democratic force:

> Remember that Seregni was imprisoned for an act of resistance in 1973, later he was released and stayed in the country, although he knew he was taking a great risk. . . . All this sacrifice is a very powerful moral value behind a political figure.[42]

What was so revealing about that interview was that Sanguinetti went out of his way to recognize the Broad Front as a valid negotiating partner, even though the military still refused to legalize it. By stressing Seregni's status as a former general and a man who had the courage to remain in the country and face the consequences of his actions and convictions, Sanguinetti also implied the contrast with Wilson Ferreira's behavior in fleeing in 1973. It was a contrast that he might hope would appeal to the generals. Above all, Sanguinetti stressed in no uncertain terms how he welcomed the moderation of the Left.[43]

The strategy that Seregni mapped out for the Broad Front after his release was one of *mobilization, concerted action*, and *negotiation*. "Mobilization" meant reestablishing the impressive street presence of the Left in Montevideo, which tended to dwarf the Blancos' efforts.[44] It also meant trying to vent the rising popular pressures, as far as possible, while preventing them from getting out of hand and derailing negotiations, although Seregni would not have admitted that openly. "Concerted action" meant maintaining a consensus with other parties and social movements regarding the correct way forward.[45] That was clear from press reports as early as April. Almost at once after his liberation, Seregni met with the president of the communists' political alliance, the old Frente

---

41 "Seregni será un pilar de la salida democrática," *Jaque*, 9 March 1984, p. 3.
42 Ibid.
43 It is interesting to note that Seregni was originally from a Batllista Colorado background and had been mentioned as a possible Colorado candidate in 1971. In the end, he allegedly had been vetoed by Jorge Batlle, and later became the candidate of the Broad Front.
44 Apart from the civic strike of 27 June, which was entirely successful, a hunger strike began in a Montevideo monastery and pastoral center in favor of amnesty, and on July 10 (the 11th anniversary of a major demonstration against the coup) 15,000–30,000 people marched down Montevideo's principal avenue demanding "general and unrestricted amnesty."
45 "Manifiesto a la opinión pública del Frente Amplio," *Ultimas Noticias*, 12 April 1984, p. 2.

Izquierda de Liberación.[46] That endorsement revealed that Seregni had the backing of the Communist party, still the strongest party on the Left, and one that had supported Wilson Ferreira until then. From that point on, Seregni and Socialist party leader José Pedro Cardoso were to represent the Broad Front in the meetings of the all-party forum, the Multipartidaria.[47] Seregni seemed determined from the moment of his release to help maintain order in Uruguay, arguing that change could come only through peace, and that peace could be guaranteed only by change. He was also anxious to integrate the Left into the mainstream of Uruguayan politics as a loyal democratic force, rather than the anti-system "popular tribune" it had been in 1971–3.

Meanwhile, Sanguinetti also took a more welcoming line toward the left-leaning sector of the Colorado party, Corriente Batllista Independiente, led by Manuel Flores Silva, who edited the progressive magazine *Jaque*. Thus, he criticized his running mate, Enrique Tarigo, when the latter publicly announced that he was ready to accept elections without full political freedoms or all candidates.[48] It was important that Sanguinetti shake off his past image as author of the education law passed under the Bordaberry administration, which had taken the first steps toward undermining the autonomy of the university. In an important address to the Colorado party convention on 7 April 1984 as general secretary and presidential candidate of the Batllista majority of the party, Sanguinetti set forth a vision of a complete return to democracy under the slogan "Revenge never! Justice always."[49]

In that masterful speech, Sanguinetti laid out the entire strategy of the majority Batllista wing of the Colorado party: the need to admit past mistakes and look to the future; the importance of avoiding any return to radicalism or personalistic politics; the refusal, at the same time, to ignore the injustices of the preceeding decade. In terms of concrete commitments, Sanguinetti emphasized that all those who had lost their jobs under the military must be rehired, that political prisoners must be released by a combination of amnesty and pardon, and that exiles must

46 "El presidente del Frente Izquierda fue recibido Seregni," *Cinco Días*, Friday, 23 March 1984, p. 3.

47 See, for example, "Multipartidaria: Diálogo Comenzará en Junio; Reunión el Próximo Martes," *Ultimas Noticias*, Wednesday, 16 May 1984, p. 3, and the accompanying photo of the meeting at which Enrique Tarigo and José Luis Batlle represented the Colorado party, and Julio Daverede and Eduardo Pérez del Castillo the Civic Union. The Blancos were not attending meetings, allegedly because they were too busy collecting signatures to force a plebiscite on the institutional acts.

48 "La posición de Sanguinetti," *Jaque*, Friday, 9 March 1984, p. 3.

49 Transcription from author's recording of the speech. See also the pullout from the newspaper *La Mañana*, Thursday, 27 September 1984, Documentos No. 85: "Dr. Julio María Sanguinetti: El Hombre, el político, el gobernante."

be allowed to return. Finally, some balance had to be restored to civil–military relations. It was a position not too far removed from that of the air-force chief, Buadas, when he had spoken on behalf of the military three weeks earlier.

Sanguinetti soon established a strong working relationship with the leader of the Broad Front, and they were the crucial political actors on the civilian side who would work out the pact for a democratic transition. The general with whom Sanguinetti would eventually forge a strong working relationship was the future army commander, Hugo Medina. Medina had been a member of COMASPO from 1980 to 1984.[50] He helped draft the statute on parties at the end of 1982, a process that increased his contacts with Sanguinetti. In that way he had accumulated a good deal of experience in dealing with the politicians. The general also had the credentials to speak in the name of all the armed forces without fear of seeming unrepresentative, given his long involvement in COM-ASPO and his promotion by seniority. When his appointment was confirmed, he told reporters, to their amazement, "as the future Commander-in-Chief of the Army it is my responsibility to think out how the Army is going to get out of this situation, and this is worrying me hugely."[51]

On 7 June, General Aranco retired, and Medina assumed command of the army.[52] That retirements and promotions continued in a regularized fashion, even at moments of crucial political tension, was testimony to the relative unity of the armed forces and the preservation of professionalism. Medina's promotion gave rise to the possibility of a new beginning, and his pronouncements were less stern than those of his predecessor. In his speech assuming command of the army, he set out his conception of the future:

I aspire to a nation confident of its Army, and an Army confident in its nation. An apolitical, fundamentally professional, Army with a single doctrine and single aim: to serve the Uruguayan fatherland.[53]

The speech was clear in its intention: The military must again become "apolitical," chaos had been "left behind," and they would defend the freedoms of the "same people" from whom they were themselves drawn.

---

50 See the long article on his career published on the occasion of his retirement in January 1987: "El pase a retiro de Medina cierra el ciclo del Comandante de la transición," *Búsqueda*, Thursday, 29 January 1987, p. 4.

51 *El Día*, 29 May 1984, p. 1.

52 General Juan Carlos Reissig took over as commander of the Third Army Region. The retirement of generals Aranco and De La Fuente left two vacancies in the junta of generals until the following year. *Mundo Color*, 21 June 1984, p. 5.

53 The speech can be found in *El Día*, Friday, 8 June 1984, p. 5.

How much power would Medina's peers authorize him to wield in negotiating, and how much ground would he be allowed to cede? Medina subsequently emphasized to me that being the commander of the army, and thus having been chosen by a secret ballot of the current army junta, his powers and responsibilities as custodian of the *proceso* were far superior to those of the president.[54] Nevertheless, as was pointed out by a leading Blanco, "President Alvarez is the only military figure to have survived from the original coup coalition. He is also the most adept at politics and the only military man who wants to try to stay on."[55] Alvarez was thus much more committed to the preservation of the military's original aims than were the younger generals. From that point on, the commander of the army would systematically oppose the obstacles that President Alvarez attempted to place in the way of the transition, pressing forward to reach an agreement with the politicians.

During his conversations with the opposition, Medina was criticized by President Alvarez regarding strategy. He at once persuaded the president to go with him before the junta of generals so that each could present his case. At that decisive moment the junta came out strongly behind Medina's insistence that negotiations with the opposition be carried forward. From that day on, Alvarez was a lame-duck president.[56] All the same, the army commander embarked on an intensive tour of military units to lecture the troops on the need for a return to democracy and to calm the fears of others regarding the possibility of subsequent trials. No one would be tried for carrying out orders, Medina promised.[57]

The crisis of the Blancos' strategy

At almost the same time as Seregni's release came a bombshell accusation from sectors of the military that in secret talks with President Alvarez, Pivel Devoto had suggested that the next president be indirectly elected.[58] Though it was a face-saving formula to allow Wilson to run, sectors of the military chose to denounce the plan publicly as "undemocratic," thus helping the Colorados make capital from the affair.[59] It was suggested

54 Personal interview, Columbia, SC, 27 March 1987.
55 Personal interview, Montevideo, 15 March 1984.
56 I am grateful to Alfred Stepan for revealing the gist of the incident to me.
57 Personal interview, Columbia, SC, 27 March 1987.
58 "Propondrían que el Presidente Fuera Electo por la Asamblea General," *La Semana Uruguaya*, Tuesday, 28 February 1984. Pivel was president of the Blanco Executive Committee, but it is inconceivable that he would have suggested that without Wilson's authority, although that was denied and Pivel was made the unwilling scapegoat.
59 The interior minister said in a radio interview that "behind all this is the proposal to insist on the figure of one person." "Rapela reiteró que las elecciones están condicionadas a un acuerdo," *La Mañana*, Saturday, 24 March 1984, p. 2.

that the Blancos had offered to sweeten the plan by allowing Alvarez two more years in office.[60] It was not so much that Wilson's proxy dealings were secret that upset other leaders, but rather the fact that they were undertaken without any attempt to consult the other parties, or even his own party. It was understandable that the Colorados would be opposed, for the plan clearly favored the Blancos, but the Left was equally negative.[61] How could Ferreira have made such a miscalculation?[62] The uncharitable said that the Blanco leader had a past history of secret dealings, but a more important factor would seem to have been his difficulties in assessing the political situation while out of the country.[63] The fragile unity of the opposition was seriously breached, and other politicians' qualms about sacrificing Ferreira were weakened.[64]

Events in March were clearly damaging to the Blancos' popular image, and they decided to announce a campaign for a popular initiative to repeal the institutional acts that still proscribed Wilson and many leftist leaders. That, however, did not solve the problem of the legal charges against Wilson, for whom an arrest warrant was outstanding.[65] Eventually the military passed an institutional act to block the Blancos' campaign for a plebiscite, which the Left's leaders had begun to find it difficult to prevent their militants from supporting.[66]

With a theatrical gesture, on 28 April Wilson made a speech in Buenos Aires offering not to run for president if there was an immediate and unconditional return to the 1967 Constitution and normal elections.[67] In exasperation, a retired general told me that the military were disgruntled by the Blancos' shifting tactics: "The National party has three tactics," he said, "the plebiscite, an alternative candidate, or a pact, *but their position keeps changing.*"[68]

60 "Sanguinetti: Elección Indirecta Supone Prórroga," *El País*, Friday, 23 March 1984, pp. 5 and 7.

61 It is less easy to see why the Frente was opposed to the idea. "Rechazo del Frente Amplio," *La Mañana*, 24 March 1984, p. 5.

62 Though the army commander was still Aranco, not Medina, it was a case of trying to talk to the wrong man under the wrong circumstances. One may almost suspect that Ferreira fell into a carefully laid trap.

63 Ferreira was still in Spain, but the following month he moved to Buenos Aires.

64 The unity of the Wilsonistas was also damaged. At the convention of Por la Patria, anger erupted at the secrecy of conversations with the military (author's notes, 17 March 1984).

65 "Rapela Reiteró Que se Detendrá a Ferreira," *El Día*, 7 April 1984. Rapela also tried to intimidate the news media into maintaining their silence regarding Ferreira's proximity. "Reiteran Restricciones a Actividad Política y Prensa," *El Día*, 23 April 1984, p. 1.

66 "Se Considera Inviable Solicitud Para Plebiscitar el Acto No. 4," *El Día*, Monday, 26 March 1984, p. 1.

67 "Ferreira Aldunate declinaría la Presidencia por vigencia de Constitución de 1967," *El Día*, 28 April 1984, p. 5.

68 Personal interview, Montevideo, April 1984. Though the retired general was very senior and

The military call for a new dialogue, and the Blancos say "no"

The eventual response of the military to Wilson's gambit was to issue a political plan on 1 May as a quarter of a million pro-trade-union demonstrators rallied at the Legislative Palace. The new plan, which came directly from the commanders in chief, proposed the election of a "Constituent Assembly" at the same time as the November elections (or its nomination by the elected Assembly) that would write a new constitution. However, it would not meet until 1986, and until it had written the new charter, existing institutional acts would continue in force. A political amnesty would be specifically banned. It thus retreated from the demand that agreement on constitutional changes be reached before elections, but it also called for prolonging the military's institutional acts. Having read through the military's May Day plan, the Colorados were guarded in their response, pointing out that for the first time the principle of putting the job of rewriting the Constitution into the hands of a sovereign and democratic body had been accepted.

According to a leader of the Christian Democratic party, the proposals caused great tensions in the Broad Front. Obviously, many sectors were inclined to reject them out of hand, given the idea of prolonging the repressive institutional acts after the elections. Others saw the wisdom of keeping a dialogue going in the hope of extracting better terms.[69] The position of Seregni seems to have been decisive in holding the Left to its moderate strategy of dialogue, regardless of the details of the latest military salvo. However, the Blancos' immediate reaction to the May Day plan was unfavorable; they argued that the plan actually toughened the conditions put forward at the Parque Hotel by extending the transition beyond 1985. A leading Wilsonista put it thus to me:

We have no confidence that there can be agreement given the harshness of the [military's] declarations. In order to vote, we have to clean up the judicial situation with a plebiscite. This has two aims: elections without legal constraints, and popular mobilization. More than 20 days ago we proposed this to the other three parties. We had to go ahead because time is running out.[70] There is no plan to destabilize [the government] – the party has no intention of promoting confrontation in the streets. But I just cannot understand the Colorados: I would prefer dictatorship to a fictitious democracy.[71]

---

still held a position of some prestige, he complained that the weekly bulletins on political affairs circulated to high-ranking officers were utterly silent on what negotiations had taken place.
69 Juan Young, personal interview, Montevideo, 27 March 1985.
70 There was a constitutional deadline for collecting the signatures if the initiative was to appear on the November ballot.
71 José Claudio Williman, personal interview, Montevideo, 4 May 1984.

When the same leader was asked if it was not in the Blancos' interests to strengthen soft-liners in the regime who could turn out to be their allies, he responded with exasperation:

We are very little disposed to compromise. The argument about strengthening soft-liners is not mad, but the price is too high. Why won't the soft-liners talk to *us*? They come out with all kinds of things. How are we to know who they are? The attempts at a dialogue failed in October 1983 because of mistaken perceptions. It is not simply a problem of communication – they have contacts. Rather, it is much more a problem of their being used to giving orders.[72]

The Blanco majority leaders began to shuttle back and forth to Buenos Aires in order to consult with Ferreira, who promised that he would give a speech in the border town of Concordia, announcing the day of his return.[73]

Some have argued that in his Concordia speech Ferreira was carried away by the mood of the crowd into inflammatory attacks against the military at a moment when that had not really been his intention. For example, he mocked the military's accusation that he intended to try to "destabilize the government" in the following terms:

We want to overthrow the government, not destabilize it. . . .[74] [W]e are not going to accept another period of transition. . . . We are not going to accept solutions cooked up by political leaders in back rooms. We are only going to accept the solutions that the people elaborate in the street by their active, vibrant and fervent presence. . . . What has to be got into one's head is that the people mobilized is master of its fate and necessarily imposes its own solution.[75]

General Rapela selectively quoted Ferreira's remarks to emphasize the charge that the Blancos were trying to destabilize the country. What he did not quote was Wilson's accusation that the military had become so isolated from Uruguayan society as its "jailers" that they were "no longer

---

72 Ibid.
73 "Dirigentes nacionalistas en Bs. As. con líder proscripto," *Ultimas Noticias*, Wednesday, 16 May 1984, p. 2.
74 At this point the version of the speech later quoted by General Rapela contains an ellipsis that distorts the original. I have added some missing text.
75 The complete text of the speech was later published as a pamphlet by Por la Patria: *Vamos a sumarnos a un gran esfuerzo nacional* (Montevideo: Documentos del Movimiento Por la Patria, 1984). It is perhaps revealing that a subsequent compilation did not include the Concordia speech, but a measured editorial from the magazine *Compromiso* dated 24 May 1984 and signed by himself and his son, which stated that "we are not returning to create obstacles in the search for a negotiated solution to the national tragedy, conscious that the future of the country can only be assured by means of understanding" (reprinted in Ferreira Aldunate 1986). Which was the real Ferreira? Would he compromise?

a part of it." But in a sense the latter accusation made negotiation nigh impossible. When the Wilsonistas attempted to publish the Concordia speech in *La Democracia*, the copies were seized and destroyed, and two of the party's most important leaders, Guillermo García Costa and Alberto Zumarán, were arrested.[76] Another reason the magazine was seized was that it contained a call to rally at the port on 16 June to receive Ferreira.[77] Attended by large numbers of supporters who crossed over the Uruguay River via the new bridge and broadcast on Argentine radio, Wilson's speech evidently induced apoplexy among the military. Its implications were summarized by an oblique headline in *El Día*, 26 May 1984: "Liberty and Security of Wilson Will Not Be Negotiated."[78]

At that point the Blancos signed their last joint plan of action with the Colorados and the Frente, ending a period of not attending the meetings of the Multipartidaria. It was supremely ironic that the key figure in securing the renewal of cooperation between the traditional parties (and the possibility of the Blancos agreeing to compromise) was General Líber Seregni, the recently released leader of the Frente. Nowhere should the message have been clearer that the crux of the problem of reaching a civil–military accord lay in willingness to allow those politicians with mass support to undertake their leadership functions, restrain the demands of the maximalists, and rebuild their party organizations. In other words, moderation could not be achieved by coercion, as was being practiced on the Blancos.

The advantages of having released Seregni were becoming clear to the military. His leadership of the Left was a major factor in stabilizing the tense political climate. Next, however, the generals had to decide whether they would treat Wilson Ferreira as generously.[79] That crucial decision rested on their perception of his likely response, and also on their estimate of the likelihood that his popularity might carry him to power. Though it seems difficult to have believed so at the time, they were to calculate that his triumphalism and maximalism could not permit them to treat him in the same manner as Seregni. Given his ambiguity regarding

---

76 "Dirigentes Blancos Continúan Detenidos," *El Pais*, Saturday, 9 June 1984, p. 1.

77 A communiqué was broadcast at regular intervals on TV and radio warning citizens to stay away. The magazine *Dignidad* was closed for eight editions for publishing the same appeal. "Gobierno y FF. AA. Aconsejan no Cuncurrir a Posibles Concentraciones o Manifestaciones," and "Clausuran Por 8 Ediciones al Semanario 'Dignidad'," *El Dia*, Friday, 15 June 1984, p. 1.

78 The same article reported that Ferreira avoided answering whether or not the Blancos would agree to take part in elections with parties or leaders still banned.

79 They often expressed hatred of Ferreira, a man who had conducted an international campaign to discredit their rule, but presumably they had as much hatred for Seregni, who had betrayed the armed forces' name by joining a political alliance that included the communists. Seregni, however, had not been able to campaign from his jail cell, and some generals may even have remembered how he had supported their demands in February 1973.

negotiated compromise, concessions might merely lead to more demands. That was fundamentally because, unlike Seregni, Ferreira might easily win an open electoral contest. And finally, the increasing strains between the parties after the events of March suggested that the Colorados and Broad Front would not risk the transition process by refusing to negotiate if he was in jail.[80]

The return of Wilson Ferreira

Time was running out for Wilson if he was to get back into the domestic political game; he was the last traditional politician without his political rights. Furthermore, the climate of opinion in the country was favorable to negotiation, and Seregni's leadership of the Broad Front was bringing it closer and closer to the moderate stance of the Colorados. The only solution seemed to be to return with as much publicity as possible, so as to make his anticipated arrest as damaging as possible to the military. He might then hope that his arrest would prevent the other parties from negotiating, and perhaps even cause the ouster of President Alvarez by the junta of generals.

On 16 June, Wilson Ferreira returned in a boat that crossed the River Plate from Buenos Aires laden with journalists, politicians, and foreign dignitaries. General Medina had to deny publicly the rumors that a coup had occurred to oust President Alvarez.[81] A massive military presence on the streets of Montevideo was unable to prevent huge demonstrations to greet Ferreira.[82] Yet it was a relatively easy matter to arrest the Blancos' presidential candidate before he got anywhere near the crowds.[83] What was significant was that the climate of fear had declined sufficiently that demonstrators dared to ignore government threats, and the government did not use violent repression, in contrast to the situation in Chile. Yet Wilson's gamble had doubly failed: The government had not fallen, and he had been taken prisoner. The following day the Blanco convention met in uproar. To riotous acclaim, Wilson's proposed running mate, Carlos Julio Pereyra, thundered:

80 This could be deduced from the Left's acceptance of Seregni's freeing without full restoration of political rights, statements made by Colorado leader Enrique Tarigo, and oblique condemnations of "personalism" by Sanguinetti.

81 El Tte. General Medina dismintió Rumores Sobre un Golpe de Estado," *El Dia*, Monday, 18 June 1984, p. 6.

82 Buses bringing demonstrators from the interior, however, were turned back.

83 Wilson Ferreira Aldunate Regresó Ayer y de Inmediato Fue Detenido," *El Dia*, Sunday, 17 June 1984, p. 1. Because the government had imposed a news blackout, the article on the inside page was ironically circumspect. Under the headline "Maritime Movements: The Ciudad Mar del Plata II Docked," the story read that the boat had arrived after a long delay and had been greeted by an unusual number of people (ibid., p. 13).

If there is anyone who thinks there can be democratic elections with a presidential candidate in jail it is because they do not know what democracy is![84]

The Blanco convention overwhelmingly voted not to negotiate with the military until Wilson Ferreira had been freed.[85]

As it turned out, Wilson's return to the country and his detention were only to worsen the Blancos' problems by making it impossible for them to enter negotiations and by creating bitter internal wrangling. Within less than a week it had been announced that there was no hope of Wilson's being freed within the two months that remained before the deadline for official registration of candidate lists at the Electoral Court, 25 August. Until the charges against him were resolved, the Electoral Court could not, under Uruguayan law, accept any ballot with his name on it.

In retrospect it is easy to fault Wilson's decision to return to Uruguay, but he was in a no-win situation. A Colorado leader commented that "Wilson was convinced that the generals would fire Alvarez, but he ruined his position with his attacks and only *reinforced the president's position.*"[86] A less sympathetic Colorado senator added, more bluntly, "Wilson gets on a platform planning to make a moderate speech and gets carried away by the crowd."[87] A young leftist leader argued that Wilson simply miscalculated: "The National party made the mistake of not acting in concert with the other parties over the plebiscite and Wilson's return in the boat. In his Concordia speech Wilson clearly did not foresee long-term imprisonment."[88]

Some Wilsonistas did seem aware of the risks,[89] however, and conser-

---

84 Author's convention notes. In a personal interview, Wilson's daughter Sylvia (who the previous day had watched her father and brother snatched away from the quayside in military helicopters) castigated the military's handling of the transition: "There is a political climate which is not free; there is no equality between the two sides. We cannot have any more censorship or accusations of subversion. There must be a climate of opening. *Nothing will be negotiated.* No National Security Council; no proscriptions; and never again any military trials of civilians!"

85 "Blancos ratificaron no ir al diálogo hasta que liberen a Wilson Ferreira," *Ultimas Noticias*, Monday, 18 June 1984, p. 2. Even Ferreira's less firm allies, such as Luis Alberto Lacalle, came out solidly backing the decision.

86 Personal interview, Montevideo, 17 July 1984. A distinguished and aged leader of the Left's "List 99" faction admitted that he, too, had believed Alvarez might be ousted in June to permit what he (tellingly) called "a serious dialogue" (personal interview, Montevideo, 5 November 1984).

87 Personal interview, Montevideo, 23 June 1984.

88 Personal interview, Montevideo, April 1985.

89 In the stormy Blanco convention of 9 June, a week before the boat was scheduled to bring him from Buenos Aires, Father Posadas had proposed the following motion, which was approved by near unanimity: "Given that Wilson Ferreira will be arrested and imprisoned [this convention] resolves that this constitutes an ineluctable obstacle to renewing the dialogue (author's notes and translation).

vative Blancos wanted to renew negotiations, along with the other parties, and then decide whether or not to take part in elections. Yet that line of reasoning led to uproar in the convention. As García Costa later put it,

> the National party argues [that] a frontal "no" can achieve a complete military withdrawal . . . the Colorados' attitude allows the armed forces to feel more confident in their demands and go further.[90]

The fundamental difficulty of the Blancos' position, however, was that with the Left favoring negotiation under Seregni's leadership, their "frontal no" would remain a vain gesture. As the deadline for registering candidates approached, all politicians were anxious for some agreement. The temptation for the Blancos eventually to take part in the elections with a different candidate would be enormous.

The end of opposition unity: the split over negotiations

Uruguay's path to democracy had come to depend almost entirely on the strategies of the politicians. The military had made it clear that they wanted to negotiate a solution to the stalemate. The question was whether or not the politicians would decide the same. In interviews with political leaders during 1984 (Table 7.6) I tried to probe their attitudes toward the best strategy for getting back to democracy. The first strategy I mentioned argued that "the only way to force those in power to give way to democracy is to intensify popular pressure and not enter negotiations." Whereas the Colorados disagreed strongly with such an assertion, almost two-thirds of Blancos agreed "a lot" or "rather a lot."[91] A chasm was opening up between the Colorados' willingness to accept some kind of negotiated reform of the regime and the Blancos' insistence that there must be a complete break.

If we consider only those interviews undertaken prior to the Naval Club pact, the Blancos showed even greater militancy.[92] The subsequent decline probably was not due to any sudden conversion to belief in negotiations, but rather to an attitude of creeping resignation to the form

90 Personal interview, Montevideo, 11 July 1984.
91 Answers were coded from 1 ("agree very much") to 5 ("agree not at all") to test the significance of the differences in means. The Colorado average was 4.5, and that of the Blancos 2.4 ($p = .001$). For ease of interpretation, the table reports only the percentage of interviewees agreeing "a lot" or "rather a lot."
92 By the same method, their score for opposition to negotiations was 1.6, taking the pre-pact interviews alone, compared with 2.4 for the full sample.

Table 7.6. *Summary of responses regarding negotiating tactics*

Response	Frente (%) (n = 10)	Blancos (%) (n = 17)	Colorados (%) (n = 18)
(a) "The only way to force those in power to give way to democracy is to intensify popular pressure and not enter negotiations."	20[a]	63	0
(b) "Though popular pressure should not cease, it must be controlled, and the time must come when the leaders of the largest opposition parties negotiate the rules of the transition with those in power."	80	79	95
(c) "In the transition, it is possible that the moderate opposition will distance itself from the most radicalized sectors and have an interest in supporting those in the regime who seek an 'opening' against the hard-liners."	22	79	63
(d) "It is going to be impossible, or very hard, to get broad sectors of the opposition to agree to negotiate the transition process with the established powers."	20	45	15

[a] Percentage agreeing "a lot" or "rather a lot" with the response.

of transition negotiated by the Colorados and the Frente.[93] For the Left, both before and after the pact, a pattern of responses closer to that of the Colorados than to that of the Blancos was detected, but with a greater spread.[94]

An assertion that might have been thought to contradict the previous assertion evaluated by respondents was this: "Though popular pressure should not cease, it must be controlled, and the time must come when

93 The Blancos' appreciation of their position was not, however, fatalistic. When asked how far they agreed with the pessimistic view that "the opposition can do nothing important or effective until after the elections," almost all disagreed strongly.

94 Although few formal interviews were carried out with leaders of the Left prior to the pact (partly because they were still legally banned), the mean score for the Frente was 3.0 ("somewhat in agreement") in the earliest interviews, compared with 4.0 for the full sample. Despite the low number of cases, this average for the earlier period was still significantly more "militant" than that of the Colorados ($p = .03$). It was also already significantly *less* so than for the Blancos ($p = .09$).

the leaders of the largest opposition parties negotiate the rules of the transition with those in power." Interestingly, in light of subsequent events, though agreement was generally rather high all round, the Colorados tended to agree with this statement more than did those on the Left.[95] Presumably the reason that the Left were less enthusiastic about this statement lay in their insistence that mobilization and negotiation were complementary rather than incompatible. There was a certain reticence among those on the Left regarding the open assertion that popular mobilization had to be controlled – whatever their subsequent tactics. A pattern of more positive evaluation by politicians from the traditional parties than by the leftists emerged when they were asked to what extent they agreed that "in the transition, it is possible that the moderate opposition (will) distance itself from the most radicalized sectors and have an interest in supporting those in the regime who seek an 'opening' against the hard-liners."[96] In fact, the Blancos were the most likely of all to agree with this view "a lot" or "rather a lot." That suggested a certain dissonance in their attitudes.

When politicians were asked if they agreed that "it is going to be impossible, or very hard, to get broad sectors of the opposition to agree to negotiate the transition process with the established powers," they were all far less inclined to agree.[97] Examination of the early interviews alone shows that the Blancos began to differ significantly from Colorados and Frentistas in their responses to this question *only after the pact*.[98] There had been no prior signs that the Blancos were less optimistic that a consensus could be reached on the terms for military extrication. In other words, though the Blancos were becoming politically isolated, they either were unaware of the fact or refused to admit it.[99]

In sum, the attitudes expressed by Colorado leaders were consistently

95 The difference between the Colorado average (1.4) and that of the left (2.1) yields a significance level of .11.
96 The Blanco average was 2.0 (agree "rather a lot"), and the Colorado 2.2 (not significantly different). The mean score for the Frente was 3.0 (agree "somewhat"), yielding a significance level when compared with the Blancos of .02, and .04 compared with the Colorados.
97 Those who had argued that broad agreement on the terms of the transition would be difficult to achieve were asked further whether those parties that could reach such agreement should go ahead or should pull out in the interest of opposition solidarity. Opinions were evenly divided in all parties on the wisdom of each path, and the differences were not significant.
98 For the whole period, the mean Blanco score was 2.9 (agree "somewhat"), compared with 3.9 for the Colorados and 4.0 for the Frente (agree "little"). The significance of the Blanco–Colorado difference was .02.
99 In the case of interviews that were carried out after the pact, I asked politicians to think back and give the answers they would have given in June of 1984, prior to Wilson's return and arrest. That obviously was not an ideal procedure. The fact that "before" and "after" differences still emerge suggests that politicians found it difficult to comply. Just like political scientists, politicians enjoy claiming prescient knowledge.

the most cautious and moderate. When directly questioned, the Blancos were the most inclined to reject negotiations, and yet they were more willing than were the leaders of the Left to countenance restraint of popular mobilization and an alliance with regime soft-liners in order to help them isolate hard-liners. This suggests that there were greater cross-pressures in the strategic approaches of both the Blancos and the Left, with neither necessarily much at ease with their respective eventual courses of action.

Another question asked leaders to rate how close they felt to the ideological positions of various other parties and factions. If we look at their evaluations of the three main parties (*lemas*), the Blancos considered themselves closest to the Frente, and vice versa. The Colorados also considered themselves somewhat closer to the Frente, but not as close as the Blancos felt; and, unlike the Blancos, Colorados aroused antipathy among Frentistas.[100] Such data would naturally lead to the conclusion that were a partial alliance to emerge among two of the three major parties, it would crystallize between the Blancos and the Frente, already working together in the exile movement Convergencia Democrática.

The vast majority of Uruguayan politicians favored a pact among the parties as part of the return to democracy (9 of 10 Colorados and Frentistas, and 8 of 10 Blancos). If one had cared to predict the future of Uruguay's transition at the end of 1983, in the wake of the traditional parties' alliance with the illegal Left and the staging of the massive rally at the obelisk, one would have foreseen the survival of opposition unity. Because the declaration read out at the obelisk committed all parties to fighting for fully free elections, with all parties and politicians allowed to take part, it seemed unlikely that there would be a negotiated pact with the military. Both of those predictions would, however, turn out to be mistaken.

Granted that the vast majority of politicians favored a pact among parties for the duration of the transition, a question that revealed a greater degree of controversy asked them whether, in general (i.e., not just during the transition), governments should rule by seeking consensus or whether majoritarianism was more desirable.

The important finding that emerges in Table 7.7 is that the Blancos were much more in favor of majoritarianism, and the Left particularly against it. Thus, the Blancos' attachment to their principle and their unwillingness to compromise again showed up strongly, as compared with the other parties (though they were divided). The corollary of the new Blanco emphasis on majoritarianism within the party seems to have been

---

100 The wording of the question was as follows: "For each of the following parties, can you tell me to what extent you consider it close to or distant from your ideological position?" Responses were coded 1 for "very near," 2 for "near," 3 for "rather farther," and 4 for "far."

Table 7.7. *Should governments rule by consensus?*[a]

Procedure	Left (%) (n = 17)	Blancos (%) (n = 24)	Colorados (%) (n = 25)	All[b] (%) (n = 70)
(a) Decisions should be reached by the majority parties and should reflect the will of the governing coalition.	12	46	28	29
(b) Important decisions should be reached by majorities going beyond the government and reflect the interests of major opposition groups.	88	54	72	71
Total	100	100	100	100

[a] The question: "There are two ways in which parties — ideally — ought to take part in political decisions. Which do you prefer?"
[b] Includes one Patriotic Union and three Civic Union leaders.

majoritarianism vis-à-vis other parties. One might have predicted that the party's long-standing opposition status, which meant that it often relied on power-sharing mechanisms, would have caused it to favor all-party consensus. Possibly that tendency reflected their predictions as to their imminent access to power. That would explain the party's high-stakes strategy. The Left's rejection of majoritarianism presumably reflected its traditional marginality and the difficulties it had in influencing policy, and also its current fear that it would be left out of the transition and remain illegal. The military remained committed to destroying it, even if the traditional parties had promised to fight for its rehabilitation.

Attitudes toward the correct strategy to be pursued in the negotiations were bound up with opinions regarding the forces that fundamentally bring about transitions and sustain democracy thereafter. This is brought out if we "cross" the responses to some of the previous questions with another question that asked whether elites or masses were more crucial for ensuring redemocratization. Table 7.8 shows that those who were averse to negotiating were more likely to see the success of democracy as depending on its acceptance by rival social interests and organizations.

Table 7.8. *Negotiating stance* × *View of the forces at work in a transition*

"What do you think is more important for a transition to democracy and its consolidation?"	"The only way to force those in power to give way to democracy is to intensify popular pressure and not enter negotiations. . . ."		Number
	(1) Agree[a] ($n = 14$)[c]	(2) Disagree[b] ($n = 32$)	
(A) The capacity of party leaders to act with some consensus, create institutions, respect minorities, be loyal . . .	7	24	($n = 31$)[c]
(B) Acceptance by different social sectors, interests, organizations, trade unions, business groups, military, foreign interests . . .	7	8	($n = 15$)

[a]Includes those who agree "a lot," "rather," and "some," with the statement.
[b]Includes those who agree "little" or "not at all" with the statement.
[c]Number of cases.

But where were the leaders of the parties distributed in this fourfold table? The Blancos were divided more or less evenly into thirds among the combinations A1, A2, and B1. Not a single Blanco leader, however, both saw the masses as the key to transition and favored negotiation. The Colorado responses had a completely different profile: Three-quarters of them both emphasized leadership over mass acceptance and favored negotiation (A2), as did the four interviewees from the Civic Union and the Patriotic Union. The remaining one-quarter saw the masses as more important, but also favored a compromise with the military (B2). No Colorados rejected negotiations, so none of them fell into category A1 or B1. The Broad Front's responses were rather evenly scattered across all four combinations, though almost two-thirds of them rejected the statement that popular pressure had to be intensified and no negotiations entered.

In sum, the observed relationship in the sample between favoring negotiation and placing importance on the role of elites in carrying out the transition was accounted for by the Colorados and politicians of the minor conservative parties. The Left was divided on these issues, and the only combination of attitudes not found in the Blanco party was that of favoring negotiations and stressing the role of the masses. It was this latter option of mobilization and negotiation that was to become the Left's slogan, but the leaders' views did not clearly support it.

Obviously, the precise wording of a question regarding issues as com-

Table 7.9. *Negotiating stance × View of the forces at work in a transition*

"What do you think is more important for a transition to democracy and its consolidation?"	"Though popular pressure should not cease, it must be controlled, and the time must come to negotiate the rules of the transition."		Number
	(1) Agree strongly* (n = 28)ᶜ	(2) Disagree or unsureᵇ (n = 18)	
(A) The capacity of party leaders to act with some consensus, create institutions, respect minorities, be loyal . . .	23	8	(n = 31)ᶜ
(B) Acceptance by different social sectors, interests, organizations, trade unions, business groups, military, foreign interests . . .	5	10	(n = 15)

*Includes those who agree "a lot" with the statement.
ᵇIncludes those who agree "rather," "some," "little," or "not at all."
ᶜNumber of cases.

plex as the strategic trade-offs between mobilization and negotiation could have a great deal of influence on the results. Therefore, I repeated the same form of analysis for this statement: "Though popular pressure must not cease, it must be controlled, and the time must come to negotiate the rules of the transition." To an even greater extent than before, we see in Table 7.9 that it was those who favored negotiation who were also more likely to see political elites as the key to a successful transition. In terms of the breakdown at the level of parties, the same scattered pattern emerged among the Broad Front politicians, whereas over three-fifths of Colorados and all of the leaders of minor conservative parties fell into category A1, as might have been expected (the remainder being evenly distributed). This time, however, the Blancos tended to "bunch" in two diametrically opposed combinations: Half of them believed in leadership and agreed that popular pressure must be controlled (A1), but 35% professed a belief in the masses and fundamental opposition to ever controlling popular mobilization (B2). That polarized situation was not found in any other party and clearly would be a source of major conflicts over strategy for the Blancos.

The conditions for maintaining unity among all parties until the military had returned to the barracks were breaking down. Uruguay's democratic transition was to be one of the few in Latin America to be based on an explicit agreement between the military and sections of the opposition, rather than one uniting the opposition against the military.

8

The Naval Club pact: party and military strategies in the transition

[I]n our country a cold war seems to have blocked the dialogue that leads to reinstitutionalization, threatening to turn into a hot war at any moment. One has the impression that in the most recent times the republic has been split in two. On one flank the government and armed forces, on the other political leaders and the expectant Uruguayan people, the only real objective of the good that must be reached, and which is the responsibility of all.

Let us abandon that exhausting vicious circle. Neither differences of opinion, nor the prerogatives of power, nor messianic fanaticisms, nor yet the idea that everything that comes from the government is detestable and inadmissible, can be grounds or sufficient handicap for not obtaining the target we have set. It is impossible to reach unanimity of thought, but it is also inconceivable not to reach a minimum honorable agreement which takes us all to the goal we desire.

Lieutenant General Manuel Buadas, 16 March 1984

By the southern fall of 1984 the political stalemate between the military and the opposition parties was coming to an end. Despite Wilson Ferreira's imprisonment, the Colorados and Broad Front were ready to renew talks with the armed forces. The options of regime continuity and complete breakdown had been eliminated as far as the Colorados, the Left, and the commanders in chief were concerned. For those opposition politicians in favor of negotiation, the issue came to be seen as simply this: how to persuade the military (which still had complete control of the country) to hand over power to democratically elected civilians. For those military leaders in favor of negotiation, the question was how to extricate themselves from rule without damaging their institution or risking human-rights trials. By July, the Colorados, the Broad Front, and the armed forces would be negotiating in earnest.

The path of Uruguay's transition was to be based on a sharp split between the Blancos and the Frente, which, under the leadership of the retired general Líber Seregni, gravitated toward the Colorado party and its decision to negotiate. It is important to remember that the risk of popular rejection was inherent in the strategies of the prodialogue parties.

Yet such a risk of isolation was minimized by the politicians' early insistence on concessions from the military. Reactions to the pact, which was finally agreed upon at the Naval Club in early August, were favorable among the supporters and voters of the parties that entered the agreement. Above all, that was the key to its eventual success.

This chapter ends by stepping back to explain the convergence of interests that made the Naval Club pact possible in terms of the successive elimination of alternatives. That gave rise to a dynamic process by which actors on both sides were able to move toward common agreement because of their aversion to all the available alternatives to a deal. In that way the opponents of a deal on both extremes were effectively neutralized. The fundamental source of convergence in such a situation seems to lie in a stalemate in the balance of power and a commitment to procedural democracy rather than substantive outcomes. Thus, the key questions are as follows: Will oppositions give up waiting for a complete regime collapse? Do they have other priorities, such as radical social change, that are more important to them than democracy? To what extent do they perceive a willingness to compromise on the part of those in power? On the other side, are power-holders afraid that a transition will lead to victory for unacceptable political forces that will jeopardize their basic interests? To what extent do they consider holding on to power a less risky alternative?

Pacts in perspective: the structure of alliances in negotiation

Leaving aside for the time being the problems of how interests come to converge, let us first focus on the pure mechanics of negotiated regime changes. Guillermo O'Donnell has emphasized the need for moderate oppositions to compromise with regime soft-liners in order to ensure a successful transition to democracy.[1] According to this model, the trick is to isolate both extremists (who oppose any compromise) and opportunists who would be too easily bought off by those in power. A further condition is that supporters remain loyal to the deal reached and the compromises that leaders are forced to accept. At the same time, soft-liners must make sure they are not outflanked by hard-liners in the regime. In essence, Uruguay would conform to this model, but with the twist of the Left, rather than the Blancos, joining the moderate opposition. In other words, one must not confuse (a) "extremes" with regard to opposition to negotiating and (b) ideological "extremes" in a left–right sense. No

---

1 O'Donnell (1979a); O'Donnell and Schmitter (1986).

		ALLIANCES	
		Inclusive	Exclusive
NEGOTIATING STANCE	Rigid	Multipartidaria circa November 1983	Blancos after June 1984
	Flexible	Colorados & Frente after June 1984	Risk of Isolation*

*Some might place the Blancos in March here.

Figure 8.1. Shifting party alliance and negotiating strategies, 1983–4.

one could have predicted this turnabout a year earlier, when all parties declared their commitment to free elections at the obelisk.[2]

Angel Flisfisch has analyzed the strategies open to parties under situations of potential regime transition in terms of two dimensions.[3] The first dimension is flexibility or willingness to compromise with power-holders; the second is the breadth, or inclusiveness, of opposition alliances. According to Flisfisch, Uruguay represented a case of a broad alliance and an inflexible refusal to negotiate. Yet he was writing late in 1983. By the middle of 1984 the Blancos had dropped out of the multiparty alliance, and the Colorados and the Frente had moved toward acceptance of a deal with the military, as Figure 8.1 depicts. Had the Colorados attempted such a deal on their own, they would have been dangerously exposed to criticism by the other parties. Some might see the fiasco of the Blancos' dealings with the president in March as a warning against such lone negotiating. However, the combination of the Colorados plus the Broad Front and the Civic Union could not be seen as having a narrow negotiating base. In fact, it was a potentially winning coalition.

Under normal circumstances, the broader the opposition alliance, the broader the level of domestic challenge to the authoritarian regime.[4] Multiparty alliances are therefore aimed at *strengthening the position of the opposition.* Coordinated opposition may offer the military stronger incentives to initiate a transition, and threaten more costly sanctions if they refuse: A pact *within* the opposition will affect military motivations by raising the relative prestige of parties and other opposition movements. Interparty competition can have an overall debilitating effect on the credibility of the opposition. Therefore, suspending it for the duration of the

2 The transition was far from "consociational," given the level of political competition between pro- and anti-pact forces. Lijphart (1969).
3 Flisfisch (1984).
4 Consider the bifurcated opposition in Chile and the blame that has been placed upon it as a factor weakening the parties.

transition is liable to mitigate this danger. However, Uruguay's transition was not based on opposition unanimity. In fact, as will be shown, opposition disunity was functional to the form of agreement that was eventually to be reached at the Naval Club. The parties that were willing to negotiate benefited enormously from their ability to point out that the alternative to a deal with them would be to play straight into the hands of Wilson Ferreira. Their negotiating position was perhaps even stronger than it would have been with all parties at the table. The pro-pact parties were also able to concentrate on their specific interests, whereas if the Blancos had been present, the issue of Ferreira's imprisonment would have repeatedly entered the agenda.

It has often been argued that transitions require that parties unite behind procedural democratic pacts, leaving contentious social and economic issues until later. The Uruguayan experience was ironic in light of that advice: Substantive policies were hardly even debated, but unanimity over procedures proved quite impossible. Divisions over future policies were rather glibly smoothed over in the talks of the Concertación Programática Nacional (CONAPRO), which the Blancos continued to attend quite happily. Thirteen years had produced a marked ideological convergence between the left and the other parties.[5] In sum, it would seem that the conditions for pacts among all parties and pacts between the parties and the military may not be the same. Indeed, the two types of pacts may fundamentally come into conflict with one another.

Politicians' differing levels of fear regarding possible regime involution and attitudes toward military demands

Because it seemed likely that the politicians had based their strategy on their perceptions of processes within the military, they were asked to assess retrospectively what risk of authoritarian involution they had perceived at various crucial junctures. Overall, the Colorados repeatedly expressed greater concern that there might have been a crackdown by hard-liners in the armed forces. Their concern was clear following the result of the plebiscite in 1980, again in 1983 when the Parque Hotel talks collapsed, and at the end of the year when the president made a speech extremely critical of the traditional parties' alliance with the Left in the Multipartidaria.[6] The level of fear on the Left was reported to have

---

5 For example, all three sent observers to a conference of the Socialist International held in Rio de Janeiro at about that time.

6 With regard to the period of crisis following the plebiscite, the Colorados reported a mean of 2.2 ("some" risk of involution), compared with 3.1 ("little" risk) according to Blancos ($p = .01$).

Table 8.1. *Perceived danger of authoritarian regression at selected critical junctures*[a]

Period	Frente (n = 10)	Blancos (n = 18)	Colorados (n = 20)
1980 When the results of the plebiscite became known	60[b]	28	60
1981 During the struggle over presidential succession	50	61	75
1982 When the results of the primaries became known	20	22	35
1983 When the dialogue between parties and military collapsed	70	39	65
1983/4 Following the hardening of positions on both sides	60	39	60

[a]The question: "The present negotiations are very tough. Do you think there was much risk of involution in the following periods?"
[b]Percentage responding "a lot" or "some."

been intermediate, though the Frentistas' mean assessment of the risk of involution in 1980 was significantly higher than that of the Blancos.[7]

The striking thing about the data in Table 8.1 is the Blancos' consistently lower estimate of the danger of authoritarian regression. The issue is not whether or not the Blancos were sincere in their confidence – given the performance of the Wilsonistas in the primaries they almost certainly were – but why. Partly their outlook was a function of inadequate understanding of the military institution, and partly an overestimate of the strength of their position: The more the Blancos saw the situation as ripe for radical change, the more they convinced themselves of the weakness of the military's hard-liners. One could also add that a certain bravura had long been part of the distinctive political style of the National party.

The intransigent line of the Blancos vis-à-vis the military was further observed when politicians were asked if they would agree to take part in elections while other parties remained banned (Table 8.2). Half the Blancos said they would not, but only one-third of Frentistas and one-eighth of Colorados.[8] When questioned regarding under what conditions they would take part in elections if the military decreed changes to the Constitution without the consent of the parties, again the Blancos were the

At the time of the collapse of the Parque Hotel talks (July 1983), fear of retrocession had slightly risen: The averages were 2.0 and 2.8, respectively (p = .01).
7 Frente = 2.4, compared with Blanco = 3.1 (p = .06).
8 The difference between Blancos and Colorados yielded a significance of .04.

Table 8.2. *Politicians' attitudes to elections with bannings still in force*[a]

Option	Frentistas (%) (n = 7)	Blancos (%) (n = 17)	Colorados (%) (n = 20)
(a) "Take part in the elections so long as they are not jeopardized, and basic freedoms are not affected."	29	18	50
(b) "Take part under protest, warning that if they win they will repeal these changes and, if necessary, call new elections."	71	59	40
(c) "Not take part."	0	25	10

[a] The question: "If the government were to decree modifications to the Constitution, should parties . . . "

most intransigent, and the Colorados the least. Underlying these Blanco attitudes was the premise that concern for the possible impact on the military of principled demands would merely play into the hands of the hard-liners. A position of weakness thus would be conceded in advance. The Colorados, in contrast, made the pragmatic assumption that the best way to achieve their aims was to take into account and anticipate the reactions they might produce on the part of their opponents. In that way they hoped to optimize their relative position.

The estrangement of the traditional parties

Unlike the Blancos, the Colorados, the Broad Front, and the Civic Union perceived the holding of elections in November as contingent on negotiations (Table 8.3). On the eve of the "civic strike" called by

Table 8.3. *The strategies of the three major parties*

Party	Mobilization	Concertation	Negotiation
Colorados	Impossible, because of lack of militants	To avoid risk of isolation	Offer the military honorable exit
Blancos	Radicalize the opposition	Despite rhetoric, isolated	Opposed until Wilson released
Broad Front	Increase presence and bargaining strength	Appear on an equal footing and raise social issues	Get back into the legal game of politics

the Intersectorial for 27 June 1984, the Multipartidaria voted to em-
power Colorado leader Julio María Sanguinetti to meet with the military commanders, who had been waiting since May Day for a response
to their call for renewed talks.[9] The military had become impatient,[10]
and the timing of the vote clearly was intended to balance the signal
of confrontation that the civic strike would imply, strengthening military moderates under Medina.[11] According to one leader who was involved in the negotiations with the military, the fact that Alvarez had
been able to survive the crisis of Wilson's return and instant arrest was
seen as indicative of an ominous hardening in the officer corps. On the
other hand, the decision of the commanders to get involved personally
in negotiations was taken to mean that they were determined to avoid
failure.[12]

Whether or not a campaign of civil disobedience might have forced
the military into granting unconditional elections is unclear, though it
would have been a risky strategy. What is certain is that it was not in
the Colorados' interests for the transition to occur in such a manner – not
just because Ferreira was a formidable electoral opponent, but because the
entire strategy of appealing to moderates would have collapsed. If politics
should flood into the streets, the Colorados would be at a great organizational and numerical disadvantage.

In protest of the decision to negotiate, the Blancos promptly withdrew
from the Multipartidaria, adamant that they could not negotiate with
Wilson in jail.[13] The interior minister, General Rapela, however, correctly
opined that talks would soon get under way.[14] The Left's decision to agree
to talks with the commanders in chief without the presence of the Blancos
was made possible by the strategy that Seregni mapped out: *mobilization*,
concertation, and *negotiation*. The decision to seek renewed talks was im-

9 "Resuelven negociar con Fuerzas Armadas," *El Día*, 27–28 June 1984, p. 1. The strike was a
total success in Montevideo, and unlike the January stoppage that the Colorados had opposed,
it had the support of all major parties: "Sanguinetti Requirió Audiencia a FF. AA.," *El Día*,
29 June 1984, p. 1.

10 The Spanish press agency EFE sent out a story over its wires on 1 June that the government
would impose a deadline, and the following day General Medina, who was about to take over
as army commander, told the press that "the silence in the face of our offer seems odd." The
Colorados deliberately tried to keep hopes alive, promising in late May that the Multipartidaria
would respond to the military's plan within a month, i.e., following Ferreira's return.

11 General Aranco had to retire on his 60th birthday early in June.

12 In contrast to the major role it played in the failed Parque Hotel talks of 1983, COMASPO was
not involved in the Naval Club pact.

13 "Multipartidaria se reúne hoy sin delegados nacionalistas," *El Día*, 3 July 1984, p. 1.

14 "Rapela: 'Pensamos estar cada día más cerca de una negociación'," *El Día*, Saturday, 30 June
1984, p. 7. Typically, the president had threatened a week earlier that there might be an imposed
alternative if agreement was not reached: "Alvarez: Si no hay acuerdo se pensará otra fórmula
para volver a un gobierno democrático," *El Día*, Friday, 22 June 1984, p. 1.

mediately supported by Victor Semproni, a member of the PIT executive.[15] The tactics of the Colorados were simply "concertation" and negotiation, given their lack of militant activists and their perception that the military would hardly be toppled by such shows of force, but possibly made more apprehensive.

Despite their isolation, the Blancos also rhetorically called for consensus (bringing out new magazines titled *Concertación* and *Unidad* to drive home the point). But having left the Multipartidaria, their entire strategy rested exclusively on mobilization against any negotiations. The only reservations expressed among their opponent parties at the decision to negotiate came from the far left and the young radicals of the Colorado party in the Corriente Batllista Independiente (CBI). As their leader, Manuel Flores Silva, said,

this dialogue cannot end up being the same as the Parque Hotel. It must concern the conditions for transferring power and nothing more, though some kind of guarantees against "revanchism" are acceptable – even Wilson renounced this in Buenos Aires. CBI can enter negotiations with Wilson and the Communist party banned, but only with the rest of Broad Front and the majority of the National party. . . . We are unhappy about negotiating without consensus. . . . Yet the Blancos have throughout their history made the most amazing turnabouts and entered pacts.[16]

In other words, the young Colorado still hoped to reconcile the National party to negotiations, but he also emphasized that the Blancos were unpredictable and unreliable, which lessened the feeling of obligation to stand by them.

A close associate of Seregni in the secretariat of the Broad Front reiterated what he saw as Seregni's crucial divergence from Wilson Ferreira:

The military project had failed, but they still had arms and foreign allies . . . the National party was too maximalist. Seregni never accepted the Convergencia. . . . It is not that we rejected an alliance with the National party – we invented the Multipartidaria, but . . . Wilson's strategy was all wrong: He imagined he could return as the country's savior.[17]

The dialogue gets under way, and public opinion is favorable

Despite reservations among their more radical youth sectors, the Colorados, the Left, and the Civic Union began the dialogue with the military. At that stage it was called a "prenegotiation," in which the parties os-

15 This information is taken from a valuable press summary: *El Marcador*, 1(1):15.
16 Personal interview, Montevideo, July 1984.
17 Personal interview, Montevideo, October 1984.

Table 8.4. *Equipos data on public opinion regarding negotiations*
with the military[a]

Group	Right/I Agree (%)	Wrong/they should wait (%)	No talks, no negotiating (%)	DK/ NA[b] (%)	Total (%)
All respondents	65	21	8	7	100
Broad Front	81	12	6	1	100
Blancos	27	49	21	3	100
Colorados	89	7	1	3	100
Undecided	67	15	5	13	100

[a]The question: "A few days ago the Multipartidaria announced its plan to begin what has been called the prenegotiation with the armed forces. The National party resolved not to take part in the negotiations so long as Wilson Ferreira is in jail. What do you think about this decision? Do you think it is right?"
[b]Don't know/no answer.
Source: Equipos Consultores, *Notas, Boletín Semanal*, No. 7 (3 July 1984), Table 2.

tensibly discussed the need to secure a climate of "opening." The Colorados made it clear that they would not negotiate without the Left and insisted on the deproscription of José Pedro Cardoso, leader of the Socialist party. Along with Juan Young of the Christian Democratic party, he was to represent the Left in the talks.[18]

A crucial factor in the decision of the Colorados to negotiate, and to some extent the Left's decision to accompany them, was the climate of public opinion. Polls strongly confirmed that the mass of Uruguayans agreed with the decision, and a majority were willing, if necessary, to settle for less than fully free elections. Gallup data suggested that there were almost no cleavages in the public regarding the necessity of renewing talks, whether in terms of gender, class, or age. Indeed, the 78% level of public support for renewing the dialogue among Blanco sympathizers, as reported by Gallup, seemed almost implausibly high.[19] However, a new polling firm, Equipos, found the support for negotiations almost as strong. At the end of July, it reported that in the first half of the month 65% of those interviewed in Montevideo approved of the Multipartidaria's decision to negotiate, though 73% of those reporting themselves as Blancos agreed with their party's line of opposing talks (Table 8.5).

The picture that emerges strongly from Tables 8.4–8.6 is that pub-

18 "Fue desproscripto el Presidente del Partido Socialista, Dr. José P. Cardoso," *El Día*, Friday, 6 July 1984, p. 1.
19 Gallup Uruguay, *Informe de Opinión Pública*, No. 343, Table 17.

Table 8.5. *Opinion on boycotting elections without all candidates (Equipos)*[a]

Group	Right/I agree (%)	Wrong/they should wait (%)	No talks, no negotiating (%)	DK/ NA (%)	Total (%)
All respondents	28	53	16	3	100
Broad Front	17	75	8	—[b]	100
Blancos	73	21	6	—	100
Colorados	4	82	13	1	100
Undecided	21	48	27	4	100

[a]The question: "Do you think the resolution of the National party not to take part in elections with Wilson in jail is right?"
[b]Zero votes.
Source: Equipos Consultores, *Notas, Boletín Semanal*, No. 7 (3 July 1984), Table 3.

lic opinion was overwhelmingly in favor of continuing the dialogue with the military. However, Equipos data suggested that Blanco sympathizers largely supported their party's refusal to negotiate while Ferreira was in jail. Some of the discrepancy between Equipos and Gallup data doubtless can be traced to their respective question wordings.[20] Gallup agreed that opinions were far more divided on the issue of whether or not to take part in elections with certain candidates or parties banned (Table 8.7);[21] a slight majority of Blancos were against (48% versus 47%), and a quite sizable minority of those in the Left (42%). Only 14% of Colorados had such qualms. Perhaps the most revealing data, nevertheless, showed that a great majority of Blanco supporters believed that elections would go ahead: 75%. That was less than the number of Colorados (86%), but more than the number of Frentistas. In other words, a fatalistic attitude was developing among Blanco supporters. The steady growth in the proportion of citizens in favor of elections, even without all candidates, was a further indicator of the mood of the country. These findings neatly sum up the dilemma of Uruguayan politics in June of 1984: The public wanted negotiations and were confident that elections would take place, but they were divided over the issue of whether or not to accept the continua-

20 Equipos did, however, find a wavering trend in both camps by the following month: Left sympathizers were less in favor of the talks than before, and Blancos more. See, Equipos Consultores, *Informe Mensual*, No. 2, 25 September 1984.
21 The question in Spanish referred to the desirability of "going to elections" (*ir a elecciones*), an ambiguous formulation that can be translated as "take part in elections" (as I have done) or "hold elections." The occupational categories used by Gallup lump together professionals with students; businesspersons with the self-employed; blue- and white-collar workers; and the retired with those working in the informal sector.

Table 8.6. *Opinion on boycotting elections without all candidates and on likelihood elections will go ahead (Gallup)*

	"With which do you agree if there are banned politicians: take part in elections or not?"				"In your view, will there be elections next November 25?"			
	Take part (%)	Boycott (%)	Don't know (%)	Total (%)	Yes (%)	No (%)	Don't know (%)	Total (%)
All	63	29	8	100	75	12	13	100
Sex								
Male	58	36	6	100	—[a]	—	—	—
Female	67	23	10	100	—	—	—	—
Class								
Upper	61	33	6	100	78	10	12	100
Middle	61	30	9	100	76	11	13	100
Lower	68	24	8	100	72	16	12	100
Age (years)								
18–29	61	35	4	100	72	14	14	100
30–49	50	39	11	100	76	10	14	100
50+	73	18	9	100	76	12	12	100
Occupation								
Prof./student	44	48	8	100	67	12	21	100
Business	55	36	9	100	82	11	7	100
Worker/employee	65	31	4	100	79	9	12	100
Retired/informal	68	21	11	100	74	13	13	100
Unemployed	65	30	5	100	70	20	10	100
Party								
Broad Front	58	42	0	100	64	12	15	100
Blanco	47	48	5	100	75	16	9	100
Colorado	82	14	4	100	86	7	7	100
None	67	20	13	100	68	14	18	100
Education								
Primary or less	71	18	11	100	—	—	—	—
Secondary & more	58	36	6	100	—	—	—	—
Interest in politics								
Much	52	46	2	100	52	46	2	100
Little	68	26	6	100	68	26	6	100
None	69	16	15	100	72	14	14	100

Note: Sample size, 756 cases; sample date, 26 June to 5 July 1984; area, Montevideo.
[a]Data not recorded.
Source: Gallup Uruguay, *Informe de Opinión Pública*, No. 343, Tables 18 and 19.

Table 8.7. *The slow growth of support for elections even with bans*[a]

	1984			
Opinion	April (%)	May (%)	June (%)	August (%)
Take part	55	63	63	69
Boycott	31	28	29	27
No response	14	9	8	4

[a]The question: "With which of these opinions are you most in agreement if there are banned politicians: take part in elections or not?"
Source: Gallup Uruguay, *Informe de Opinión Pública*, No. 345, p. 16.

tion of proscriptions on leaders such as Wilson Ferreira. The success of the prenegotiations and the eventual Naval Club pact would help persuade them that the proscriptions were lesser evils.

Early achievements of the prenegotiations and their momentum

At each step, the *dialoguista* parties extracted concessions in order to avoid attempts by the Blancos to outmaneuver them, while walking a narrow line between demanding too much and too little.[22] According to one participant, Socialist party leader José Pedro Cardoso's first speech at the talks at the headquarters of the Estado Mayor Conjunto was designed to relax their hosts and show a positive intent to dissipate military fears. Nevertheless, the *dialoguista* parties attempted to impose five conditions at the first meeting:

1 press freedom,
2 repeal of institutional acts No. 7 and No. 14,
3 lifting of the decrees of 2 August 1983 that banned political activity,
4 "significant" liberation of political prisoners, and
5 deproscription of leftist parties and leaders, with the express right of the Broad Front to run as a coalition.[23]

These were scarcely radical demands to make as a precondition for dialogue. The decree of 2 August 1983 was already a dead letter, and the vague demand for "significant" freeing of prisoners in effect implied that

22 "Sanguinetti: Aplicar medidas que mejoren el clima político," *El Día*, Saturday, 7 July 1984, p. 5.
23 "Políticos plantearon 5 puntos a los militares," *El Día*, Saturday, 7 July 1984, p. 1.

Wilson Ferreira need not be one of them. By way of contrast, a full-scale political amnesty for all political prisoners had been declared by the authoritarian rulers of Brazil and Spain as part of their own projects for liberalization. It should not be forgotten that politicians were still being arrested in Uruguay.

Repeal of Institutional Act No. 4, the original decree banning politicians and parties, was *not* made a condition for the dialogue by the Multipartidaria.[24] Although the military were quite happy to repeal Institutional Act No. 7, which had led to purges of civil servants, and Institutional Act No. 14, which had allowed new proscriptions, they refused to countenance releasing Wilson or legalizing the extreme Left.[25] Though they were evasive on the question of freeing political prisoners – which they insisted was a matter for the military courts – they hinted that some might be released once they had completed half their sentences. In addition, the Christian Democratic party would be legalized. Prodialogue sources therefore insisted that they detected "a change of climate" that suggested the "receptivity of the military to all suggestions."[26] As one negotiator for the Left put it, "the freeing of Wilson was not a condition because that would have meant no talks, which was what the National party wanted."[27]

Defending the Left's decision to negotiate, Seregni later said that it was their line to say no to the dialogue, but yes to discussion of the "climate" necessary to negotiate. That meant not only winning political space for the Broad Front but also winning space for freedom. They took the liberty of recommending to their militant comrades that they read the record of the *Parque Hotel*, and also the press of just a few months earlier, when there had been those who came forward to accept proscriptions, and others were offering a pact with the armed forces to make elections indirect.[28]

Table 8.8 sets out the legal decrees that established the rules for the transition throughout the middle four months of 1984. The first decrees

24 As a Blanco leader remarked bitterly, "Seregni was the arbiter of the pact. Why did he ask for derogation of AI 7 and AI 14 instead of AI 4? They should have dug in their heels" (personal interview, Montevideo, 30 August 1984).
25 "Militares analizan problema: Frente crea diferencias," *Mundo Color*, Monday, 2 July 1984, p. 1; "Desproscripciones y Amnistía totales 'no resultan viables'," *El Día*, Tuesday, 10 July 1984, p. 1
26 Ibid., p. 18.
27 Personal interview, Montevideo, 27 March 1985. Speaking from memory, it is interesting that the same leader was momentarily unable to remember the third condition: repeal of the 2 August decree "suspending public political activity." Instead, he mentioned the need for an end to attacks such as that which had led to the death of a doctor in the Roszlik case.
28 In return for this allusion to Wilson Ferreira's alleged underhand dealings in March, the Blancos replied with a vicious attack in their ironically titled magazine *National Unity*, dredging up Seregni's role as military commander of Montevideo in strike-breaking during 1968.

Table 8.8. *The last institutional acts and laws*

Act or decree	Date	Substance
Institutional Act No. 15	23 May 1984	Blocks the Blancos' plebiscite campaign to have all institutional acts repealed
Institutional Act No. 16	4 July 1984	Permits deproscription of Left leaders on a case-by-case basis
Institutional Act No. 17	16 July 1984	Repeals Institutional Act No. 7 (no new civil-servant firings) and Institutional Act No. 14 (no new bannings)
Institutional Act No. 18	27 July 1984	Legalizes the Broad Front and its constituent parties, except for communists and Tupamaros; un-bans their leaders unless tried for subversion; restores the vote to the military
Institutional Act No. 19	3 August 1984	Embodies the Naval Club provisions regarding elections, transfer of power, civilian trials, military promotions, and constituent powers

Source: *Actos Institucionales* (*1 al 17*) (Montevideo: Editorial Técnica, 1984); *Diario Oficial*, 3 August 1984.

were designed to block the Blancos' strategy of refusing to negotiate, and subsequent decrees were aimed at rewarding the *dialoguista* parties. Most notable of all was the long-awaited rehabilitation of the Broad Front as a legitimate political actor on 27 July.

Generals Aranco and Rapela began to threaten that any parties that refused to accept an eventual pact would be excluded from the elections.[29] Military impatience began to grow in some sectors, and on 14 July the leader of Uruguay's most conservative party, Juan Vicente Chiarino, was forced to reject suggestions from opponents of the negotiations inside the military itself that the parties were wasting time. He then added, revealingly, "with regard to mobilizations, nobody can imagine what we are holding back. No one takes this into consideration because it does not appear in the press. We cannot go out and say we are restraining this and containing that."[30]

Chiarino's comments implied that there were great strains among the Left and the Multipartidaria, presumably coming from the grass roots and from social movements that did not like the turn of events. That was

29 Such incidents showed that there still were differences between the generals regarding the strategies for negotiation. Significantly, however, Rapela and Aranco were by then both retired. Medina had the greater weight as spokesman for the interests of the military institution.
30 *El Día*, 10 July 1984, p. 21. Actually, to go out and say it to the press was exactly what he had done in *El Día*, 24 July 1984, p. 5.

in effect the symmetrical counterpart to the military's earlier warnings that the parties must not push too hard lest they strengthen the hardliners. If the military tried to make the political leaders move too fast, they might lose control over their supporters and even be ousted.[31] The commanders seemed to appreciate that problem: To create a political climate of relaxation it was announced that exiles could return home (as long as they were not subject to arrest warrants). Three journalists who had been imprisoned and tried were acquitted and released.

The Colorados chose 16 July to proclaim Sanguinetti and Tarigo as the candidates of the Batllista majority of the party, to emphasize their confidence that elections would be held.[32]

Dénouement: the Naval Club negotiations

The prenegotiations had brought significant progress regarding opposition demands: Individual leftist leaders were being restored their rights and allowed to join the talks, and a change in the political atmosphere could be sensed. At that point, Civic Union leader Juan Chiarino stated that negotiations were, in effect, under way. With Tarigo and Seregni, he produced a plan for the next phase of the dialogue, which would take the form of an unwritten agreement, as the politicians were unwilling to sign their names to any de facto revisions of the Constitution. When the PIT labor federation, the ASCEEP students' association, and the FUCVAM cooperative housing movement proposed another day of popular protests, the prodialogue parties of the Multipartidaria rejected the idea as inopportune.[33] The significant thing was that the Broad Front already had regained enough control to block that idea, which might have upset the delicate state of talks. Despite the secrecy regarding the negotiations, which had shifted to the more neutral territory of the Naval Club, official communiqués kept up the climate of optimism.[34]

In actual fact, the conversations with the commanders in chief reached the brink of collapse over the question of rehabilitating the Broad Front,

---

31 The Christian Democrats, for example, had earlier ousted their leader, Juan Pablo Terra, for attempting to take the party out of the Broad Front.

32 On the same day, Adolfo Suárez and General Guttiérrez Mellado, among other Spaniards, arrived to take part in a widely publicized seminar on negotiated transitions to democracy, at which politicians from all parties were quite visible – and the Blancos were visibly uncomfortable. High-ranking military leaders did not attend, however. General Medina told me that he did not revise his unfavorable opinion of Spain's "democratic General" until after his retirement (personal interview, Columbia, SC, 27 March 1987).

33 *El Día*, 25 July 1984, p. 28.

34 "Políticos califican de positivo encuentro con Fuerzas Armadas," *El Día*, Friday, 27 July 1984, p. 1. The politicians refused to negotiate in an official military building, but agreed to meet in the naval officers' club.

which the Multipartidaria insisted come before, and the commanders after, the final agreement.[35] The army commander, General Medina, publicly stated that negotiations might break down as a result of the declarations of politicians and press reports, in a manner similar to the collapse of the 1983 Parque Hotel negotiations.[36] As a result of that, the Broad Front voted to require all its leaders to remain silent until after the next meeting with the military on 27 July. On that day, according to a participant in the talks, Sanguinetti's insistence on immediate legalization of the Broad Front finally caused the commanders in chief reluctantly to give in and announce Institutional Act No. 18, which legalized the Christian Democratic *lema* under which the Broad Front could be reformed. The right to constitute a *lema* had great advantages for the leftist parties in terms of allowing them to run competing slates for each party, maximize the number of seats they would win, and run a joint presidential candidate. It was inconceivable that all leftist parties could have agreed on a single joint candidate list. Under the terms of Institutional Act No. 18, about 6,500 leftist politicians had their democratic rights restored, with about 3,000 remaining banned. A verbal commitment was made to release 411 prisoners who had served more than half their prison sentences. The same evening, downtown Montevideo was jammed with a jubilant demonstration by the Left that seemingly had been planned in advance. But the act also restored the vote to the military, adding 70,000 (probably conservative) voters to the electorate.

In the subsequent days the Naval Club talks moved toward a successful conclusion. On 30 July they agreed that the National Security Council would be retained as an advisory body meeting at the president's command, that military justice would apply only during periods of emergency, and that the latter would be more closely defined.[37] The following day it was agreed that from 1 July 1985 the National Assembly would have the powers of a constituent assembly and that any constitutional reforms would be submitted to plebiscite in November of that year. It was also agreed that each armed-forces commander would be chosen by the president from a list of three put forward by the junta and then subjected to Senate approval. Those two points were breakthroughs of the utmost importance. The decision to give an elected body the power to accept or reject constitutional revisions meant that whatever transitory provisions were agreed upon could be undone. Thus, the parties felt that they were risking very little. Furthermore, the principle that the president would

35 Personal interview with a delegate of the Multipartidaria to the talks, Montevideo, 27 March 1985.
36 *El Marcador*, 1(1):29. "Medina: manejo de la información puede hacer fracasar negociación," *Ultimas Noticias*, Wednesday, 25 July 1984, p. 8.
37 "Políticos coinciden que está cerca el acuerdo," *El Día*, Tuesday, 31 July 1984, p. 1.

have a choice when it came to top military promotions and that the Senate would have to agree to his choice was a fundamental step toward reestablishing civilian supremacy (even though the Blancos complained it was not enough).

Finally, on 1 August, a formula was agreed upon for suspending civil rights in time of emergency, baptized a declaration of a "state of insurrection," to distinguish it from the military's previous proposal for a "state of emergency" at the Parque Hotel.[38] Although such a state could be declared only by the president, it would result in the military courts having jurisdiction over those arrested. According to a leading Colorado negotiator, that latter point, too, nearly caused the talks to collapse: "The principal obstacle was guaranteeing liberties. Holding suspects for 10 days before seeing a judge was unacceptable. But in 1983 we were not sure they wanted to leave power. This time General Medina did."[39]

The Broad Front negotiator previously cited agreed that the question of military justice had caused a crisis in the discussions, but he emphasized that the compromise not only limited military trials of civilians but also stated that the military themselves would be tried by their peers only for actions taken "within the exercise of their duties." In his (controversial) view, that would mean that civil courts could try officers for torture or corruption, a point that the commanders in chief definitely did not accept, which apparently caused serious criticism of their actions inside the armed forces.[40] They were, of course, adamantly opposed to any "revenge trials," but Sanguinetti had already promised to oppose those in his nomination speech. Meanwhile, Medina justified the lack of a specific clause granting the military immunity by saying that that would have been tantamount to admitting guilt! The Blancos charged that a secret deal had been made that there would be no human-rights trials, but it is not clear why such a deal would have been of more use to the military than would Sanguinetti's word before the Colorado convention.

One of the things that made the Naval Club pact possible was precisely such ambiguity. Ambiguity was actually functional in debating such highly charged issues: One of the lessons that was learned after the 1983 Parque Hotel talks was that insistence on total resolution of differences was unrealistic. Some issues may not even have been raised. None of the participating groups has ever admitted that the issue of military immunities was discussed, precisely because it was too delicate. The great difference, according to a Civic Union negotiator, was that "talks were cordial and respectful, unlike the Parque Hotel. Furthermore, both sides abandoned 'positional bargaining':[41] The military's May plan was hardly even discussed."[42]

The major thing that had been decided was not articulated: Elections would go ahead without all candidates permitted, and specifically without Ferreira. The rehabilitation of the Broad Front allowed the possibility of splitting the antimilitary vote and allowing the Colorados to win the election. Finally, a number of substantive compromises had been reached regarding military prerogatives. Otherwise, the provisions for various possible constitutional changes and continuation of the institutional acts were devices to tie up loose ends and permit the commanders to avoid too much loss of face in the eyes of their subordinates, rather than guidelines to the future form of democracy. Sanguinetti made it clear that if he won the election, there would be no more banned parties the day he took office. The pact, in sum, represented not the continuation of the *proceso* but the prospect of continuity with the elected government that would be its undoing. It was somewhere between a negotiated reform and a negotiated rupture.

The terms

Although no formal document was signed at the conclusion of talks in the Naval Club, the participating parties implicitly subscribed to Institutional Act No. 19, published on 3 August 1984.[43] The basis of the pact (or the "accord," as the participants preferred to call it) was the following:

1 Institutional Act No. 1 suspending elections was repealed.
2 Army promotions to the rank of commander in chief would be made by the president from a list of three candidates provided by the generals; for the other services, from a list of only two candidates.
3 The National Security Council would survive in an advisory capacity, meeting at the request of the president alone, and including a majority of cabinet ministers over the military.
4 At the initiative of the president, Parliament would have the right to vote a "state of insurrection" to suspend habeas corpus.
5 A new protective legal mechanism (*recurso de amparo*) would allow appeals against government decisions or military actions.
6 Military courts would continue to try civilians only when Parliament had voted a "state of insurrection."

41 See Chapter 6.
42 Personal interview, Montevideo, 13 April 1985.
43 The full text appeared in *Ultimas Noticias*, Saturday, 4 August 1984, p. 3.

7 The National Assembly elected in 1984 would act as a constituent assembly to consider permanent incorporation of the provisions of this last institutional act into the Constitution.
8 If amended, the new text of the Constitution would be submitted to plebiscite in November 1985.[44]

The plenum of the Broad Front voted in favor of these terms, 31 to 14, with 6 abstentions – only the extreme Left refusing to endorse the agreement. Of the 15 members of the Blanco executive, only 2 voted in favor (Silveira Zabala and Zorrilla de San Martín), and even a former anti-Wilsonista voted against (García Pintos). Colorado support for the pact was unanimous.

Army commander General Medina, the single most important man in ensuring that the pact was accepted, made the following statement to the press:

The Armed Forces have come out of this process upright. . . . But for democracy not to break down again depends on many things. Above all that the Armed Forces appreciate fully that the times we are living through have changed. That politicians elected to public office behave with probity, with honesty and do the best for the country. That the Armed Forces, when all is said and done, be respected as those who gave themselves to their country deserve. . . .

However, Medina went on to add a stern warning:

The Armed Forces are not going to accept rough handling, or anything like it. They are disposed to accept justice done to elements in their midst who have shown themselves to be dishonest, who acted on their own behalf. But those who acted to follow out orders . . . from superiors, these are going to merit our widest support.[45]

Medina's declarations can be read as a clear warning to the hard-liners in the military not to flirt with any "putschist" plots. But the commander clearly was trying to allay the fears of the military institution and its junior officers regarding the future possibility of trials.

Reactions to the pact

On 8 August the decree banning political activity was lifted, long after it had ceased to be applied. When the Blanco *directorio* (executive) met

44 The legal advisers to the commanders in drafting the act were the president of the Supreme Military Tribunal (Court), Colonel Silva Ledesma, and the education minister, Juan Bautista Schroeder. A week later the latter resigned in frustration at being unable to put through liberalizing reforms in the university that he favored.
45 *El Marcador*, 1(1):41; "Medina: cumplar con objetivos," *Ultimas Noticias*, Saturday, 4 August 1984, p. 2.

again on 9 August, it denounced the pact as illegitimate, because the armed forces should have had no role in such matters, and because it would lead to elections with proscriptions and to institutional instability.[46] They continued to insist that the pact was repressive and equivalent to a prolongation of military rule (*continuismo*). As Pereyra said, "negotiations were unnecessary. The government was exhausted and could not go on. It had no support and was in an unsustainable position."[47] Wilson went out of his way to denounce the pact in the most vitriolic terms, smuggling a letter from his jail cell that was read out during a television debate. Among other barbs, it referred to the Naval Club accord as the "Sanguinetti-Medina Pact."[48] Sanguinetti retorted (live): "What about the Alvarez-Ferreira pact which he attempted, sending the unfortunate Professor Pivel Devoto to the commanders in chief!" In the same debate, Christian Democrat Juan Young added, with irony,

[Wilson] has not given us any other paths to follow . . . he came in the Ferry, intending to overthrow the dictatorship with the tactics of a naval war which never happened. We were there in solidarity with Mr. Ferreira when he arrived, but this mechanism did not overthrow the dictatorship and the National Party offered no other way forward.[49]

In his letter from jail, dated 5 August 1984, Wilson Ferreira laid out the basis for his opposition to the Naval Club pact:

The pact seeks for the first time to have Uruguayans take on responsibility for the dictatorship and transform what until now had been imposed upon them into a valid system, expressly accepting the point of agreeing to its prolongation and de facto institutional survival. . . .

For the first time in our history, it has been accepted that the Constitution be modified without prior popular assent.[50]

According to Ferreira, what the pact meant was "not the risk of a military coup, but something much more dangerous: no more need for a coup."[51] Responding with fury to Ferreira's letter, Sanguinetti vehemently rejected that thesis:

46 Two leaders who supported the pact stayed away. Luis Alberto Lacalle voted against the motion, considering it too strong, even though he opposed the pact.
47 Personal interview, Montevideo, 12 December 1984.
48 Notice that Ferreira did not mention Seregni's name, although he had been very much involved in the negotiations. Because Seregni was still banned, the commanders would not allow him to come to the talks, but he attended the breakfast meetings held at Sanguinetti's home prior to each negotiating session and contributed massively to the parties' strategy.
49 *El Marcador*, 1(1):45–6.
50 The full text of the letter was published in *Ultimas Noticias*, Friday, 10 August 1984, p. 6.
51 In that phrase, Ferreira implied that military rule would, in effect, continue, and he referred to the future president's lack of freedom to determine military promotions. However, the thought that coups might become "unnecessary" might have been welcome to some.

The legitimacy [of the pact] will not be given by Ferreira nor any of us present. It will be the people who give it. And if in fact all parties take part in the election, they will accept its legitimacy. . . . Nobody left the National Party out. The National Party chose to marginalize itself.[52]

Public-opinion polls suggested that there was support for the terms of the deal despite the fact that Medina made it clear that there would be no more "deproscriptions." Wilson would not be allowed to run, and about 5,000 citizens would be both banned and disfranchised, with about 300 political prisoners remaining in jail. On the other hand, all curbs on the news media were lifted at once, and politics flooded television and radio, while demonstrators crowded the streets. The Blancos continued to threaten to cast blank ballots or abstain if Wilson, who had received the overwhelming nomination of their convention, was not allowed to run. Nevertheless, the charge that the terms of the deal amounted to a disguised continuation of military rule through manipulated elections lacked plausibility, given that even the communists and extreme left were allowed to run proxy lists within the Frente – as Democracia Avanzada and Izquierda Democrática Independiente, respectively.[53] When the communists' leader, Rodney Arismendi, returned from exile in Moscow, he was greeted by a vast rally, a motorcade from the airport, and a platform from which to speak. The irony of his reception compared with that for Wilson only a few months earlier could hardly have been lost on anyone.

The data in Table 8.9 show clearly that public opinion had been doubtful in June regarding the decision of the Colorados and Left to renew the dialogue, but by August it had come out strongly backing the pro-dialogue parties. (The August data were collected in the same week that the details of the Naval Club pact were made public.) The most interesting fact was the great increase in support for the Colorado party's actions among its identifiers, and the marked wavering among Blancos. The popularity of the military also increased as a result of the pact.

The core interests of the military: amnesty and immunity

One of the most fundamentally contentious issues of Uruguay's transition was what to do with the country's imprisoned guerrillas: those who had robbed banks, planted bombs, shot at soldiers and policemen, and kidnapped ambassadors and businessmen. The regime put the number of deaths that the guerrillas had caused at 35. That was slightly more than

52 "¿Qué tendría que decir de Alvarez-Ferreira?" *Ultimas Noticias*, Friday, 10 August 1984, p. 7.
53 The fact that both chose to incorporate the word "democracy" in their titles was an interesting sign of the Left's evolution, at least in rhetoric.

Table 8.9. *The evolution of opinion regarding party and military tactics*

"Do you think the parties are acting well or badly?" Party evaluated	May (%)	June (%)	August (%)
Evaluations by all interviewees			
Broad Front			
Well	42	32	59
Badly	15	26	21
No reply	43	42	20
Total	100	100	100
Blancos			
Well	45	32	36
Badly	30	40	50
No reply	14	28	14
Total	100	100	100
Colorados			
Well	49	39	62
Badly	30	32	26
No reply	21	29	12
Total	100	100	100
Each party's sympathizers			
Broad Front			
Well	88	82	80
Badly	6	6	15
No reply	6	12	5
Total	100	100	100
Blancos			
Well	74	65	64
Badly	12	18	22
No reply	14	17	14
Total	100	100	100
Colorados			
Well	75	64	91
Badly	13	23	6
No reply	12	13	3
Total	100	100	100

"Do you think the military are acting well or badly?" Group	May (%)	June (%)	August (%)
All interviewees			
Well	12	15	25
Badly	75	66	65
No reply	13	29	10
Total	100	100	100

Note: Sample size, 772 cases; last sample 2–8 August 1984; area, Montevideo.
Source: Gallup Uruguay, *Informe de Opinión Pública*, No. 345, pp. 1–25.

Table 8.10. *Politicians' views on an amnesty for terrorists*[a]

Option	Frente (%) (n = 10)	Blancos (%) (n = 17)	Colorados (%) (n = 19)
(a) "The amnesty should include everyone who took action (including violence) against the government, prior to the breakdown of democracy."	90	71	21
(b) "The amnesty should be limited to political crimes of opinion, supposed attacks on the Constitution, but cannot include violent crimes, kidnapping, bombing, etc."	10	12	58
(c) "All those imprisoned by military courts should have the right of retrial by civilian courts."	0	18	16
(d) "No type of amnesty is acceptable."	0	0	5

[a]The question: "Some say that an amnesty is needed to pacify the country. With which of these alternatives are you most in agreement?"

the number of Uruguayans who had "disappeared" at the hands, it is assumed, of the security forces.[54] Regarding the need for an amnesty, which the military strongly rejected, there was a convergence between Blancos and Frente leaders on a relatively radical stance (Table 8.10). On the other hand, a majority of Colorado interviewees actually opposed any amnesty for those who had been convicted of "crimes of blood" – a major point in their favor for the military. References by Wilson's son to "beloved" Tupamaros must have produced horror among the military, and many Blancos. However, the personal statements of politicians who favored negotiations showed a desire to reach agreement with other sectors on that issue. One close aide to Seregni said that "the National party insisted on a general and unrestricted amnesty, but we know this was impossible. It is not a problem of their [the Blancos] being extreme but inflexible."[55] By contrast, a leading Colorado stated that "I prefer that the country err on the side of generosity."[56]

54 Estimates of the numbers who disappeared in Argentina range from 10,000 upward. In Uruguay the figure is nearer 30, though five times more Uruguayans died in Argentina, probably as a result of joint action by the Uruguayan and Argentine security forces.
55 Personal interview, Montevideo, 12 December 1984.

Table 8.11. *Politician's views on immunity for the military*[a]

Opinion	Frente (%) (n = 10)	Blancos (%) (n = 16)	Colorados (%) (n = 19)
(a) "Immunity should include whoever committed alleged errors and excesses in the exercise of public duties so long as this was in the framework of combating subversion."	10	6	5
(b) "Immunity should include only those who committed alleged excesses in the course of carrying out orders from their superiors."	0	25	16
(c) "Immunity should include those officers who ordered the fight against subversion, independently of possible excesses committed."	0	6	5
(d) "No type of immunity is acceptable, and those responsible must be subjected to sanctions."	90	63	74

[a]The question: "With regard to the security forces in their fight against terrorism, with which of these alternatives do you agree?"

The danger that they might be subject to trial for violations of human rights, as was happening just across the River Plate in Argentina, was also of particular concern to the military. Surprisingly, as Table 8.11 shows, the Blancos were the least tough on that issue when interviewed individually. Though all parties were circumspect, it was clear that the Left had the strongest feelings on the subject. Wilson (who had narrowly escaped a death squad in 1976) had also adopted a tough line in his speeches, yet other Blancos apparently were anxious to appear reasonable.

What the data show is that the Left did not have any deep-seated agreement with the Colorados, and the Blancos did not have any particular divergent attitudes regarding the political substance of the restored democracy. The Left was not agreeing to negotiate for the same reasons as the Colorados, and it did not come naturally to them, just as the Blancos were not particularly at ease with their stance. Rather, the pro-pact parties were responding to the incentives as the military had laid them out, dividing the dangerous multiparty coalition they had faced at the beginning of the year. The real determinants of party strategies were the

56 Personal interview, Montevideo, 14 December 1984.

incentives of power. Excluded from winning "first prize" (i.e., the presidency), the Blancos chose to denounce the rules but still take part.

In short, the fight between the parties was centered on the procedures and personalities as much as on principles. Luckily, that suggested that the estrangement of the National party might not last long, once their leader was released from jail. Nagging doubts remained, however, that they would accept the legitimacy of the elections, particularly if the Colorados were to win narrowly, as they had done in 1971.

The incentives and disincentives for playing the negotiations game

As a result of the pact, the Blancos charged the other parties with "opportunism," and they, in turn, retorted that the Blancos were "free-riding" by leaving the "dirty work" to the other parties. In fact, though altruism was not in evidence on any side, there was advantage for all in the Blancos' intransigence, in that it greatly strengthened the position of the other parties. Furthermore, the incorporation of the Left had a potential bonus in their future commitment to democracy.

Beyond the tactical convergence of the Colorados and the Frente, many ties continued to bind the traditional parties, despite the vitriolic election campaign that began. The Frente clearly was not ideologically predisposed to negotiations, but it had the most to gain from them in that continued marginalization might have caused it to break up (as its most moderate parties sought legalization) or go into a decline (if progressive voters turned to Wilson Ferreira). Under the right circumstances the Blancos were willing to negotiate, as the previously cited questionnaire replies and the mysterious events of March suggested. What was true, however, was that they were less amenable to arm-twisting than were the Colorados, while Wilson indulged in triumphalist rhetoric, implying he would "teach the military a lesson."

Few politicians would admit that contacts with the military had been a source of tension in their political sectors. Indeed, few would admit that much contact had taken place, and the numbers declining to answer the question on that matter were very high (especially for Blancos). Quite simply, any sort of dealing with the military was regarded as suspect and not legitimate (Table 8.12). Nevertheless, the military were a political reality, and contacts were unavoidable. What was revealing, however, was that it was the Broad Front leaders who reported the greatest strains, whereas the Blancos were not significantly more likely to find that a source of controversy than were the Colorados. That was further evidence that the Left–Colorado alliance was in some sense "unnatural," based on a temporary convergence of interests.

Table 8.12. *Repercussions of dealings with the military*[a]

Party	Affirmative (%)
Broad Front (*n* = 14)	28.6
Blancos (*n* = 7)	17.3
Colorados (*n* = 11)	14.3
All[b] (*n* = 36)	19.4

[a] The question: "Have any contacts or collaboration with the regime that have occurred produced divisions within your *sublema*?"
[b] Includes one Patriotic Union and three Civic Union leaders.

The central concern of the military became to block Ferreira's election, and in that they were to be successful. That they were willing to undo their carefully crafted repression of the Left at a stroke in order to block Wilson suggests, however, the measure of their peculiar aversion to him.[57] In a sense, they trapped the Blancos into an ultimately fruitless campaign against the pact by depriving them of a candidate on whose charisma they were especially reliant (unlike the Colorados and Frente, who did not have any such leaders). The Blancos did not have a weighty organization to substitute for their leader.

For reasons that perhaps will become fully clear only when their memoirs are published, Seregni and Sanguinetti had no faith or trust in Wilson Ferreira. With regard to the distant past, one might invoke Seregni's Colorado origins, or Sanguinetti's memories of Ferreira's role in the 1973 crisis. More recently, there had been the unpredictable swings in the Blancos' strategies and Ferreira's propensity for making radical speeches after his arrival in Argentina. Yet the leaders of the Colorado party and the Broad Front were co-opted, not coerced, into abandoning their rival. There seems to have been some truth to the accusation that had the other parties held firm, eventually the military would have had no choice but to release Ferreira. However, neither group was favorable to his radical call for complete rupture with the military, and both feared that his program for demilitarization might provoke rapid reentry into politics by the armed forces. They also realized that his chances of winning the presidency would have been greatly boosted by the adoption of his model for the transition.

Perhaps most important of all the factors facilitating the Colorado–Left strategy was the evidence that Ferreira aroused antipathy in major sections

57 The reasons for the mutual detestation of the military and Ferreira are discussed in the third section of Chapter 6.

of the population. According to Gallup, 58% of Blancos thought that the party should take part in the elections, even without their main leader.[58] Thirty-one percent of those interviewed in all parties described Wilson Ferreira's return as a "bad thing" for the country, and a surprising 33% thought that the armed forces had done "well" to arrest him.[59]

The structure of military interests in the transition

The fundamental situation prior to the Naval Club pact was one of stalemate: The military maintained their monopoly over coercion, and civil society had reorganized enough to demonstrate its capacity to resist, without setting off antagonistic social conflicts. Although united, the military were unwilling to use massive force, as they showed when they ceased to repress illegal demonstrations. The costs of repression were seen as too high. Yet what mattered were not the actual costs, but the *expectations* as to the potential costs, and to no small extent those were influenced by the behaviors of other actors. Thus, the negotiating parties attempted to convince the military that extrication was fully in the military's interests and that the consequences of failure to reach agreement would be dire. Recall, for example, the conservative Chiarino's remarks that the parties were heroically holding back the radical opposition forces.

The generic motives for any such military withdrawal that have been suggested by Finer could almost all be detected in Uruguay: belief in the superiority of a civilian administration; widespread demoralizing opposition; a pact for at least minimum guarantees (with the insurance policy of possible reentry if they were not respected); and a rather suitable party to form a government that also was capable of winning a nearly fair election.[60] The Colorados offered the military a suitable force to which to hand over power, as well as certain guarantees that their interests would be respected thereafter. The added weight of the Left simply meant that the deal could be reached without the Colorados becoming isolated.

But what of the internal interests of the military corporation and how they were perceived? The most practical analysis to date of military corporate interests in transitions has been undertaken by Alfred Stepan. His emphasis is on the bottom-line commitment to surviving as a hierarchical

---

58 See Gallup Uruguay, *Informe de Opinión Pública*, No. 345, Table 3. Interviews were undertaken from 30 July to 1 August 1984.

59 Only 13% thought it was a bad thing that he had returned, but 21% thought the military had done the right thing in arresting him! Source: Gallup Uruguay, *Informe de Opinión Pública*, No. 343, Tables 20 and 21. Such survey results must be treated with caution, but they were borne out by the polarization of feelings regarding Ferreira on the "thermometer" of the rival firm Equipos.

60 Finer (1985).

institution, which can require a retreat to the barracks if factional disputes lead to irreconcilable conflicts. Here the feared symptoms are a subversion of the top-down command structure (which happened in Portugal after 1974) or even armed combat (which pitted "blues" against "reds" in Argentina in the early 1960s). Stepan has distinguished "transition initiated by the military as government" from "extrication by the military as institution." This distinction implies the possibility of dyarchic situations under military authoritarian regimes, where the commanders in chief of the different services remain distinct from the general(s) in control of the government.[61] Recall, for example, the statement by Jorge Batlle that the military should realize that their interests were separate from those of Alvarez. The failure of the military to endorse the president's plan for a new party was striking confirmation that the generals in active service had appreciated the wisdom of Batlle's remarks.

Stepan maintains that extrication led by the military as institution is the most common path to democracy, as the relative autonomy of military governments vis-à-vis their own armed forces is closely circumscribed. In Uruguay, the clear differentiation of the government and the military survived Alvarez's attempts to draw them close together: The commanders in chief were members of the National Security Council, but not the cabinet. Given increased military autonomy and strict promotion by seniority, the commanders were not subject to control by the president. Furthermore, the economic consequences of the government's policies offered a particular incentive for dissociating the military as institution from its record. The continual affirmation of the commitment to returning power to elected civilians by active-service generals during 1984 was another sign of the split between President Alvarez and the junta of commanders he faced.

The Uruguayan transition closely followed Stepan's pattern of extrication by the military as institution. The most dramatic evidence of the split that had emerged between President Alvarez (who had retired) and army commander General Medina (whose interests were those of the military institution) was that the president had to try to find out what was going on at the secret Naval Club talks by sending bogus representatives from an allegedly new party. To the immense surprise of politicians and armed-forces chiefs alike, those friends of the president demanded a seat at the negotiating table, presumably so that they could report back on what had been said. That was the clearest indication of the paralysis of communication within the regime and the estrangement of the military institution from the government of President Alvarez. Medina and the other commanders began to see the benefits of continued rule accruing

61 Stepan (1986).

only to the president and his cronies. The long-term costs, however, would clearly be imposed on their institution.[62]

Toward a more dynamic model of coalitions and negotiations

O'Donnell and Schmitter distinguished the regime soft-liners from the most extreme hard-liners, as we saw. However, it is possible to break that down even further. The original hard-liners in the military were eliminated by Alvarez, but he and his followers ultimately were willing to see only an evolution of the authoritarian regime. It fell to Medina, at the Naval Club, to agree to a radical reform much nearer to a negotiated rupture. The military wanted elections without the Left, but they eventually abandoned that original goal in the interest of defeating Ferreira. How can we account for that strategic retreat? A useful model has been developed by Albert Hirschman, who has proposed a complex typology of political actors based on their preference order regarding reform.[63] The most extreme conservatives are those who would risk revolution or, let us say, a "rupture" of their regime rather than accept reform. These are the members of what the Chileans refer to as the "bunker," and in Uruguay they were defeated in three stages: in 1976, with the ouster of the civilian corporatists; in 1977, under the pressure from the United States to adopt a timetable for elections; and in 1981, when the defeat of the plebiscite led to Alvarez's rise to power and the ouster of the *gorilas* (hawks).

Less extreme are those who are resistant to reform, but nevertheless prefer it to the risk of disorderly regime rupture. One might call these the reluctant accepters of reform. In this category we may place the Alvarezistas, though their behavior came close to that of the bunker group at times in 1984. Closest to the center of the spectrum among power-holders are those who have a positive preference for reform over the status quo. These we may call enlightened or farsighted reformists: General Medina was the clearest example in Uruguay.

Among the opposition, the most extreme are those who are so committed to a major revolutionary break that they will positively oppose any reform pact. At times, certain Blancos and leftists appeared to fall into this category, but, crucially for the ultimate acceptance of the Naval

---

62 They did not trust him after his exposés of corruption in 1981, his attempt to launch a political career, his increase in the fiscal deficit in 1982, and the installation in late 1983 of a new mayor in Montevideo who attempted to buy votes by hiring new employees. Nor could they have liked the secret negotiations that he allegedly entered into with Wilson Ferreira in March 1984, regarding which military sources alerted the Colorados.

63 See the Hirschman (1965) discussion of "reform-mongering." I am very grateful to Professor Juan Linz for pointing out the relevance of that essay.

Club pact, Wilson Ferreira did not take his party into this maximalist ghetto.[64] Rather, we may say that though the Wilsonistas preferred the idea of a rupture to a reform of the regime, they would settle for reform as their second choice, rather than getting nothing at all. Hence the Blancos' eventual decision to take part in the elections. The most moderate opposition elements are those with a positive preference for a reform of the regime, not a rupture. These reformists par excellence included many Colorados, who knew well that they stood to gain from political stability and continuity. By a temporary convergence, the Broad Front chose this line, too, but only on the strictly pragmatic grounds that its true preference for a complete rupture was impractical. Putting these preferences all together, we get Table 8.13.

There are two caveats regarding the preceding form of analysis. In the first place, the preferences are not static over time, but dynamic, and they depend on the strategies of other actors. Second, abstract preferences are less important than practical preferences, which depend on what is deemed feasible more than on what is ideal. The dynamic component is the most interesting factor in this otherwise static model. It seems probable that few generals who were still near the apex of power had a deep desire to see democracy return under any circumstances. They typically were reluctant reformers. However, they became convinced by the opposition's tactics and by events elsewhere in the region that the risks of the status quo were becoming serious, given Wilson Ferreira's continuing pressure for a complete breakdown of military rule. Generals such as Medina thus came to appear and behave as "enlightened reformers." By a symmetrically opposite process, Alvarez became more and more opposed to restoration of democracy, and ended up in the bunker.

The Colorados' strategy was more consistent than that of any other major party: They placed themselves in the reformist opposition for as much of the time as they found possible. After the collapse of the Parque Hotel talks, however, they joined the radical alliance of parties and social movements in demanding a complete democratic rupture. They thus moved for a time into the pose of reluctant reformists, preferring a complete break to a negotiated reform of the regime that would amount to little more than prolongation of military rule. By mid-1984, however, they had resumed the stance of reformist opposition. The Broad Front also shifted from its pose of radicalism to reformism under the leadership of Seregni. His fundamental consideration seems to have been the ambition

---

64 The only party really to do so was the Trotskyist Partido Revolucionario de los Trabajadores, which, despite the same TV time as the other parties, received only 488 votes in Montevideo. It linked the demand for socialism to the demand for democracy in an immediatist way that the Broad Front strongly rejected.

Table 8.13. *Preference rankings for reform versus rupture*

Preferences regarding regime	Power-holders			Opposition		
	Bunker	Reluctant reformers	Enlightened reformers	Reformist opposition	Radical opposition	Ghetto
1st preference	Status quo	Status quo	Reform	Reform	Rupture	Rupture
2nd preference	Rupture	Reform	Status quo	Rupture	Reform	Status quo
3rd preference	Reform	Rupture	Rupture	Status quo	Status quo	Reform
Actors of tendency	Gen. Queirolo	Gen. Alvarez	Gen. Medina	Sanguinetti, Seregni?	Wilson Ferreira	PRT, IDI?

to transform the movement from a permanent opposition force with anti-system overtones to a loyal democratic opposition.

The Blancos' strategies were the most difficult to classify, because they shifted among all three of the possible opposition categories. Fundamentally they were reluctant reformists; that is, they preferred rupture to reform, particularly after Wilson was imprisoned. At times, however, they seemed more ready to negotiate, and they even (according to some) countenanced a delay in the transition as the price for a full return to civilian power. In the immediate aftermath of the pact, they sometimes claimed that they would have preferred dictatorship to fraudulent democracy. However, they did not stay in the "ghetto," but entered the elections, with the warning that they did not feel bound by the agreements reached at the Naval Club.

At any given time, the strategies of political actors are influenced by the previous actions of other actors. Arrival at a path for transition to democracy thus becomes a process of successive elimination of alternatives. This narrowing of alternatives meant that transition would occur, but the election still lay ahead. No one believed that the Naval Club pact alone could assure democratic consolidation. No one could tell to what extent the factors that had come together to produce the transition would have a positive impact on the legitimacy of the new democracy.[65] Above all, what remained to be seen was the verdict of the people.

65 A third level of conflict management that went on has been little discussed here: that of attempting to reach a social pact through concerted action (concertación). The talks had effectively been turned into a means for postponing consideration of economic demands, given the preoccupations of the transition. The issue of labor demands returned to the fore under the new democracy and is discussed in the last chapter.

PART III

Political parties and democratic consolidation

9

The competition for support: leadership strategies and electoral behavior before and after the 1984 elections

Responsibility for the future lay squarely in the hands of Uruguay's parties. Their leaders had determined the course of the transition from authoritarianism, and now they would be the central actors in determining the success of democracy. The overwhelming issue became the Naval Club pact, and the Blancos' accusation that it presaged a continuation of military power. Political tensions were enormous: Democratic consolidation depended not only on party strategies in the elections but also on reactions to the results and the parties' patterns of cooperation and competition once the new government had been installed. Would the Blancos abide by the results, or would they impugn the legitimacy of the new democracy from the start? How much had politicians learned from the past? How much, if at all, had parties' leadership and internal structures changed since the unhappy days of the breakdown? How deep was their willingness to compromise to protect civilian rule?

Pressures for change in the Uruguayan party system came from three sources: from the military, with their undying ambition to root out "subversion"; from the electorate, as voters punished those politicians whom they blamed for the country's ills; and from inside the parties, as young Uruguayans became activists and new leaders arose. However, all too often those three types of pressures pulled in different directions. Addressing the Colorado convention, Sanguinetti stated the challenge:

The country can only democratize by means of a party functioning democratically internally. The country does not want to see the old style of politics return. The country does not want personality conflicts.[1]

The bitter competition for votes after the pact with the military

The 1984 election campaign began immediately after the Naval Club talks, the Electoral Court having imposed a deadline of 25 August for

[1] Author's notes, 7 April 1984.

the registration of candidates. In the Colorado party, two presidential tickets had emerged: Sanguinetti-Tarigo in the center, and Pacheco-Pirán on the right.[2] A bitter struggle broke out in the Blanco party: Should they boycott the elections in protest of Wilson's imprisonment? If not, who should run in his place? The abstentionist option would have risked splitting the party and might even have allowed the anti-Wilsonistas the legal right to use the Blanco name forevermore. Pressure to take part in the elections had been building up all year, particularly from rural politicians, for whom access to public office was crucial to their survival. As early as March, some had complained to the national leaders: "How can we mobilize without candidates?"[3]

At the close of 1983, President Alvarez had begun attempting to penetrate the Blanco party by the appointment of a renegade ex-Wilsonista, Juan Carlos Payssé, as *intendente* (mayor) of Montevideo.[4] With hindsight it can be seen that the major reason for re-creating a progovernment faction in the Blanco party (where they had been largely wiped out in the primaries) was to prevent the Wilsonistas from controlling the party label (*lema*) and threatening to boycott the elections.[5] An amendment to the "Second Fundamental Law" was passed by the Council of the Nation in April 1984 stipulating that as long as 10% of any party's conventioneers wished to take part in the election, they could do so under the party's banner.[6] That sophisticated strategy was often misunderstood, as all Payssé's votes (he also ran for president) would end up accumulating with those of Wilson's supporters under the system of the double simultaneous

---

2 Sanguinetti and Tarigo ran separate lists for the Chamber of Deputies ("15" and "85," respectively), but agreed on a joint list of senatorial candidates and formed a *sublema* known as Batllismo Unido. Accompanying the Sanguinetti-Tarigo formula from the left of the party was Manuel Flores Silva's Corriente Batllista Independiente ("List 89"), which had a separate slate for each house. A large number of lists supported the Pacheco-Pirán ticket.

3 Author's notes, Por la Patria convention, Montevideo, 17 March 1984.

4 Over the next year, Payssé shamelessly swelled the municipal payroll to win friends and influence people.

5 The Wilsonistas engaged in a bitter struggle to oust fellow travelers of the regime from the party. The Colorado convention did vote to suspend certain conventioneers from the interior who had agreed to become *intendentes* (provincial governors) for the military, but in general the split between left and right was less antagonistic among Colorados.

6 The vast majority of all those politicians interviewed were against the lowering of the established hurdle. However, the Colorados were less strongly opposed (75%) than the Left (which was unanimously hostile). The Blancos were 83% against: p(Left > Blancos) = .13. Whereas 44% of Blancos were against allowing parties total freedom to regulate their forms of democratic internal organization, only 17% of Colorados agreed they should be regulated, and no Frentistas. Only the difference between Colorados and Frentistas was of low statistical significance (p = .24). The Blancos' opposition to a free-for-all presumably was based on the irony that the military's statute had strengthened the hands of the radical Wilsonistas.

vote.[7] Finally, other military mayors were also replaced by civilians, and the cabinet was reshuffled to make Bolentini minister of labor.

The Wilsonistas issued contradictory announcements regarding whether or not they would take part. Their initial call for abstention soon gave way to statements in favor of taking part in the elections and calling new ones if they won.[8] Then came yet another letter from Wilson Ferreira, this time resigning as candidate in order to allow a proxy ticket to be chosen. On 19 August, with less than a week to go before candidates had to be registered, the convention voted to reject his resignation.[9] Finally, after frantic behind-the-scenes dealing, a surprise proxy ticket was announced to the convention on 23 August: Alberto Zumarán and Gonzalo Aguirre.[10] A conservative but anti-regime ticket was put up by Ortiz and Ferber, and the Montevideo mayor, Juan Carlos Payssé, headed the frankly pro-military lists. Much of the crisis had been generated not by whether to have alternative presidential candidates, but whom to pick. Movimiento de Rocha leader Carlos Julio Pereyra apparently was angry at being denied the nomination and, according to informed sources, vetoed Por la Patria's García Costa (whom he saw as too close to Wilson) in retaliation.

The Blancos' difficulties were not over. Many of them wanted to let Wilson out of jail and immediately call new elections if they won. However, when they suggested that Zumarán would merely be a "caretaker" (the so-called *provisoriato*) they came under a barrage of criticism. A long-time Wilsonista justified the idea thus: "New elections are indispensable. Two out of three major political figures in the country are banned: Seregni and Wilson."[11] The Left, however, refused to endorse the idea of new elections, and Colorados were frankly hostile: "We cannot have new elections because people need solutions to their economic problems" was the comment of one long-standing leader.[12] One Colorado even claimed that "the two elections idea was just an excuse to cover up the U-turn."[13] Given the very negative public reaction, the Blancos began to downplay the proposal. In any case, the military would hardly have tolerated such

7 As it turned out, he did very poorly, but that was almost preferable!
8 "Los Blancos no votan," *El Nuevo Tiempo*, 1 August 1984, p. 1; "Los Blancos no votan con Ferreira preso," *El Nuevo Tiempo*, 6 August 1984, p. 1.
9 "Rechazaron las renuncias: la Convención dijo que No," *El Nuevo Tiempo*, 20 August 1984, p. 1. At the same convention, the architect of Spain's transition to democracy, Adolfo Suárez, called for Wilson's release. Suárez was expelled from the country the following day.
10 "Acuerdo," *Ultimas Noticias*, 23 August 1984, p. 1.
11 Personal interview, 31 August 1984.
12 Personal interview, Montevideo, 24 September 1984.
13 Personal interview, Montevideo, 3 August 1984.

a complete overturning of the strategy agreed upon with the Colorados and the Left at the Naval Club.

The biggest handicap the Blancos faced was the absence of their charismatic leader. The military's decision to release his radical son, Juan Raúl, may have been a deliberate ploy to sow discord in the party's ranks. With his support for land reform he was a constant cause of controversy in the conservative interior. Quarreling on the Blanco campaign bus that was to transport candidates across the country broke out before it had left Montevideo. In a theatrical gesture, Lacalle (leader of the most conservative pro-Wilsonista faction) publicly disembarked – a literal case of jumping off a bandwagon![14]

The strategy of radical Wilsonistas was to appeal to the segments of the young radical electorate who were traditionally supporters of the Left. However, Carlos Julio Pereyra tried to play that down:

[We went for the votes of] progressives but not militants. We hoped they would vote for us because we could win. . . . I believe the mobilization strategy was correct. Our problem was to convince people that the problem was not just to put an end to the dictatorship; not just a political problem, but also a social and economic one. The main thing needed is structural reform to redistribute wealth and increase production.[15]

Nevertheless, less than a month before the elections, a rising star of the Wilsonista camp, with a particular specialization in the new social politics,[16] admitted that things were going badly: "We are suffering the disadvantages of too long a mobilization. The plebiscite campaign, the ferry boat, and rallies were very expensive, so now we are concentrating on press interviews and TV debates."[17] Such debates, however, tended to risk showing up the party's ideological incoherence and internal frictions. Discussion inevitably returned again and again to the Naval Club, underlining the Blancos' isolation, and effacing the differences between the Colorados and the Left.

The restoration of the Left

The Broad Front entered the elections with just one presidential formula: Juan José Crottogini (a respected doctor of medicine), with José D'Elía (the former president of the CNT union federation) as candidate for the

---

14 He was later persuaded to rejoin the bus farther along its route.
15 Personal interview, Montevideo, December 1984.
16 Apart from organizing the Blanco effort to establish a union presence, as a delegate to the CONAPRO (National Programmatic Concertation) talks, he had privileged contacts with the unions.
17 Personal interview, Montevideo, 4 November 1984.

vice-presidency.[18] Many leftists remained deprived of their political rights, either under the terms of judicial sentences or because they were members of parties that were still banned (such as the Communist party and former allies of the Tupamaros).[19] Nevertheless, both the communists and the far Left were able to run lists by forging alliances with legal groups and finding new faces. Despite such handicaps and the lateness of its legalization, it was soon clear that the Broad Front had by far the most active and committed organization. So-called base committees, with a minimum of 50 members, were set up in each neighborhood or ward section, bringing together militants from every party in the Broad Front. Those committees were a remarkable testimony to the grass-roots cooperation of the Left. The Colorados and Blancos also set up local offices, but those had a less high-minded atmosphere and typically spent much of the day blaring campaign songs into the streets. The same tunes were picked up in sophisticated TV commercials.

The renovators in the Broad Front faced the disadvantage of their late rehabilitation. Those who saw the Front evolving in an avowedly electoralist and democratic direction – especially "List 99" – were to be handsomely rewarded by the voters. Yet it would be difficult to say that the moderation of the Uruguayan Left was a product of some spontaneous mellowing at the grass roots. In fact, there had to be an intensive campaign of explanations as to why the leaders were talking to the military, and even agreeing to elections with Wilson in jail. The problem remained that the balance of opinion among the militants was not necessarily the same as that among the Front's voters (an affliction that spread to the Blanco party). The Broad Front, however, was able to draw on its far superior organizational and ideological resources to ensure greater discipline and internal cohesion than could the Blancos.

Given that the alienation and radicalization of the Left was a major factor in the breakdown of democracy, the question arose of what the Italians call *aggiornamento*. The three major attempts to create a new leftist force all failed. Convergencia Democrática, founded in exile by Blancos and leftists, broke down because all of its components feared they might end up being used by their rivals. The Izquierda Democrática Independiente (IDI) never became the broad synthesis of democratic socialist

---

18 There were five electoral lists within the Broad Front: Democracia Avanzada (communists and allies), Izquierda Democrática Independiente (an ultraleft alliance, including some former anarchists), the socialists, the Christian Democrats, and "List 99" of ex-Colorados led by Hugo Batalla. In August 1986, "List 99" was refounded as a political party with the name Partido por el Gobierno del Pueblo (Party for Popular Government) or simply PGP.

19 About 500 people could not vote or run for office because they were still in prison, bringing the total disfranchised to about 5,000, according to the Peace and Justice Service, a human-rights organization.

currents designed to support Seregni that its founder, respected radical economist Danilo Astori, had envisioned. The final hope for a new leftist force would have been a social-democratic amalgamation of the Christian Democratic party (PDC) and the "List 99" of ex-Colorados. During the dictatorship, while "List 99" moved to the right, the PDC eventually veered to the left.[20] However, crude organizational rivalry, rather than ideology, seems to have dictated the decision of "List 99" not to renew its 1971 *sublema* with the PDC. Instead, it chose an alliance with the far more radical Socialist party.[21] Unlike the Christian Democrats, "List 99" benefited from an image of being uncompromisingly anti-*proceso* and the closest option to Seregni, who maintained formal neutrality. As one "List 99" leader argued, "militants of the Broad Front's base committees favor '99' if they consider themselves just supporters of the Broad Front as a whole."[22]

To what extent had the impact of authoritarianism altered the two largest Marxist parties in Uruguay: the Socialist party (PS) and the Communist party (PCU)? The Socialist party had normally been the smaller, with a relatively larger number of middle-class and intellectual members, and it had tended to be quite radical. During the 1960s it was heavily influenced by Castroism and even Maoism, before voting to adopt the principles of Marxism-Leninism at its 1972 congress.[23] Unlike its Chilean counterpart, however, it avoided internal schisms under the military. The party increased its vote in 1984 appreciably – the only sector to do so apart from "List 99." However, it was by no means a foregone conclusion that it would smoothly evolve toward some variant of social democracy. It did, however, seem unlikely to become infatuated with guerrilla tactics again.

The Communist party at times found itself in the moderate center of the Broad Front during the early 1970s. It was also a bitter enemy of the guerrillas, and its leader, Rodney Arismendi, criticized their tactics in

---

20 A distinguished and aged leader of "List 99" admitted that had it not been for the Naval Club pact, many of its cadres might have ended up back in the Colorado party, which they had left in 1971.

21 The double simultaneous vote allows groups of lists to form a *sublema* in order to increase their chances of winning a seat when competing against rival lists. As it turned out, the PS–"99" deal caused the PDC to win only one Senate seat.

22 Personal interview, 30 November 1984.

23 When I asked a young leader, who reputedly was an admirer of Felipe González, if the declaration of Marxism-Leninism should remain in the party's statute, he avoided answering directly: "We want all the Marxist heritage – Mariátegui and Trotsky as well. We certainly don't want a Soviet-style model" (personal interview, Montevideo, 27 September 1984). A committed exponent of Marxism-Leninism, when asked if he saw the PS as revolutionary, replied: "Yes, but as an object, not a method" (personal interview, 26 April 1985).

various books.[24] However, beginning in late 1975 the party suffered a most terrible repression in which the security forces effectively disarticulated its apparatus by means of arrests and systematic torture. The impact on the leadership seems, amazingly, to have been to confirm its commitment to working through democratic institutions. A Communist Central Committee leader who had been sent into exile argued that "though the choice is democracy or fascism, with the same capitalist state in each case, only an idiot would say it does not matter."[25] The communists had long favored unity of the Left, and a Central Committee leader saw three main priorities during the democratic transition:

First, to maintain the unity of the Broad Front as the great path to reconquering democracy in Uruguay and to move as well toward Socialism. Second, to confront the permanent problem of relations with the traditional parties, but these are changing [improving]. Third, to keep the ultraleftists outside the Broad Front.[26]

This latter comment revealed the deadly struggle for hegemony within the Left. At first the party found its trade-union support difficult to regain. Too many of its leaders were of the older generation, and it seemed to lack new ideas. Though it attempted to stabilize democracy, as a leading figure hastily assured me, "we are far from being Eurocommunist."[27]

Perhaps one key to the renovation of the Left lay in the central apparatus of the Broad Front, the team surrounding Seregni, which maintained itself independent of party affiliation. When I asked Seregni if he would call himself a socialist, he was surprisingly careful in his response: "a democratic and advanced Frenteamplista" was all he would say.[28] Had eight years in jail changed his thinking? "No, I believe in self-criticism and realism, but they affirmed my way of thinking. What are needed are grand solutions and political formations to go forward out of our country's structural crisis."[29] In other words, Seregni maintained his commitment to Left unity, meaning alliance with the communists. As a close aide argued, "we need to maintain the alliance of Marxists and democrats,

24 See his major treatise, *Lenin y la Revolución en América Latina* (1971), and my own research note (Gillespie 1985).

25 Personal interview, Montevideo, 18 April 1985. The popular union leader Jaime Pérez, who suffered terribly under the regime, was equally eager for peace: "If there is to be a solution in this country, it has to be free of hatred and rancor" (personal interview, Montevideo, 7 November 1985).

26 Personal interview, Montevideo, 18 April 1985.

27 As a noncommunist intellectual argued at a seminar attended by politicians and social scientists, "the Left is entering a crisis. The Leninist model is being abandoned but there is much confusion about the alternatives" (presentation by César Aguiar, CIEDUR, June 1984).

28 Personal interview, Montevideo, 30 April 1985.

29 Ibid.

though one day our paths may separate."[30] The fact that he distinguished Marxists from democrats was, however, revealing.

The evolution of the rival campaigns

In the Blanco party, the process of agreeing on an election manifesto was accompanied by intense conflicts, many embarrassingly public. It seems undeniable that the new leaders shifted the party to the left of its traditional electorate and (unlike the Colorados) led it from the left rather than the center. That meant that the party was in greater danger of disequilibrium whenever disputes broke out. Wilson's capacities for acting as arbiter were sorely missed. The Colorados' program was deliberately vague about actual policies, stressing principles rather than proposals. That probably was an advantage, compared with the Blancos' painful commitment to specific measures, which chained the party to controversy. Although the Wilsonistas consolidated their hold over the party, the cost in lost votes probably was high.

Meanwhile, the Colorados were anxious to occupy the center of the political spectrum. The image projected by their campaign was deliberately one of experience, moderation, and capable leadership. Sanguinetti's slogan summed up the message: "For a Change in Peace." The Blancos' image was less well groomed, and more emotional: It emphasized intransigence, principles, and radical reforms to rid the country of the scourge of authoritarianism and poverty. The Colorados issued a long program for a new government that attempted to move back toward their progressive past, without necessarily espousing statist economic principles, and emphasizing ends rather than means. The Blanco election manifesto included nationalization of all banks that wanted to continue to take deposits from Uruguayans, land reform, and state control of foreign trade to alleviate the debt crisis.[31]

Ideology was deliberately downplayed by the Colorados. When asked to define what it meant to be a Colorado, a distinguished leader resorted to a string of negatives: "antidogmatic, anti-Marxist, rationalist, but antipositivist." Because he was a leading apologist for neoliberal economics, he also added a less representative opinion: "We need to slaughter some social-democratic sacred cows . . . left and right no longer matter."[32] When asked what the Blancos stood for, a radical replied that "the Na-

---

30 Personal interview, Montevideo, n.d.
31 The list struck horror into the hearts of even many pro-Wilsonista Blancos from the interior. They attempted to limit the incongruity of their positions by claiming, for example, that bank "nationalization" did not necessarily mean "statization," but merely the end of foreign ownership.
32 Personal interview, Montevideo, 23 June 1984.

tional party is integrally antiimperialist and antidictatorship, including the dictatorship of the proletariat."[33]

The ethos of the traditional parties consisted in rejecting class struggle in favor of less easily defined "isms." Batllism in 1984 was a style of politics more than a particular program: pragmatism, responsibility, statesmanship – in short, the typical blend of a party of government. Wilsonism, on the other hand, was also more a style than a coherent ideology or project: intransigent opposition to militarism and authoritarianism, mobilization and protest, intense loyalty to a leader. That was also rooted in the party's tradition of oppositionism. The only fundamental ideological difference between Batllism and Wilsonism was the greater nationalism of the Wilsonistas – their attachment to radical economics, like the Batllistas' attachment to conservative economics, was in many ways only skin-deep.

The Broad Front tried to keep ideology out of their campaign as well. Ironically, the Left hardly mentioned their program at all, emphasizing instead the demand for a full-scale political amnesty. Seregni's image was one of reconciliation and moderation, and he appeared often in the campaign, although he was, in theory, still banned from political activity. Within the Front, the communists attempted to cast themselves as the most militant and martyred sector, causing serious upset by their decision to open parallel committees alongside the joint committees of the Broad Front. The strategy of "List 99" was the exact opposite: almost no visible organization, handing out leaflets or demonstrating, but a skillful cultivation of its leader's image. Hugo Batalla managed to combine an air of moderation with impeccable credentials as Seregni's former defense lawyer.

As the campaign entered its last phase in November 1984, the tone of the Colorados' pronouncements became much more antileftist, as if to suggest that they were less worried about defeating the Blancos at the national level than about the possibility that the Broad Front might win Montevideo's *intendencia*.[34] Sanguinetti attacked the Broad Front for supporting the military rebellion of February 1973. Then he went on to blame the PIT for the failure of the CONAPRO talks, which had been suspended until after the elections, as a result of their rejection of an industrial "truce." The Frente was quick to respond in kind, reemphasizing many Colorados' close links to the dictatorship.

Although the Left adopted a strategy of moderation during the cam-

33 Personal interview, San José, 23 November 1984.
34 Their own polling (admittedly biased by the fact that interviewers identified themselves as working for Sanguinetti's magazine, *Correo de los Viernes*) had shown the Colorados overtaking the Blancos by August, but it had also shown the Front growing rapidly, and the commercial polls seemed to report a Left lead in the capital.

Table 9.1. *Radicalism, reformism, and conservatism*[a]

Attitude	Left (%) (n = 17)	Blancos (%) (n = 21)	Colorados (%) (n = 23)	All (%) (n = 65)[b]
(A) "The whole way our society is organized must be changed radically and rapidly."	58.8	19.0	8.7	24.6
(B) "Our society must be gradually improved by means of appropriate reforms."	41.2	71.4	87.0	70.8
(C) "The present organization of our society is satisfactory overall and should be consolidated as it is."	0.0	9.5	4.3	4.6
Total	100.0	100.0	100.0	100.0

[a]The question: "Of the following attitudes to Uruguayan society, which is the closest to your own opinion?"
[b]Includes one Patriotic Union and three Civic Union leaders.

paign, few Uruguayans could have been unaware of the fundamental differences between it and the traditional parties. When asked to describe their attitudes to the status quo, leftist leaders unsurprisingly emphasized the need for radical change. The vast majority of Colorados expressed reformist views, as did almost as many Blancos, though it was noticeable that both their radical and conservative flanks were twice as large as those in the Colorado party. Once again, that was evidence of the Colorados' relative unity and the difficulties that the radicalization of the Wilsonistas had entailed for the Blanco party (Table 9.1).

When interviewees were asked about the degree of conflict in society (a veiled reference to doctrines of class struggle), the same divide between the traditional parties and the Left emerged. As Table 9.2 shows, there was a particularly consensus-oriented view of society among Blancos, and a conflictual emphasis among leftist leaders. That was thus one of the cases in which the Colorados held the middle ground. Perhaps revealing a certain Catholic and organicist legacy, the Blancos saw the least conflict

Table 9.2. *The perceived importance of social conflict*[a]

Characteristic	Left (%) (n = 17)	Blancos (%) (n = 23)	Colorados (%) (n = 23)	All (%) (n = 67)[b]
(A) Consensus is much more common than conflict.	6	17	4	10
(B) Consensus is more common but there are conflicts.	6	13	22	15
(C) Both are common, and neither one predominates.	29	39	35	34
(D) Conflict is more common, but some consensus exists.	59	30	39	40
Total	100	100	100	100

[a] The question: "With respect to the interaction among the different groups that make up society, which do you think is the most relevant characteristic?"
[b] Includes one Patriotic Union leader and three Civic Union leaders.

in society, yet another belief that may have clashed with their strategy of radical mobilization against the military.[35]

Commitment to conflict management among politicians

A major determinant of the path of the regime transition and the subsequent attempt to consolidate democracy was the degree to which politicians kept their conflicts within certain bounds and emphasized a common commitment to preserving the system. It has been hypothesized that to preserve opposition unity in periods of democratic transition, parties may have to avoid divisive debates on contentious issues. As Table 9.3 shows, a majority of leaders in all parties favored promoting debates. However, significant minorities of Blancos and Colorados did favor suspending controversies until democracy was consolidated, whereas those leftist politicians who favored postponing debates apparently had a somewhat shorter time frame.

35 The Blancos' relative disunity was also suggested when politicians were asked to locate each *lema*'s factions on a 10-point left–right scale. In terms of the distance between the extreme wings of each *lema* seen by all respondents, the Blancos spanned the greatest range of the left–right spectrum: 4.0 points, on average, compared with 3.6 points for the Colorados and 1.5 for the Left.

Table 9.3. *Unity versus debate*[a]

Option	Left (%) (n = 10)	Blancos (%) (n = 15)	Colorados (%) (n = 19)	All (%) (n = 48)[b]
(A) Avoid debate until democracy is consolidated.	10.0	26.7	21.1	22.9
(B) Avoid debate until after the elections.	20.0	0.0	15.8	10.4
(C) Promote debate, as long as it is not hostile.	70.0	73.3	63.2	66.7
Total	100.0	100.0	100.0	100.0

[a]The question: "Do you think parties have to postpone excessive debates on problems of concrete policy in order to maintain a united front? Or is it better to discuss the issues and put forward alternative solutions to the crisis?"
[b]Includes one Patriotic Union and three Civic Union leaders.

When asked about the future priorities for the democratically elected government, the Left placed much more emphasis on freeing political prisoners than did the leaders of the traditional parties, the vast majority of whom saw strengthening democracy as the number-one priority. Most politicians also placed emphasis on job creation, but where the Left saw the need to increase wages and salaries, the Colorados emphasized economic restructuring. About one in five traditional politicians (but no leftists) mentioned the need to maintain peace, order, and security.[36] However, whereas politicians were especially preoccupied with the problem of democracy and political freedoms, the general public seemed overwhelmingly concerned with jobs and wages.[37] That was especially true of the less educated, and the preponderance of economic concerns clearly was related to lower social class and occupational status. The figures emphasized the practical challenge that the new democracy would face: The mass of the people did not seem to see democracy as their leading goal in and of itself, but part of a broad concern for their living standards.

Ideology and issues are of limited direct importance in distinguishing between the traditional parties. Presumably, therefore, they can have only secondary influence on voter choices between the Colorados and Blancos – particularly in more "normal" circumstances than 1984 – though they

36 Consonant with their traditions of welfarism, the Colorados were strongly concerned with improving health care. Given Wilson's experiences, and perhaps also their innate nationalism, the Blancos seemed especially committed to bringing home exiles.
37 Aguiar (1985, p. 48).

may well be important in determining the support for different tendencies in each party. Voters may be influenced by their predictions as to which broad ideological tendency will predominate in a given party. The position of the Left in terms of its radicalism and leftism, as well as (to a lesser extent) its stance on specific issues, was quite distinct. Not only did the Left have a more conflictual view of Uruguayan society, but it had a more immediate interest in the release of political prisoners and a clear agenda of pro-labor policies. Nevertheless, in the critical juncture of the transition, the Left was willing to postpone divisive debates.

Electoral behavior in 1984

Soon after the first results filtered in late on 25 November, computer predictions began to show Sanguinetti as the next president, with the Colorados heading for a major victory over the Blancos. The Blancos' hoped-for margin of victory in the interior quite simply failed to materialize, and it had long been known that they would come in third in Montevideo. In the capital it was a close race between the other two parties, but by the middle of the night it was clear that the Left had lost. Six days later, Wilson Ferreira was at last released from jail, following a decision by the military courts to drop the charges against him.[38] Immediately upon his return to the capital he addressed a subdued open-air rally. Rationalizing his party's defeat (and, by implication, his intransigent strategy), he declared that the nation had failed to realize the gravity of the crisis facing it. Instead of the "surgeon's scalpel," which it had needed, it had chosen "sticking plaster."

What had happened in the two years after the primaries to turn an apparent Blanco lead into a convincing Colorado victory? One of the reasons for the shift was that voting was compulsory in the general election, unlike the primaries. Whereas in 1982 the turnout had been 56% in Montevideo and 65% in the interior, in 1984 it was 86% and 89%, respectively. Table 9.4 shows that the Colorado vote share was almost exactly the same as in 1971.

The straight national percentages show the stability of the Colorados' vote, and the slide of over five points in that of the Blancos from 1971 to 1984. Over the same period, the Broad Front grew about three points; continuing the trend toward a three-party system. Though the Civic Union quintupled its share of the national votes, it remains a much smaller entity. Table 9.5 compares the evolution of the major parties' votes in Montevideo and in the interior.

Whereas the percentage Colorado vote actually fell in the capital, it

38 News that he would be released had been leaked a week before the election.

Table 9.4. *Uruguayan election results, 1954–84*

Party	1954	1958	1962	1966	1971	1982[a]	1984
Colorados	50.6	37.7	44.4	49.4	41.0	39.7	41.2
Blancos	35.2	49.7	46.6	40.4	40.2	46.4	35.0
Civic Union	5.0	3.7	—	—	0.5	1.1	2.4
Communists	2.2	2.6	3.5	5.7			
Socialists	3.2	3.5	2.3	0.9	18.3[b]	6.6[c]	21.2[b]
Christian Democrats	—	—	3.0[d]	3.0			

Note: A dash indicates that the party did not exist at that time; a blank space means that the party was running under the umbrella of the Broad Front. The Civic Union became the Christian Democratic party in 1962. In 1971, when the Christian Democrats joined the Broad Front, the right wing of the party split off and ran under the old Civic Union name.
[a] Primaries.
[b] Broad Front.
[c] Blank voting.
[d] New name of Civic Union.
Sources: Julio Fabregat, *Elecciones Uruguayas* (various years); Corlazzoni (1984).

rose in the interior enough to compensate. The Blancos, on the other hand, registered a serious decline in the interior, which many immediately blamed on their radical electoral manifesto. The Left pulled far ahead of

Table 9.5. *Comparison of voting trends in Montevideo and the interior*

Party	Montevideo		Interior	
	1971	1984	1971	1984
Percentages				
Colorados	39.5	36.0	42.0	45.8
Blancos	29.7	27.0	47.9	42.1
Broad Front	30.1	33.7	9.6	10.3
Civic Union	0.6	3.2	0.5	1.8
Turnout	87.6	86.0	89.4	89.6
Votes				
Colorados	278,392	318,588	403,232	459,113
Blancos	209,651	239,080	459,171	421,693
Broad Front	212,406	297,490	91,869	103,614
Civic Union	3,911	27,953	4,933	17,888
Blank ballots	2,524	18,838	3,615	20,663

Sources: Uruguay, Corte Electoral, *Elecciones Generales 28 de Noviembre 1971. Elecciones Generales 25 de Noviembre 1984* (mimeograph); Solari, "Algunas reflexiones sobre los resultados electorales," *La Semana de El Día*, No. 301, 1 December 1984.

Table 9.6. *Comparison of traditional party candidates in 1971 and 1984*

1971	%	1984	%
Total Colorado *lema*	41.0	Total Colorado *Lema*	41.2
Bordaberry	22.8	Pacheco	9.7
Batlle	14.0	Sanguinetti	31.5
Vasconcellos	2.9		
Total Blanco *lema*	40.2	Total Blanco *lema*	35.0
Aguerrondo	13.7	Payssé	1.2
Ferreira	26.4	Ortiz	4.0
		Zumarán	29.3

Note: Totals do not sum to 100% because of minor candidates and votes for the *lema*.
Sources: See Table 9.5.

the Blancos in Montevideo, and their seeming stagnation in the interior can be explained by the abolition of absentee balloting by the military. Previously, quite large numbers of migrants had cast votes in Montevideo that were tallied in their native departments. Once in contact with urban politics, they were more likely to vote for the Left than were those who remained encapsulated in the rural and small-town environments.

Because of the restoration of the double simultaneous vote to the electoral system, and the factionalism that it encouraged in the major parties, the significance of the results lay as much in the shares for each *sublema* and list within each *lema* as in the overall result. Table 9.6 compares the performances of the major presidential candidates in the 1971 and 1984 elections,[39] showing how support for the traditional parties was built up in terms of blocks of votes for each candidate.[40] The first thing that shows up clearly is the collapse in the strength of the right wings of both parties – to less than half their former shares. The moderate wing of the Colorado party almost doubled in strength, but the Wilsonistas in the Blanco party grew only 2.5 points, not nearly enough to compensate for the hemorrhage of votes on their right. As one radical Blanco, who jokingly used to enjoy

39 In 1971, the candidate of the Colorado right wing was Bordaberry (because Pacheco's simultaneous bid to revise the Constitution in order to be re-elected did not gain the necessary two-thirds majority). The moderately conservative candidate was Batlle, and a more center-left figure was Vasconcellos. The progressive candidate in the Blanco party, who also had a lot of centrist support, was Ferreira, and General Aguerrondo represented the Right.

40 The percentages are based on the shares of valid votes and exclude some very minor Colorado candidates in 1971 and those votes cast for the *lema* rather than for any specific candidate. By putting two lists in their voting envelopes, citizens may vote for the whole party without expressing a preference for any particular list, but few do.

Table 9.7. *The sociodemographic basis of voting in Montevideo*

Parameter	Left (%)	Blancos (%)	Colorados (%)	Other[a] (%)	No reply (%)	Total (%)
Income (pesos)						
Up to 6,000	15.6	32.8	35.9	6.3	9.4	100.0
6,001–12,000	31.4	25.7	38.1	2.9	1.9	100.0
12,001–20,000	47.1	25.9	17.6	5.9	3.5	100.0
More than 20,000	36.2	15.5	25.9	19.0	3.4	100.0
Occupation						
Prof./white-collar	34.2	20.5	27.4	12.3	5.5	100.0
Skilled workers	43.1	29.4	13.7	9.8	3.9	100.0
Laborers	31.4	25.5	37.3	2.0	3.9	100.0
Unemployed	42.3	23.1	23.1	0.0	11.5	100.0
Students	52.2	17.4	26.1	4.3	0.0	100.0
Housewives	27.6	19.7	38.2	6.6	7.9	100.0
Retired	9.9	37.0	35.8	11.1	6.2	100.0
Age (years)						
Less than 30	44.1	27.5	15.0	8.6	3.6	100.0
30–39	42.7	20.2	25.0	7.3	4.8	100.0
40–49	33.5	19.7	34.6	7.4	4.8	100.0
50–59	20.0	20.7	34.9	7.4	17.0	100.0
60+	18.4	26.8	36.1	6.2	12.5	100.0
Education (years)						
Less than 3	7.3	32.7	45.5	7.3	7.3	100.0
4–6	22.5	35.5	31.9	6.5	3.6	100.0
7–9	39.2	15.2	29.1	6.3	10.1	100.0
10–12	43.8	20.3	23.4	6.3	6.3	100.0
13+	50.0	12.5	18.8	14.6	4.2	100.0

[a]Includes minor parties and nonvoters.
Source: Unpublished data supplied to the author by Equipos Consultores.

describing himself as a "Marxist-Wilsonist," gloomily commented on the result, "the Batllistas won in every party" (i.e., the moderates).[41]

Survey data suggest that the broad sociodemographic characteristics of the main parties' voters in Montevideo were similar to those of 1971.[42] What emerges from Table 9.7 is the relative weakness of class voting in Uruguay: Leftism is fundamentally an intellectual and youth phenomenon.[43] The victory of the Colorado party was made possible by its ability

41 He was referring particularly to the growth of Carlos Julio Pereyra's Movimiento de Rocha relative to Wilson's Por la Patria.
42 I am very grateful to César Aguiar and Agustín Canzani of Equipos Consultores for providing me with these data in advance of publication.
43 On the weakness of class voting in 1971, see Chapter 2. One caveat that emerged in 1984, however, was the conspicuous strength of the Left (and the weakness of the Colorados) among

to advance in the countryside, while retaining a broadly based urban spectrum of support, particularly among the middle-aged and elderly. In a country with an aging population (due to comparatively low fertility and emigration), their inability to appeal to youth was not as damaging. However, the ideal typical Colorado voter, a retired woman living on a state pension, was not necessarily a "renewable political resource."

The components of Colorado victory and Blanco defeat

The rough equality in Zumarán and Sanguinetti's shares of the poll was turned into a strong Colorado lead by the far better showing by Pacheco than by Payssé and Ortiz combined in the Blanco party. That has led many to argue that the Wilsonistas' biggest campaign mistake was to drive away conservative voters with the radical election manifesto and speeches. As a leading conservative Blanco put it,

the National party is a broad party with diverse currents. People who want to close it off will inevitably cause others to leave. If Wilson continues to support the young radicals, there will be an unavoidable decline.[44]

Another conservative Blanco put the emphasis more on strategic errors:

The National party got chained to too many bad ideas. I am not scared of agrarian reform, but the co-mixtures are rather disconcerting, for example, Juan Raúl's "dear shaven friends."[45] I would have preferred a deal with the Colorados. We should have negotiated in order to demand Wilson's freedom. But his big mistake was not to soften his line once the political "opening" began.[46]

In fairness, one should say that the manifesto of the Blanco majority in 1984 was not necessarily more radical than Wilson's 1971 program. However, it came at a different political juncture, in which the Wilsonistas had fully hegemonic pretensions within the party.[47] What is more, reforms were presented not as the ideas of one faction but a position of the party

---

skilled manual workers and the unemployed. Multivariate analysis was not possible, but for a far more detailed discussion than can be entered here, see González (1988).

44 Personal interview, Montevideo, 8 November 1984.

45 A reference to Juan Raúl Ferreira's defense of amnesty for the Tupamaros.

46 Personal interview, Montevideo, 8 November 1984.

47 Nevertheless, one progressive Colorado leader came to Juan Raúl's defense (relations between "youth sectors" in the traditional parties had always remained cordial throughout the acrimony of the campaign): "Juan Raúl's mistake was not his ideas, but his *style*. He scared away small savers, rather than bankers, and saw the land reform in Central American terms" (personal interview, Montevideo, 7 December 1984).

as a whole, dissent being ridiculed and excoriated. However, the voting system punished them for attempting to found a more coherent and programmatic party. As an intellectual Blanco put it,

the National party is a middle-class and bourgeois party – its rural weight imparts a conservative impulse. The trade-union and student strategies try to dispute the Front's electorate and disregard its traditional electorate. If the party wants to win, it will have to balance modern and advanced ideas with old. Unless the double simultaneous vote goes, the Wilsonistas need a strong Right.[48]

One symptom of the failure of the Wilsonistas' strategy was the poor showing of the joint Por la Patria–Corriente Popular Nacionalista list in Montevideo ("W"), which attempted to fuse young militants and faithful old allies. It received 92,348 votes, about the same as the total for its predecessors in 1971. Carlos Julio Pereyra's Movimiento Nacional de Rocha ("List 504") surged ahead compared with 1971, from 17% of the Blancos' votes in Montevideo to 29%.

Whereas many Wilsonistas privately accepted some of the previously cited criticisms, they also emphasized the difficulties they had faced:

In 1982, Terra, Zumarán, and Rodríguez Labruna were jailed – this helped our "ACF" list a great deal. This time, Wilson's being in jail did *not* help. No one had really heard of Zumarán. The National party lost more in image than it gained in sympathy. We wrongly thought Seregni would cause a rebellion in the Broad Front.[49]

The moderation in the mood of the electorate also affected the Left. Within the Broad Front, the communists' share of the vote fell from 33% in 1971 to 28% in 1984. The share of the moderate ex-Colorado "List 99" shot up from 10% to 40%, and that of the socialists with whom they formed a *sublema* went from 12% to 15%. The Christian Democrats' share fell from 20% to 11% of the Front's votes, and the IDI picked up just 6%, compared with the 22% of the Patria Grande *sublema*, its close ancestor in 1971. The net result was a striking shift in the center of gravity of the Front toward the middle of Uruguay's political spectrum. That was a case of an electoral trend reinforcing an ideological trend among the party leaderships, as opposed to the reverse, which had befallen the Blancos.

48 Personal interview, Montevideo, 12 December 1984.
49 Personal interview, Montevideo, 6 December 1984. A young militant of the Movimiento de Rocha had a simpler (if fundamentally contradictory) view: "We lost because Wilson was in jail and because Carlos Julio [Pereyra] should have been the candidate. Also, all the to-ing and fro-ing about whether or not to take part in the elections. . . . I favored abstention" (personal interview, Montevideo, 12 December 1984).

The internal elections of 1982 shifted the traditional parties to the left with respect to 1971, and the trend was confirmed in 1984. But the kinds of citizens who in 1982 were politically aware and involved enough to turn out in a noncompulsory election were not representative of national opinion as a whole. Half again as many voters turned out to vote in 1984, many of them conservative or apathetic. At the level of the party as a whole, and its factions, the Colorados' nationwide pattern of support was largely the same in 1984 as it had been in the primaries; that is, the distribution did not change, despite the marked growth over two years.[50] By contrast, the pattern of support for Zumarán across departments did not correlate with support for the Wilsonistas in 1982. These findings suggest two important things: First, the new shift to rural support for the Colorados began before 1982. The winning coalition of 1984 was already there in 1982, but it was not activated. Victory required getting out the vote of the "silent majority" for cautious consolidation of democracy. What helped was that nonvoters were threatened with a fine of 250 pesos by the Electoral Court unless they could produce medical certificates.[51] Second, the lack of correlation between Zumarán's vote in 1984 and the Wilsonistas' strength in 1982 supports the hypothesis that the latter had indeed been inflated and distorted by support from those leftists who chose not to cast blank ballots or abstain.

The Blancos' defeat was the product of a fundamental misreading of the 1982 primaries, yet one should not belittle the Batllista leaders' skill. The thorny debates over how statist to be in economic policy were settled in theory (if not in practice). The new sectors were particularly opposed to neoliberal economics, but the party may never have been so united during this century.[52]

---

50 We can see this by regressing the 1984 vote share in each department on the 1982 primaries:

$$\text{Colorado } 84 = 17.24 + 0.658(\text{Colorado } 82)$$
$$\text{beta} = .794$$
$$\text{adj. } R^2 = .608 \qquad t = 5.38$$

The same stability was true of Sanguinetti's support:

$$\text{Sanguinetti } 84 = 18.18 + 0.585(\text{Batllism } 82)$$
$$\text{beta} = .789$$
$$\text{adj. } R^2 = .600 \qquad t = 5.29$$

Only the pattern of Blanco support as a whole was equally stable:

$$\text{Blanco } 84 = -1.28 + 0.833(\text{Blanco } 82)$$
$$\text{beta} = .839$$
$$\text{adj. } R^2 = .687 \qquad t = 6.36$$

51 The fine was equal to about five dollars, which meant that it was an average day's pay for most Uruguayans.

52 The program was published as *Por un Uruguay para todos: programa de principios y carta orgánica del Partido Colorado*, Montevideo, *El Día*, 1984.

To many, it came as a surprise that Tarigo's new "List 85" should overtake the old "List 15" in Montevideo, to become the most-voted list of the Batllistas proper. It has been suggested that the spread of television and sophisticated advertising meant that candidate presentation was far more important than before.[53] "List 85" deliberately advertised the fresh faces of their young senatorial candidates in the hope of catching floating voters. Apart from Sanguinetti, the leaders of "List 15" seemed old and unattractive by comparison. Those people who were voting Colorado for the first time, particularly those having broken with the Blancos, found it easier to choose this new option. One leader also claimed that "85" had used Sanguinetti's picture to a far greater extent than had his own "15" – perhaps because of the Batlle–Sanguinetti rivalry.[54]

Despite the relative lack of experienced politicians in "List 85," it made a significant difference to the internal functioning of the Colorado party, imparting an unaccustomed degree of participation and leadership accountability to its movement.[55] For example, though during 1984 Tarigo had merely favored suspension of Colorado politicians in the interior who accepted posts as *intendentes* under the military, he had bowed to the wishes of the "List 85" General Assembly, which voted for their expulsion. He was further overruled when the General Assembly decided that there should be a joint Senate list with "15."[56] A young leader pointed out that "85" mobilized young voters, not through the old-style clubs but through magazines, particularly *Opinar*.[57] That new type of politics also typified the more radical Corriente Batllista Independiente ("89"), which originally was allied to Tarigo, but then fell under the influence of the Colorado Left, led by Manuel Flores Silva. If "85" was moderately Keynesian and rather technocratic, "89" was frankly social-democratic and in favor of participation and mobilization. It, too, grew dramatically in 1984, partly as a result of emphasizing its independent Senate list.[58]

---

53 "List 85" made a special effort to present a well-groomed image of its leading Senate candidates on full-color posters all over Montevideo. They contrasted with the drab red-and-white posters of "List 15."

54 According to one young "85" leader, the competition forced the old-line Batllistas to find new faces themselves, such as Vásquez Romero and Fernández Faingold.

55 Also important, of course, was the decline of Pachequismo, which was the most personalist and clientelist sector of all.

56 Personal interview, Montevideo, 12 December 1984.

57 Nevertheless, the magazine Tarigo had founded in 1980, as the first to oppose the regime, did eventually close for lack of funds, having been eclipsed by CBI's popular *Jaque*.

58 "15" and "85" had joint Senate lists headed by the unpopular Batlle. Flores Silva was also rather adept at forming alliances in the interior of the country with minor lists that promised to adopt the Senate list that he headed, instead of the mainstream Batllista list.

Table 9.8. *Party system changes following authoritarian regimes*

Country	Remmer discontinuity index
Uruguay, 1971–84	10.5
Colombia, 1953–7	8.5
Honduras, 1972–81	20.9
Honduras, 1963–71	45.3
Argentina, 1966–73	48.3
Venezuela, 1948–58	59.4
Argentina, 1976–83	63.7
Peru, 1963–80	65.6
Ecuador, 1972–8	97.4
Peru, 1948–56	108.6
Argentina, 1946–58	118.9
Bolivia, 1964–82	147.9

Source: Remmer (1985) and author's calculations.

The dilemma of stability

At the heart of the future success or failure of democratic consolidation lay the dilemma of stability versus innovation. On the one hand were those who argued that avoidance of a return to the past and repetition of the same mistakes was the overriding priority. Some stressed the need to reform the democratic *process*, particularly the process of internal party democracy. Others emphasized the need for new *policies* in order to confront not only the country's long-standing economic decline and social tensions but also the catastrophic legacy of military rule. An even more fundamental question, however, was whether to seize the historic opportunity for reforms or seek to maintain consensus among all political sectors by postponing contentious proposals for change.

In a strictly numerical sense, Uruguay's party system had been remarkably stable, as seen by comparing the 1984 election results with those of 1971. On the simple index developed by Karen Remmer to measure shifts in party systems associated with the impact of authoritarian regimes in Latin America (Table 9.8), Uruguay shows less fluctuation than do 10 of the 11 cases she examined.[59]

Such aggregate stability, however, may be misleading. In the Uruguayan case, for example, although the Colorados' percentage of the na-

---

59 Remmer (1985). It is interesting to check the hypothesis that discontinuity is a function of the duration of the authoritarian regime. The simple correlation between Remmer's index and the duration of the regime in years yields an *r* value of .556. The figures for Argentina are somewhat misleading because of the banning of Perónists from 1958 to 1973.

tional vote was almost exactly the same in 1984 as in 1971, it had fallen significantly in Montevideo and risen in the interior. Furthermore, it is also necessary to emphasize the qualitative aspects of the party system, as defined by the evolution of party programs, alliances, and ideological polarization.

Party "renovation" has several different components: emergence of new leaders, shifts in parties' and factions' electorates, reforms in party organization, renewal of electoral platforms, and changes in the decision-making processes inside parties. The emergence of new leaders had occurred to some extent in spite of the military's attempts to force out the old politicians with the Fourth Institutional Act. The changes in the parties' electorates were traceable more to the climate of reaction against extremism than to the military's heavy-handed pressures. Little policy renovation had been attempted by the parties – the Blancos adopting a radical program somewhat transiently, and the Colorados pulling back toward the center from the right, also as part of their electoral strategy.

To take an important example, even the largest new faction to emerge in the Colorado party, Tarigo's "List 85," did not offer renovation along the dimensions previously mentioned, apart from leadership and organization: Its program and electorate were clearly within the (historical) mainstream of Batllism.[60] The major source of renovation came from electoral shifts between factions. Yet the country was not necessarily returning to the old stalemates and crises. There seemed to be a subtle learning process at work that had taught major political actors certain lessons about how to avoid the kind of chaos that might bring a return to military rule. That was very clear in the Broad Front under Seregni's moderate strategy.

There was no denying that Uruguay's transition had led to a restoration of the status quo ante in most respects. Could political behavior nevertheless evolve in ways favorable to democratic consolidation without fundamental reforms?

60 Nor was Sanguinetti, originally a stand-in for Jorge Batlle, such a new face; he had been education minister before the coup. Although he had somewhat outgrown Batlle's "List 15," he remained identified with the list, whose leading candidates were, without exception, survivors from pre-coup politics.

10

The legacies of authoritarianism and the challenges for democracy

The main danger is that Uruguay is going straight back to 1970. The Left has not changed at all. PIT, ASCEEP, the Rural Federation and Chamber of Industries are all doing exactly the same things as before. Wilson and the Front are the same. . . . The Colorado party is the only party to have really changed in abandoning Pachequismo.

A young Colorado, 12 July 1984

Whoever wins, there will be a huge political crisis between president and Parliament. Demagogy will be massive in order to defeat the government and win the 1989 election. Institutional breakdown will result. The president may dissolve Parliament. Subversion would return – not just terrorism but coordinated leftism, including demonstrations, strikes, and bomb attacks. Sooner or later there will be another coup.

An air-force colonel, November 1984

Sanguinetti is a very intelligent, enormously able and cultured statesman. And definitely a conservative. He will have a major place in Uruguayan history, I am sure of that. I have great respect for Wilson Ferreira, but Sanguinetti has a more global view.

A Broad Front candidate, 17 April 1985

Though Sanguinetti soon did show himself to be a capable, cultured, and tough president, the challenges he faced were huge: most urgently, the military refusal to countenance any trials of those accused of human-rights violations and the continuing economic crisis. The Colorado administration presented a typically Uruguayan reaction to problems that other Latin American nations often have attempted to fight by more dramatic efforts. The new government had no particular ideological ax to grind: It was fiscally conservative, but mildly committed to greater social justice; favorable to the private sector, but not ideologically opposed to state intervention. For most Batllistas, the era of social reforms was largely over, because lack of resources was judged to have limited the capacities of the state to meet every social need. However, that conservatism was pragmatic rather than ideological.

The Colorados' overriding priority was the consolidation of democracy, but that brought with it a host of political dilemmas: the trade-off between stability and justice (e.g., with regard to past military crimes), the conflict between government by majority and government by consensus, the tensions between strong government and democratic liberties, and the balancing of reforms with institutional continuity. These formal political questions impinged on Uruguay's perennial search for an elusive balance between distributive politics and economic growth. In the face of dire obstacles, democratic *convivencia*, or peaceful coexistence, was promoted by three types of conflict-regulating mechanisms:

1   *concessionary* pacts between military and politicians,
2   *corporatist* pacts between parties, government, and unions, and
3   *consociational* pacts among parties.

The deal with the military in 1984 was achieved at the cost of rupturing the unity of the parties. The government then sought a pact with the unions in 1985, but an initial wave of strikes drowned all hopes for early progress. Following a year-end crisis over the budget, the government's attention shifted in 1986 to the need to consolidate cooperation among the parties, though the results again fell short of a coalition government or "consociational democracy." This chapter thus examines the three great issues facing Uruguayan democracy: the military question, the social question, and the political question. These correspond to the three previously discussed levels of conflict regulation, but the analysis will discard the assumption that avoiding conflict is necessarily the best long-term solution for democracy.

The military question

Ensuring loyalty on the part of the armed forces is the first priority of any newly inaugurated leader of a fledgling democracy. Two questions are constantly immanent: Will they fully relinquish the prerogative of influencing government policy? Are they prepared to tolerate interference in their institution, which, under the authoritarian regime, has become accustomed to defining its own goals? National-security doctrine had the effect of adding many branches of state activity to the list of military concerns – even as far afield as education. In Uruguay, it was a measure of the military's retreat that they relinquished all attempts to influence policies other than those most directly impinging on the internal functioning of their corporation.

Many generals, and colonels especially, were far from happy with the

Naval Club pact and subsequent developments such as the March 1985 amnesty. As one military thinker put it,

the new government is going to completely dismantle the legacy of the *proceso* and throw away all the good with the bad. The Constituent Assembly is going to throw out the whole Naval Club accord. There has been no learning from past mistakes. Instability will return, and the government won't have the tools to act.

The same analyst went on to make two predictions, one regarding the future behavior of the military, the other the fundamental danger to democracy:

The armed forces could accept both amnesty and revisionism as long as they are not projects sponsored by the government. The big problem is going to be cabinet instability, strikes, subversion, shortages, and conflicts among politicians.[1]

The same officer was, however, able to alleviate his *Schadenfreude* momentarily when he admitted that "Uruguay will have the safest return to democracy [in the region] because of the traditional parties."

Despite military apprehensions, the new government trod carefully. Above all, it decided to retain the same commanders bequeathed by the dictatorship, which Blanco leader Wilson Ferreira Aldunate argued constituted an implicit commitment made at the Naval Club.[2] Throughout 1985, denunciations of human-rights violations under that military government increased in the press, through judicial channels, and in parliamentary investigating commissions. The government, however, attempted to buy time. An arrest warrant for two officers issued by a civil judge was held back in official channels until military courts could file suit disputing jurisdiction. The Supreme Court then was asked to decide whether that and other cases would be aired in civil or military courts. Sanguinetti ruled out mass trials of armed-forces institutions in the Argentine manner,[3] declaring that "the best thing that can happen to the past is to leave it to the historians." Meanwhile, military sources expressed confidence that penalties for crimes committed during the repression would not be imposed.[4] On the other hand, the government did reduce

1 Personal interview, Montevideo, 14 December 1984.
2 This section draws heavily on unpublished notes by Miguel Arregui that were incorporated into our jointly authored essay "Uruguay" (Arregui and Gillespie 1988).
3 In an interview with a French newspaper he said, "Listen. Some of our military have perhaps certain responsibilities, but so do the terrorists, and weighty they are. Now, we gave them an amnesty. It is natural to have amnestied the military, too." See "Un entretien avec le Président Sanguinetti," *Le Monde*, 3–4 November 1984.
4 Unattributed remarks made to Arregui in interviews with the military.

the military's bloated share of the budget, cutting troop numbers by 5,000 to their pre-coup levels.[5]

The authorities were obliged to impose sanctions on several officers for making political statements.[6] They also had to put up with resignations, as a result of the decisions to release the Tupamaros and to rehabilitate officers who had been stripped of their rank, such as Seregni. Nevertheless, the majority of the military maintained a grudging calm. The government did not meet major obstacles to its conciliatory policy from the opposition, which generally acted with discretion when handling military affairs. Ferreira even agreed to meet in secret with the high command to clear up their differences. At the beginning of March 1986, Institutional Act No. 19, negotiated at the Naval Club, ran out. The government immediately sent a bill to Parliament reestablishing previous civil–military conventions, fortifying civilian authority, and purging the dictatorship's concept of "national security" from military legislation. It did not, however, alter the mechanisms for promotion, except at the very highest levels.

In May of 1986, Defense Minister Juan Chiarino admitted publicly that he had no control over the armed forces' intelligence arm, but was attempting to bring them under his authority.[7] The unpopular Chiarino's handling of the military became decidedly controversial, however, when he turned over to the military courts the evidence gathered by a parliamentary commission investigating the assassinations of exiled politicians Michelini and Gutiérrez Ruiz. That decision produced a storm of criticism from Blancos and the Left alike. When, in June, the government finally introduced its proposed bill to grant members of the armed forces immunity from prosecution for past violations of human rights, polls showed that an overwhelming majority of Montevideo voters in all parties favored punishing the guilty members of the security forces. However, only a slender minority believed that they would in fact ever be sanctioned.

The Colorados' first proposed bill to close the book on human-rights prosecution was defeated by the combined opposition of the Blancos and the Broad Front. Then a Blanco compromise bill that would have allowed certain trials to go ahead was defeated by bilateral opposition from the Colorados and the Left. Finally, after a long hiatus during which the military began to threaten that they would boycott any civil trials that were attempted, the majority of the Blancos introduced a new bill that would grant immunity in the form of a statute of limitations. Passage of

5 Boeker (1990, p. 82).

6 The most serious incident concerned General Alfonso Feola, who was stripped of his command for having implied that Medina was failing to protect the interests of the armed forces.

7 Chiarino, it may be recalled, was the leader of the Civic Union.

the law, known as the *ley de caducidad*, at the end of 1986 led General Medina to thank the politicians personally. In early 1987 he retired as army commander, but before the end of the year President Sanguinetti had named him minister of defense.

The Left and some Blancos voted against the law, which they called a "law of impunity," rather than "immunity." They immediately began a campaign to collect the half-million signatures necessary to force a referendum on the law. That referendum was finally held in April 1989, but the law was upheld.

Any attempt at a series of civil trials of high-ranking officers on the Argentine model probably would have been more dangerous than giving in to the pressure from the military. The circumstances of internal military feuding in Argentina that weakened the armed forces also made the trials of the junta leaders possible; the scale of their crimes and incompetence not only increased the pressure to try them but also made it politically easier. Such conditions clearly were lacking in Uruguay, where the issue was not trials of former leaders, but of those lower down, who carried out torture and "disappearances." Even Argentina finally enacted a law limiting prosecution to those who gave orders.

Politicians had to be wary of undermining those sectors of the military that had originally agreed to the extrication – particularly since Medina had been attacked by his subordinates for allegedly allowing the name of the armed forces to be tarnished. As one colonel put it,

denunciations of fraud or economic mistakes greatly weaken the high command. The military is not just its commanders in chief. There is a great deal of discontent at their high-handedness. . . .
   All the politicians are in agreement over attacking the morale of the armed forces, but when the violence returns, they'll have no one to help them.[8]

One experienced Colorado, who had retired from public life, pointed out that "the generals are scared of their colonels."[9]

To assess the costs and benefits of Uruguay's negotiated path to democracy with respect to the military question, we are forced to confront a paradox. The fact that the military retired to the barracks "less defeated" meant that they retained greater potential influence, but their relatively gentle treatment also meant that they had less reason to be discontented. It is simplistic to argue (as did some Blancos) that their position was strengthened by the mode of transition. Such a view inverts the real causal sequence. There is no doubt that the potential for justice to be meted

8 Personal interview, Montevideo, 15 April 1985.
9 Personal interview, Montevideo, 29 September 1984.

out to torturers was highly circumscribed, given the threatened refusal of the military to recognize civil courts. By comparison with Uruguay, the Brazilian military retained influence in government even under the new republic.[10] The benefits for Uruguay's new democracy from the Naval Club pact were that direct military participation in government and state enterprises was brought to an end, and meddling on grounds of "national security" was abolished. Most important, and uniquely in the Uruguayan case, the high command became wedded to the success of the new government, and even to democracy itself.[11]

The social question: economic stress

Like the other southern-cone countries' economies, Uruguay's economy had been devastated by the military's neoliberal experiments. From its peak level at the beginning of the decade, GNP had fallen more than 15%.[12] The impact of the same policies dramatically boosted unemployment, forced workers into the informal sector, and eroded the percentage of the labor force covered by social insurance.[13] From 1970 to 1980, the fraction of the labor force in the informal sector grew from 23% to 27%, and social-security coverage fell from 95% to 83%.

In the first year of the new democracy, workers' real wages grew about 15%, though that, of course, did not compensate for the severe declines registered during the preceding decade. Unemployment fell from about 13% to 11%. Investment nevertheless continued to fall until September 1985, showing that business confidence was still low.[14] "Trade unions are elated, and businessmen depressed," Sanguinetti stated in an interview.[15] The president insisted that he would not give in to "irresponsible populism," but publication of a restrictive five-year public-spending plan, which would have kept public-sector wages low, led to a wave of strikes and deteriorating relations between the government and the opposition. However, unlike Argentina or Brazil, Uruguay never suffered triple-digit inflation during the transition to democracy.[16]

Declining world interest rates caused Uruguay's debt service to fall in

---

10 Schneider (1987).
11 Stepan (1988) has stressed this comparative dismantling of military prerogatives, which were scarcely more ex.ensive than prior to 1973.
12 Inter-American Development Bank (1986, Table 3).
13 Mann and Sánchez (1985).
14 In 1985, Uruguay's economic growth was a modest 0.7%, but that was the first time since 1981 that it had not actually fallen, and growth was an excellent 4.5% in 1986 (mainly because of an export boom to Brazil).
15 *Le Monde*, October 1985. He added that entrepreneurs "must be coaxed into investing and producing while, at the same time, we must calm the unions."
16 Stallings and Kaufman (1989).

1985,[17] and an agreement between Colorados and Blancos led to a law on refinancing private-sector debts to local banks.[18] Nevertheless, Uruguay's foreign debt remained an astronomic $5 billion. The Blancos avoided demagogic opposition to the government's handling of the debt crisis. Because of rising tax revenues, the government was able to cut the fiscal deficit, which the Alvarez administration had pushed up to 28% in 1984, back down to 16% in 1985. However, the struggle between Parliament and president over the budget left a legacy of tensions regarding the conduct of the economy.

The social question: union response

Many of Uruguay's labor organizations inherited a strategic conception of unions as revolutionary weapons of resistance to the state and the employers, as well as tools for the defense of economic interests. Almost at once the PIT-CNT campaigned directly against the Colorados' economic policies. Of all the southern-cone military dictatorships, that of Uruguay had produced the most savage compression of real wages.[19] There are no data on deteriorating working conditions, but it may be surmised that they had been equally neglected under the military government.

How would labor react to the sudden restoration of its full freedom to organize and strike for higher wages and better conditions? Would it exercise restraint in the interest of stabilizing democracy? Grass-roots labor militants were ill-disposed to such an idea, and from late 1984 an escalating wave of strikes and factory occupations broke out. But, more important, would parties (especially on the Left) do their best to hold conflicts to a manageable level, or would they encourage and exploit them? Overall, there was relatively high agreement among Blanco and Colorado politicians that unions must consider the impact of their demands on the new regime, and even 35% of those in the leftist parties agreed, though a clear majority of Frentistas saw the defense of labor's interests as more important. Things were even more harmonious when it came to the duties of business, revealing once again the traditional parties' reticence about appearing as full-blown conservatives (Table 10.1).

After the return to democracy, strikes spread to the public sector, where wages had fallen the most under the military, repeatedly paralyzing the courts, posts, and customs. The first general strike took place six months

17 The falling price of imported oil also had the potential to save the state oil corporation $80 million or more each year.
18 That included ranching, industry, commerce, and services, and it removed much of the uncertainty facing businessmen and improved the liquidity of firms.
19 Taking 1970 as an index of 100, real wages had fallen to 62 in 1982. See Mann and Sánchez (1985, p. 29).

Table 10.1. *Labor and capital's responsibilities under democracy*

Response	Left (%) (n = 17)	Blancos (%) (n = 23)	Colorados (%) (n = 22)	All[a] (%) (n = 67)
View of labor's demands[b]				
Yes, above all, consequences must be taken into account.	35.3	65.2	77.3	59.7
Up to a point, but defense and protection of their interests is more important.	58.8	30.4	22.7	37.3
No, unions' principal obligations are toward workers.	5.9	4.3	0.0	3.0
Total	100.0	100.0	100.0	100.0
View of business demands[c]				
Yes, above all, consequences must be taken into account.	93.8	95.2	91.3	92.5
Up to a point, but defense and protection of their interests is more important.	6.3	4.8	8.7	7.7
No, business success is a necessity for the country.	0.0	0.0	0.0	0.0
Total	100.0	100.0	100.0	100.0

[a] Includes one Patriotic Union and three Civic Union leaders, plus a nonparty high-ranking officer.

[b] The question: "Regarding labor's demands, do you think unions should take into consideration their consequences for the advent, stability, and consolidation of the future elected government?"

[c] The question: "Regarding business demands, do you think businessmen should consider their consequences for the advent, stability, and consolidation of the future elected government?"

into the Sanguinetti administration. Many stoppages were beyond the control of union leaders, who found themselves completely overtaken by the militancy of middle and lower activists in the labor movement, where the political balance was difficult to measure, or in mass assemblages of workers and employees, where it often was irrelevant. Only sizable wage increases, following agreements in "wage councils," allowed strikes to abate after mid-1985. As Arregui has pointed out, in destroying union cadres, the military had upset a delicate balance of power that had been painstakingly created over decades. As one leading communist commented,

many trade unions have changed. The working class is different now. So many people have retired or gone into exile for economic reasons. . . .

Many factories have very young workers and increasing participation by women. The number of workers has fallen a lot in the packinghouses due to new technologies and increased exploitation.[20]

Other changes in the union movement came with the advent of white-collar radicalism and the expansion of the PIT-CNT to include all unions, where some had previously been independent.[21]

Competition between different sectors of the PIT-CNT gave rise to the identification of each group according to its party affiliation (*partidización*). At first the communists lost their hegemony, but they quickly fought back. The radical Marxist Left ("ultras") seemed to weaken, and a new alliance of socialists, Christian Democrats, and "List 99" emerged. Blancos achieved some union gains, but remained much in the minority, and the Colorados were even more outnumbered. A moderate member of the Broad Front expressed support for a more open union movement, but was cautious regarding the likely extent of change: "It is salutary that unions be pluripartite, but the Wilsonistas cannot easily rob workers in the way Batlle or Perón once did."[22] Old cadres, many of them communists who had been in exile or in prison, found it difficult to win the backing of the new grass-roots militants. However, the defeat of various unions after prolonged strikes, the strengthened position of the communists, and the consolidation of leadership all eventually contributed to reestablishment of control "from above" and greater industrial peace.

20 Personal interview, 18 April 1985.
21 An example of a union that fell into both categories was the civil servants' union (COFE).
22 Personal interview, Montevideo, 17 April 1985.

The social question: government response

Although public-sector wage increases were fixed administratively, in the private sector the government reestablished the tripartite wage councils, with representatives from unions, employers, and government. Every four months they were to negotiate wage increases in their respective areas of activity. However, that soon led to massive economic disruption, so in February 1986 the government bypassed the councils. It also abandoned its policy of linking wage increases to past inflation and switched to its own projection of *future* inflation. That led to a second general strike on 12 March that was totally successful in Montevideo, but patchier outside the capital.[23] Incomes policy was managed on an ad hoc basis, without any sustained attempt to build institutions that might stabilize labor relations.

The Colorado party remained divided over how to regulate strikes and unions. Whereas the right wing held dear the idea of legislation, Labor Minister Hugo Fernández favored voluntary "self-regulation," arguing that no law could work unless it had at least the tolerance of the unions.[24] The first moves of the government had been to repeal the military's repressive labor law, and Fernández at first adopted a vague progressive tone. In a May Day radio broadcast he promised that

we want workers to retain a greater percentage of what they produce, to democratize firms and protect the rights of organization. But today it is not so easy; there is a war economy. However, we are very interested in going beyond routine ideas; for instance, we plan to promote co-ops.[25]

In fact, the communists' cautious strategy and opposition to militant strikes led to an increasing convergence of interests between them and the government, which saw them as less threatening than the "ultras."

During 1984 the concept of concerted action had become a buzz-word on the lips of every politician, but the Colorados attached their own particular meaning to the term. As Sanguinetti said,

concertation does not mean a social pact, but that the country should for once understand itself. The [proposed] National Economic Council is a totally different thing – not

23 A third general strike on 17 June proved less successful and was opposed by the communists.
24 In contrast, a conservative Colorado commented that "we must have democratic unions even if the grass roots are more radical than the leaders. It is compatible with 'concertation' . . . we want secret ballots and no career leaders" (personal interview, Montevideo, n.d.).
25 Radio broadcast, Radio Sarandí, 1 May 1985.

corporatist but participatory. It represents the road that has been shown by Sweden and Germany.[26]

With all-party support, the unions took part in the *concertación* talks on negotiating joint policies prior to the Colorados taking office. They also participated in the abortive discussions on a "social pact" in mid-1985, suspended in August when the government claimed that the unions' attitudes were proving dangerous and "antidemocratic." Yet the 1986 talks on a "national accord" did not include the unions, only the political parties. The accord was thus consociational rather than corporatist in intent. Hopes for a "neocorporatist" solution to Uruguay's distributive struggle foundered on the internal political turbulence of the unions and their distance from the major parties.

The government's relatively conservative economic policies were feasible because of a political conjuncture in which popular mobilization was limited and party competition was not so cliff-hanging as to induce irresponsible outbidding. What the form of a closely guided transition based on elite pacts seemed, above all, to have achieved was control over inflation. Even though talks over a "social pact" failed, the Left continually found itself *structurally* committed to restraining labor's demands. Expectations were never raised that democracy would immediately solve economic deprivation. Had the transition been more "triumphalist," or had the Blancos won the election, the moderate strategy of the Left might have collapsed. Wilson then would have faced a hard choice between carrying out the radical economic proposals made to win votes from the Left in a new Left–Blanco alliance or creating a conservative axis with the Colorados and risking an eruption of social protest given the rapid elevation and betrayal of expectations.

Argentina's disorderly military retreat and rising popular expectations fueled the near hyperinflation of 1984–5. The subsequent stabilization ("Plan Austral") was all the more harsh as a result. Brazil followed a similar pattern, though even more of its inflation was inherited from the last days of the authoritarian regime. What was striking was that neither of those countries was able to achieve a neocorporatist wage pact with organized labor. Perhaps the economic parameters were simply too unfavorable. However, Uruguay's incorporation of the Left into the transition provided a crucial respite from popular pressures that might otherwise have generated the boom-and-bust cycle experienced in Argentina and Brazil.

---

26 Colorado convention, 7 April 1984, author's notes and translation. Calls for concertation were also heard at the Por la Patria convention on 15 March. To some extent that was a rhetorical commitment to expressing the solidarity of parties in opposition to the military.

The political question: immobilism or centripetal democratic consolidation?

Democratic consolidation repeatedly raises the dilemma of government by majority versus government by consensus. This, in turn, involves the problem of the proper role of loyal oppositions in a democratic system. The uncomfortable fact remains that Uruguay experienced a return to the politico-institutional status quo ante. The fact that the authoritarian regime did not produce any significant structural or political innovations, apart from a new democratic spirit, means that Uruguay's fundamental problem may be *too much stability*.[27] A historical opportunity for political innovation provided by regime discontinuity was missed; indeed, it was structurally blocked by Uruguay's negotiated path of transition. Though many politicians acknowledge the potential advantages of various reforms, too many interests are at stake. The nature of the Uruguayan political future seems destined to remain transformist, and largely shackled by the requirements of reaching consensus within the existing configuration of interests.

President Sanguinetti's mistrust of corporatism, and only limited endorsement of policymaking by consensus, held out the possibility of executive-led reforms. But it equally heralded the danger of a Colorado government attempting a hard-line majoritarian form of rule that could produce the same confrontations and democratic erosion seen during 1968–73. The cost of relative stability in Uruguay, during the transition, and during the attempted consolidation of democracy, may be a stalemate.

Controversy over the Naval Club pact might have produced a permanent polarization of politics, but the election result contributed to a return to competition for the center ground. Would those trends continue once the strain of substantive decision making fell on the government, and opposition frustration reemerged? President Sanguinetti's first decrees legalized the Communist party and scrapped several repressive laws and remaining institutional acts. The Colorados compromised by agreeing that all former Tupamaros be released, the Left by accepting legal formulas that, unlike true amnesty, did not exculpate their actions.

In the first years of the new democracy, the behaviors of all major parties contrasted healthily to their egoism and polarization prior to the 1973 military intervention. Hardly had he been released when Wilson Ferreira introduced the term "governability" to Uruguay, hinting that he would ensure Sanguinetti a grace period of two or three years. During that time the National party would refrain from systematic opposition

---

27 González (1985a) has argued that the real solution to Uruguay's political and economic stagnation will require abandonment of an electoral system that foments factionalism in the parties, preventing global solutions to problems.

Table 10.2. *Distribution of seats in the House of Deputies and Senate*

Seats	Broad Front	Blancos	Colorados	Civic Union	Total
Senators	6	11	13	0	30
Deputies					
Interior	5	22	23	1	51
Montevideo	16	13	18	1	48
Total	21	35	41	2	99

Source: Juan Rial, *Uruguay: elecciones de 1984* (Montevideo: EBO, 1985).

and ease the legislative passage of government policies. Although the president's desire to form a multiparty cabinet proved impossible, two Blanco sympathizers did accept positions in the government.[28] Nevertheless, the administration did not pay much attention to fulfilling what had been agreed upon in the "concerted action" talks before it came to power, and political crises erupted over key questions such as the budget and immunity for the armed forces.

Sanguinetti responded with toughness to those crises that threatened the stability of his cabinet. Although the Colorados had only just over two-fifths of the seats in the legislature, which exposed their ministers to censure, they had enough to prevent the Assembly from overriding an executive veto. The pressure for compromise was thus built into the structure of political competition. When the opposition altered the administration's financial plans, increasing expenditures in various areas, Sanguinetti vetoed 75 clauses of their amended budget to cut the projected fiscal deficit.[29] However, the Supreme Court declared the executive veto of the budget for the judicial branch to be unconstitutional, precipitating an abrupt moderation in the president's strategy.[30] In January 1986, following a summit meeting with Wilson Ferreira, Sanguinetti switched to proposing a "national accord" on specific policies and called for opposition participation in his government.

Once the new Parliament met, the Colorado–Broad Front axis quickly broke down, and the two parties instead occupied opposite poles in the legislature, while the Blancos tended to oscillate between them, acting as arbiter (Table 10.2). Sanguinetti always sought consensus when he encountered steadfast opposition and sensed that the nation was deeply

28 They were Enrique Iglesias as foreign minister and Raúl Ugarte as minister of health. The difficult job of defense minister was given to the aged but spry leader of the Civic Union, Juan Vicente Chiarino.

29 *Búsqueda*, No. 316, 23–29 January 1986. General Seregni later described the president's leadership as "tough, almost authoritarian."

30 *Búsqueda*, No. 317, 30 January to 5 February 1986.

divided. In practice, that meant allowing a great deal of influence to Wilson Ferreira. A drawing together of Blancos and Colorados put the Left at risk of being totally eliminated from political decision making, but it attempted to avoid being marginalized by also appealing to the center of politics. Indeed, one of the most important symptoms of the competition for the center ground among parties was the strategy of the Left. Seregni insisted on the need to convert the Broad Front into a "real alternative for power," abandoning its traditionally contestatory role. For example, agreements with the other parties in 1985 meant that the Left was for the first time allotted seats on the boards of directors of some industrial and commercial state enterprises.[31]

When the proposal for a "national accord" between government and opposition was first discussed, Blanco and Colorado sources were surprised to find that the Frente adopted the idea. The Left took an active part in the negotiations and showed an unusual degree of tolerance toward future economic policy, by abandoning specific demands for reflation or a moratorium on debt repayments. Seregni's strategy, which had the explicit backing of the Communist party, showed a desire to break the Left's classic image as a politically inefficient sector more interested in playing the role of popular tribune and radical opposition than in being a constructive force for government. Support for the *acuerdo* might be seen favorably by moderate reformist sectors to which the Broad Front planned to appeal in the 1989 elections.[32] Such agreements could be seen as either a triumph of immobilism or a stepping-stone to real reforms. However, the importance of the accord lay more in its symbolic implications than in its practical implementation. Shortly thereafter, the divisive issue of the military's amnesty was to alienate the Left.

By late 1986 the majority of Blanco leaders favored political compromise. The rationale for cooperation with the Colorados had been espoused early on by one of Wilson's leading allies, who argued that: "Colombia's pact seemed like a dirty trick to me at the time, but not nowadays. We need to unify against the regime and the Latin America military international."[33] The strategy of moving toward the center and supporting the government complemented the attempt to rebuild the party's appeal among right-wing voters. As a radical Colorado had surmised following the elections,

---

31 In addition to that new role in the *entes autónomos* (para-statals), the Left won back much of its former influence in the nation's largely state-run educational system. Efforts to win posts in the Supreme Court, the diplomatic corps, and various state agencies proved fruitless, however.

32 Unpublished notes by Miguel Arregui.

33 Amazingly, those sentiments were privately expressed right in the middle of the other parties' prenegotiation with the military (personal interview, Montevideo, 14 July 1984).

Wilson now wants to reverse Juan Raúl's homogenization of the National party and ask the conservatives to return. He also called for democratization of the unions to undermine the Left. Wilson wants to create a kind of populist nationalism.[34]

The centripetal dynamic of electoral competition was the major factor in promoting the abrupt return to a search for elite consensus. Leadership strategies and public opinion (as revealed in regular polls) interacted in ways that were politically stabilizing. Wilson's moderation was driven by a desire to become president in 1989.

The evidence of political learning

An absence of institutional innovation need not necessarily mean a lack of *political learning*. Democratic restoration alone is insufficient unless accompanied by such political learning by leaders and citizens if the danger of authoritarian cycles is to be avoided. But some lessons do seem to have been learned in all three parties. The first danger to democracy is the failure of political elites to cooperate. The Broad Front's abandonment of anti-system behavior, the self-criticism and isolation of the Tupamaros, the Blancos' electoralist moderation, and the Colorados' search for consensus are all genuine and healthy. The dangers of mass praetorian mobilization are more clearly recognized on all sides than in 1971–3. As we have seen, Uruguay's party system has proved highly stable and resilient.

A second potential danger to democratic consolidation is the survival of an undemocratic Right. One of the few blessings of the recent Latin American authoritarian regimes was that none of them was ultimately very effective at solving economic problems, even as they themselves defined those problems. In Uruguay, the antidemocratic right wings have certainly gone into retreat in both traditional parties. The Pachequista wing of the Colorado party lost its controlling position, as compared with 1971. Nevertheless, it retained a certain leverage over the government, for without it, centrist and progressive Colorados could have no hope of winning an election. Mindful of the electoral imperative, the Wilsonistas welcomed the revival of the Herrerista wing of the Blanco party, which captured the presidency in 1989. The interests of capital are thus well represented in both the Colorado and Blanco parties, thereby, from the

---

34 Personal interview, Montevideo, 7 December 1984. A Blanco leader nevertheless rejected the analogy with Perónism when I put it to him: "Ferreira is far more internationalized – he subscribes to European ideas. He seeks a movement which is less proletarian and massified" (personal interview, 12 December 1984).

standpoint of the business community, making the benefits of participating in the democratic game greater than the costs.[35]

A third danger to democracy comes from the antidemocratic Left; yet
experience of authoritarianism has led to a revalorization of democracy by
almost all the Left.[36] Furthermore, the dynamic of electoral competition
in 1984 rewarded those sectors of the Broad Front that had moved closest
toward the center. This centripetal pattern of electoral competition is very
stabilizing for liberal democracy, other things being equal.

A fourth problem concerns the need for party strengthening, particularly regarding the linkages between parties and organized systems of
interest representation. The great challenge to Uruguay's new democracy
(even more than the military) was to deal with the demands of labor.
However, despite attempts by the Colorados in the 1950s, and the Blancos
in the 1980s, to develop links with labor, the union movement remains
strongly allied to the Left.

The balance of trends in the first five years of Uruguay's restored
democracy was favorable. The victory of conservative Blanco Luis Alberto
Lacalle in 1989 and the peaceful transfer of power was viewed as normal
rather than remarkable. The Left captured control of the city government
of Montevideo, giving rise to tensions between central and local authorities, but those were no worse than in, say, Britain. In order to assess
the longer-term prospects for democratic survival, however, we must
therefore again delve into the processes by which democracies collapse.
In 1973, as now, the vast majority of Uruguayans remained solidly committed to the abstract principle that democracy is the most legitimate
form of government; nevertheless, political practices can threaten that
system in three ways. First, there are actions that are both legal and
consonant with what are normally considered the fundamental rights of
citizens in a democracy, but that tend by their interplay to lead to
irreconcilable crises. At a second (inferior) level of legitimacy are those
actions that are more or less legal but are not agreed to by everyone to
be in keeping with fundamental democratic values, leading in many cases
to fierce disputes about their "constitutionality." Finally, at a third and
still more dubious level of legitimacy there are political actions that are
unambiguously illegal and yet are appealing because of allegedly "higher"
democratic principles.

35 Przeworski (1986) has argued that the acceptance of democracy requires the acceptance of "uncertainty" by capitalist elites. However, stable functioning democracies seem to produce quite
predictable policy outputs, as compared with unstable authoritarian regimes. It is thus not
democracy per se that produces uncertainty, but the transition.

36 To take a random example, consider the self-criticism by Oscar Bruschera (1986), a Christian
Democrat who made the mistake of coming out in favor of the military demands of February
1973.

As examples of political actions that produce crises, but are both formally legal and substantively democratic, we might mention demonstrations that are designed to bring pressure on the government to resign, or inflammatory propaganda. Although such acts may be made illegal by legislation, the right to free expression is fundamental to democracy, and thus its limitation is clearly unconstitutional. Equally, however, repeated paralyzation of the streets, obstruction of parliamentary business, and incitement to violence will undermine the stability of the democratic system, generating many forms of dangerous political reaction, including calls to curtail the "abuse" of democratic rights.

The major posttransition example of an unimpeachably democratic demand that posed a potential threat to democracy was that of the human-rights movement for trials of those responsible for the disappearances.[37] In 1987 it engaged in a campaign to have the law on military immunity reversed by plebiscite. However, the scale of the movement remained far smaller than, say, the student movement of the late 1960s. The Left's centripetal tactic of negotiating with the military and seeking moderate voters weakened all popular movements – not only those in favor of human rights. Seregni seemed anxious to avoid an antimilitary stance that might have contributed to democratic instability. The fundamental disagreement with the Colorados over immunity for the armed forces had more to do with form than substance: As had been the case for the terrorists, judgment should precede eventual pardons, the opposition argued.

In the second category, we have the more dubious situation of political actions that arguably are legal, but may be held either by government or opposition to violate the spirit of a democratic order. It is often argued that the advent of military rule in Uruguay was made possible by a period of substantive democratic values. The Right argued, for example, that political strikes against a democratically elected government were intolerable,[38] and the Left attacked the militarization of strikers by President Pacheco as a violation of civil rights.[39] Mercifully, under the new democracy the problem of general strikes (as opposed to sectoral strikes), which is the only form that would come near to falling into this second category, did not nearly reach the scale of the early 1970s. Neither trade-

---

37 Another such movement was the successful initiative to raise and index social-security benefits by referendum in 1989.

38 As Uruguay before 1973 showed, the disruption caused by general strikes can produce an authoritarian reaction well beyond the capitalist class. Members of the middle sectors, small businessmen, those dependent on pensions or other state benefits, and even workers themselves where they are not fortunate enough to be employed in industries with strong unions tend to be left behind in the inflationary spiral.

39 Once "militarized," workers who refused to return to work could be tried by military courts as "deserters."

union mobilization nor the government's response could be characterized by either side as violating the spirit of the Constitution by abusing democratic rights or authority.[40]

Finally, the third type of challenge to democracy is the symmetrically opposite problem of actions that are agreed to be illegal, but are pursued in the name of a "higher" or "more substantive" democracy. Into this category would fall the past actions of the MLN-Tupamaros. Those who rightly point out that the guerrillas were not by themselves "to blame" for the military coup (not least because they were defeated by 1972) cannot deny the fact that the MLN contributed to the collapse of democracy by their unrepentant hostility to Uruguay's "bourgeois democracy," which they denounced as perpetuating the rule of an "oligarchy."[41] It is a measure of the current strength of Uruguayan democracy that since the transition, no salient illegal activities have occurred in the name of political ideals, and most Tupamaros have renounced violence. An ultraleft leader, who had survived in exile, suggested to me that "armed struggle is a method like any other, to be used when there is no alternative." But when asked if there had not been alternatives before 1973, he replied "yes, I think so. Armed struggle was misconceived – it was almost an interelite conflict."[42] When the Christian Democrats and "List 99" left the Broad Front in 1989, the Tupamaros were allowed to join. A milestone was thus reached in the process of their transformation into a democratic opposition.

The parties still disagreed over the correct response to terrorism, yet the data in Table 10.3 are highly encouraging from the point of view of democratic consolidation, in that the most extreme responses listed were rejected by all interviewees. The next most extreme responses also received little approbation. The Blancos, for once, had the most consistent and central position, symbolizing the role they were to play in the Parliament from 1985 on.[43] The Colorado minority tended toward a tough response, whereas the Broad Front was perfectly split down the middle on the merits of negotiation.

40 However, though Fernández Faingold remains popular, the skillful and progressive minister of labor has his enemies. Were he to be replaced by someone favoring strict union legislation, a serous eruption might ensue.

41 The three categories are not necessarily chronological; it is essentially fruitless to attempt to identify "which came first." Furthermore, the particular political actors that we have identified in our examples of each category (unions, executive, guerrillas) often were responsible for creating problems of other types. For example, the executive began to abandon even a formal democratic façade, while claiming allegiance to a different model of democracy, and in that sense used methods similar to those of the terrorists.

42 Personal interview, Montevideo, 3 May 1985.

43 Although Wilson and most Blancos voted for the 1972 law regarding state security, which was designed to confront the guerrillas by such means as suspending habeas corpus and instituting military trials, Wilson has since recanted and admitted that that was a mistake.

Table 10.3. *How should the government respond to terrorism?*[a]

Response	Left (%) (n = 10)	Blancos (%) (n = 17)	Colorados (%) (n = 19)	All[b] (%) (n = 51)
The government should accept the terrorists' demands.	0.0	0.0	0.0	0.0
Negotiation and dialogue should be held with the terrorists.	50.0	11.8	5.3	15.7
The government should maintain law and order while respecting basic human rights.	50.0	76.5	73.7	68.6
The government should declare war on terrorism with all available means, but still maintain its control.	0.0	11.8	21.1	15.7
The government should put the matter in military hands.	0.0	0.0	0.0	0.0
Total	100.0	100.0	100.0	100.0

[a]The question: "If in the future terrorism should recur, what action would you support?"
[b]Includes one Patriotic Union and three Civic Union leaders, plus a nonparty high-ranking officer.

Many of the objective problems faced by the country, such as its foreign debt, stagnation, unemployment, and inflation, were aggravated by the authoritarian regime. But what of the characteristics of Uruguayan political society? There are signs of an enduring increase in democratic *convivencia*, of a return to reformist politics rather than to the polarization of the 1960s. The Broad Front has been incorporated as a legitimate form of "loyal" and democratic opposition, and the balance of the traditional parties has shifted toward the center. Although the problem of the disjunction between trade-union power and political power has not been solved, politicians from the Left do not see Uruguayan politics as particularly polarized (Table 10.4). Even the rather polarized view of Uruguayan politics found among Blancos probably was a product of their isolation from the other parties and confrontation with the military at the time of the interviews in 1984–5.

Table 10.4. *Political antagonism*

Parameter	Broad Front (*n* = 8)	Blancos (*n* = 11)	Colorados (*n* = 18)	All[a] (*n* = 41)
Percentage responding "yes" to the first question[b]	37.5	55.6	27.8	36.6
Percentage responding "yes" to the second question[c]	100.0	75.0	87.5	85.0

[a] Includes one Patriotic Union and three Civic Union leaders.
[b] The question: "Frequently, political polarization in Argentina is described in terms of Peronism versus anti-Peronism, while in Chile the polarization is seen as socialism versus capitalism. Do you think that an equivalent polarization has existed in Uruguay?"
[c] The question (only for those answering "yes" to the first question): "Do you think this polarization remains?"

Thus far, we may safely say that the second and third forms of threat to democracy are not present in Uruguay. The government has been tough, but it pulled back decisively when its budget veto was deemed unconstitutional. The opposition has not been tempted into disloyal obstruction, mobilization, or conspiracy. Everything, therefore, hinges on the degree to which the lawful exercise of democratic rights continues to breed discipline, responsibility, and *convivencia*, rather than egoism, crises, and instability.[44] In formal theoretical terms, political actors must see a stable democratic regime as a "public good." As long as they perceive the current alternative of mass praetorian mobilization as not only bad for the system but also not in their own interests, they will seek to cooperate. This requires learning that the aggressive pursuit of short-run self-interest can be self-defeating when it provokes retaliatory strategies from opponents. For example, if workers repeatedly strike, capitalists will refuse to invest. The potential for this classic "prisoner's dilemma" conflict can be mitigated only by historic memory, negotiation, law, custom, and political intermediation.

Overall, as Table 10.5 shows, politicians were relatively optimistic about the parties' capacities to learn to stabilize democracy. The only

44 To those who charge that attention to democratic "survivability" is tantamount to capitulation before conservative interests, the government has but one reply: What alternatives exist? It is to be hoped that memories are not so short that the gruesomeness of the authoritarian possibility fades. Many now recognize that by guaranteeing the autonomy of popular movements, democracy is the best hope for those with radical visions of the future.

Table 10.5. *The parties' capacities to contribute to democracy*[a]

Party evaluated	Party of respondent			
	Broad Front (*n* = 23)	Blanco (*n* = 22)	Colorado (*n* = 17)	All[b] (*n* = 67)
Broad Front	1.3	4.4	4.7	3.8
Christian Democrats	1.1	3.5	3.9	3.1
Socialists	1.6	4.3	4.7	3.9
Communists	1.9	6.3	6.0	5.3
Blanco	1.8	1.7	3.5	2.4
Ortiz	5.1	3.1	3.9	3.9
Consejo Nacional Herrerista	2.8	1.2	2.6	2.1
Movimiento de Rocha	1.6	1.2	2.9	2.0
Por la Patria	1.9	1.8	4.0	2.7
Corriente Popular Nacionalista	2.3	2.5	4.8	3.3
Colorados	2.1	1.7	1.2	1.6
Unión Colorada y Bat	6.8	4.2	3.5	4.4
Unidad y Reforma	2.6	1.7	1.2	1.8
Libertad y Cambio	2.2	1.7	1.2	1.7
Corriente Batllista Independiente	1.4	2.2	2.3	2.1

[a] The question: "How would you judge the capacities of the political parties after the 1984 elections to behave according to the rules of the democratic game and contribute to political stability?" (1 = maximum, 10 = minimum)
[b] Includes one Patriotic Union and three Civic Union leaders, plus one nonpartisan military officer involved in government.

political sectors to be seen as frankly unhelpful for democratic consolidation were the right-wing Colorados and Blancos, who did very badly in the elections, and the communists, who stagnated. However, it is noteworthy that both traditional parties remained suspicious of the Left, as did the Colorados of the Blancos, to a lesser extent. Perhaps the most encouraging thing is to compare the figures in Table 10.5 with the figures reported in Chapter 3 regarding loyalty to democracy in the crisis. No clearer indication of perceptions of political learning among politicians exists. If we adopt the same criterion as we did then, and call any score between 4 and 7 "semiloyal" to democracy, and any score above that "disloyalty," we find that even the average score for the Broad Front no longer falls into the semiloyal region. In fact, the only groups to do so are the communists and the Pachequistas. Even more important, no group scored more than 6, meaning that no group was seen as outrightly disloyal to the new democracy.

Commitment to democracy at the mass level

Political learning must occur not only at the level of leaders but also among citizens as a whole. They are the final judges of whether a regime is worth preserving. Here Linz has drawn a crucial distinction between the intrinsic legitimacy of a democratic system and its performance.[45] Regimes that face severe economic crises and major social disruptions do not always collapse if democracy is valued as an end in itself by leaders and citizens, and if the alternatives are perceived as less desirable or inviable.[46]

Opinion data in the late 1980s suggested that Uruguayans did perceive Linz's distinction between regime performance and legitimacy. There is no doubt that few Uruguayans considered the country to be progressing economically, and economic issues were those that concerned them far more than any others.[47] However, when asked about the meaning of democracy, only 28% mentioned satisfaction of economic needs; rather, the overwhelming majority emphasized the value of freedom and participation.[48] Furthermore, though by 1989 the popularity of the Sanguinetti administration had seriously declined, across a broad range of policy areas it was rated vastly higher than all four preceding administrations, two of which had been dubiously democratic, and two outright authoritarian.[49] Fully 87% of interviewees believed that a democratic government was better than a military government from the point of view of solving economic problems, with 81% giving it the edge in fighting poverty, and 71% favoring it on the issue of corruption. Similar proportions even saw democracy as better able to maintain security in the streets, an extraordinarily revealing indicator. Even when asked the relatively sophisticated question of whether majorities should ever be allowed to take rights away from minorities, only 21% agreed.[50]

In sum, survey evidence suggests not only that Uruguayans have a sophisticated and liberal vision of democracy but also that they are able to distinguish its intrinsic value from its contingent ability to solve the country's deep problems. Yet they also see it as performing far better than military rule with regard to these challenges.

45 Linz and Stepan (1978, pp. 16–23).
46 Linz (n.d.).
47 González and Rius (1989, Tables 1 and 3). The findings were summarized in a series of articles in *Búsqueda* during January 1989.
48 González and Rius (1989, Table 19).
49 González and Rius (1989, Table 12). Only on the question of growth had a previous administration come close to the Sanguinetti administration in interviewees' perceptions of performance: that of Jorge Pacheco, from 1968 to 1972.
50 González and Rius (1989, Table 17).

Conclusion: Parties and regime change – some lessons and comparisons

What lessons can the examination of a single (at times singular) case produce for the study of comparative politics? The implications of this study regarding the importance of parties, and their specific roles in regime change, are broader than they might appear. Detailed case studies often can reveal important issues that have been neglected in previous theoretical discussions or broad comparative works. But the divide between case studies and comparison can be overstated: Serious comparative work cannot proceed without the richness of empirical evidence that case studies generate, and case studies in turn are immensely more interesting when informed by theories and comparisons. This conclusion therefore seeks to blend the specific lessons of the Uruguayan transition with broader comparisons to other cases.

The role of Uruguayan parties in the rise and fall of authoritarianism

By the early 1970s, the behaviors of at least some sections of all major Uruguayan parties were semiloyal (or even disloyal) to democracy. Abdication of responsibility by politicians eventually occurred in the form of refusal to form coalitions, as well as failure to come to the aid of the president when he was faced by a military rebellion. Indeed, most political sectors at one time or another encouraged military role expansion, hoping it would work to their advantage. It is plausible that despite the wave of authoritarianism that was sweeping Latin America in the 1960s, different strategies by political leaders might have prevented a military coup in Uruguay. One alternative would have been a quasi-authoritarian but civilian interlude based on a pact between the traditional parties, akin to that which occurred in 1933. Of course, such a pact was quite impossible given Wilson Ferreira's ambitions to turn the Blanco party into a vehicle for his populist leadership and oust the Colorados from power.

If the political parties share a heavy portion of the blame for the military intervention, they also contributed to the eventual defeat of military rule.

Their situation under the authoritarian regime may be likened to one of "suspended animation"; however, their predicted marginalization did not occur. The regime soon showed itself to lack a "foundational" project in the social or economic sphere, as opposed to merely a desire to return to Uruguay's past (i.e., restoration of conservative politics in a two-party system). Contrary to many expectations, however, the parties resisted manipulation by the military and began the difficult task of renovating their leadership and programs. The refusal of most politicians to collaborate meant that reliance on state patronage (one of the traditional ways of generating support) was blocked. Rather, politicians built their appeal on demands for the rule of law, fundamental freedoms, and the restoration of democracy.

As was demonstrated by the extraordinary defeat of the military in the 1980 plebiscite, a failed attempt to seek legitimation was the major background condition preventing institutionalization of the authoritarian regime. Yet that did not determine either how or when democracy would be restored. In the event, the transition was to take a further five years. What factors did then determine the course and timing of the transition?

The failure of economic policy was one reason that power-holders were anxious to extricate, but that did not determine how they would do so. Whereas analyses rooted in political economy throw light on the class bases of support for authoritarian rule, in Uruguay the dominant economic interests were loath to take the political stage during the transition. The most militant business protests came from the ranchers, but those seem to have stemmed as much from their political opposition to the growth of the military's power as from their economic interests. In short, the economic crisis of the 1980s played a major role in undermining the effectiveness of authoritarian rule, but it, too, was not a sufficient condition for transition. Comparisons with other cases of authoritarian breakdown suggest that economic slumps are neither necessary nor sufficient conditions for transitions to democracy. Some regimes that have achieved high rates of growth, such as Spain and Brazil, have nevertheless become unstable. The case of Chile (where the crisis of the early 1980s was even worse than in Uruguay), furthermore, suggests that economic crises can perversely solidify support for an authoritarian regime.[1]

Popular movements can, under certain circumstances, force structural change in regimes.[2] Yet such groups as labor unions, student associations, and community organizations are only rarely able to launch successful

---

1 Huneeus (1985, p. 66). An English version appears in Enrique Baloyra, ed., *Comparing New Democracies* (Boulder, CO: Westview Press, 1987).

2 Apart from violent overthrow of an insurgent kind, popular demonstrations, rioting, and disorders may reach a pitch at which power-holders will abdicate. However, that requires an extreme degree of governmental isolation and a loss of will by the security forces.

frontal assaults on modern, professionalized military regimes. In Uruguay, their leaders shrank from attempting to make the country "ungovernable," under pressure from the political parties. Their role was precariously subordinated to the negotiation strategies the leftist parties pursued. Although early on they may have accelerated the pace of transition, ultimately it was their demobilization that permitted the *reforma pactada* (negotiated reform) path of transition. As the case of Chile also shows, popular protest movements may solidify support for military rule where they are perceived as antagonistic to dominant-class interests (and even middle-class interests).

A fundamental feature of the Uruguayan transition was that despite personal rivalries, the unity and hierarchical command structure of the military ultimately held up. When the military attempt to govern, there arises a confusion between the deliberative roles of the regime and the administrative functions of the state. After 1973, real power lay with the junta of generals and the commanders in chief, and thus state and regime were in some sense fused. The decision to initiate a transition to democracy thus represented a desire on the part of the armed forces to return to a clearer delineation of responsibilities between politicians and generals. Two major hypotheses regarding the interest calculus of power-holders have been confirmed by this study: Military extrication was facilitated when the interests of the armed forces as an institution began to diverge from those of the president, and the strategies of the opposition strongly influenced those calculations.

The military as institution frequently see certain advantages in withdrawal from government, but oppositions rarely find themselves able to force the military from power. Yet negotiations between the two sides are by no means easily started, nor always successful. In Uruguay, it was only the successive exhaustion of alternatives that belatedly brought the Left into the dialogue and produced the commitment to successful negotiation on both sides in 1984. Incorporation of the Left into the transition pact produced a minimum winning coalition behind a negotiated path to democracy. It also facilitated a restraint on popular expectations, particularly regarding the immediate economic benefits the transition would bring.[3] Though the pact between the parties and the military reached at the Naval Club in August 1984 eventually paralleled the model of convergence between moderates as described by O'Donnell, it was by no means consensual. Yet even with a major party opposed to them, the plans laid at the Naval Club bore fruit.

3 The final milestone in the incorporation of the Broad Front into the democratic system as a loyal party, and its ultimate reward for the responsibility with which it acted during the transition, came when it captured municipal power in Montevideo in the elections of November 1989.

The conclusions regarding the prospects for democratic consolidation must be more tentative. However, the occurrence of political learning was confirmed in the preceding three chapters. The authoritarian experience restored the cohesion of Uruguayan politicians as a "political class," although that was not apparent until Wilson Ferreira was released from jail. The balance of the evidence regarding party renewal is that, though internal change was limited, the crucial transition elections of 1984 greatly strengthened the most democratic parties and factions and produced a centripetal pattern of competition.

The failure of political engineering from above and of radical efforts to change the system from below led to negotiated military withdrawal, but peace was bought at the price of severe limits on the potential for structural change. Innovative reforms – of parties, government, and society – are extremely difficult if political elites are seeking to dissipate conflict and establish mutual guarantees. The clear view of the Colorados after they came to power in 1985 was one of skepticism regarding whether power-sharing arrangements could prove flexible enough to create the "moving consensus" required to provide adaptive responses to governmental challenges, rather than degenerative "pluralistic stagnation." Yet a major irony of democratic restoration was that the earlier pact with the military subsequently limited the possibilities for innovation in politics and policy, producing a probably unhealthy return to the political status quo ante.

Six conditions for negotiated transitions to democracy

Political parties and party systems have played rather different roles in democratic breakdowns elsewhere in Latin America, but in cases such as Argentina and Chile they have proved equally important.[4] They have also played quite different roles in the demise of authoritarianism. By way of comparison, let us begin to see how the foregoing analysis of the Uruguayan case can help throw light on the fate of other neighboring military regimes. An enriched case study does not substitute for systematic comparison. However, we can already draw certain lessons regarding the paths of democratic transition that will hold for those regimes that consist of professional military-technocratic alliances that came into being to exclude relatively well developed and democratic political parties.

The speed of onset of authoritarian crisis in the 1980s varied in Argentina, Brazil, and Chile, and so did the paths by which they made the transition to democracy. Only in Uruguay did the parties sit down with

4 For a discussion of the weakness of Argentina's party system as a factor in democratic breakdown, see Cavarozzi (1986). On the role of parties in the polarization of Chilean politics, see Valenzuela (1978).

the military and negotiate the formal rules of the transition; the business elite did not play a major role in that process, and nor did social movements or foreign actors.[5] That pattern of relatively high political autonomy was somewhat less clear in the neighboring cases of transition, but in no case were parties marginal to the transition process. In Brazil, the democratization process was more controlled by the military and thus was based on an oblique pattern of regime initiative and response by opposition parties that, nevertheless, some have seen as equivalent to implicit negotiation.[6] In Argentina it was the refusal of the parties to negotiate with the military and their insistence on the military's unconditional withdrawal from power that determined the path of the transition.[7] One can also see the failure of the Chilean opposition to secure a transition in 1984, which led to prolongation of the authoritarian regime for a further five years, as in many ways rooted in the polarization of Chile's party system.[8]

Whether parties choose to negotiate or not, in countries with some prior experience of democracy and established party systems they can play a major role in closing off certain paths to democracy, and opening certain others. This is, of course, not to say that parties and their strategies are the only factors in the breakdown of authoritarian rule. This study has shown how lack of legitimacy, economic crisis, and popular mobilizations contribute to the failure of authoritarianism. In those cases where there is no convergence between the regime and the opposition on a negotiated transition, these factors can escalate to the point at which they force military withdrawal (as in Argentina in 1983), or they can be deflected and repressed (as in Chile in the same year). Nevertheless, parties are clearly central to the achievement of a negotiated transition.

What, then, are the conditions under which pacts are and are not possible between authoritarian regimes and oppositions? The Uruguayan case suggests that the following six perceptions (three on each side) must be present for a negotiated transition to democracy to be feasible:

1 The perception by opposition leaders that
   (a) regime collapse is not imminent, and military hard-liners are still an obstacle,

---

5 International factors, such as external economic shocks and the foreign policies of other states, nonstate actors, and international organizations, were of only secondary importance in southern-cone transition and nontransitions. The second oil shock and rising world interest rates dealt an equal, or worse, blow to Chile's military regime, but it held on. No one has shown that external actors were more than an irritant to the military, though regional events provided encouragement to the opposition.

6 Share and Mainwaring (1986).

7 Fontana (1984).

8 González (1985b).

(b)   nevertheless, the dominant sector of the military sincerely wishes to extricate if the terms are right, and

(c)   liberal democracy is more important than any long-run agenda for radical social change, and indeed democracy is the only hope for such change.

2   The perception by regime leaders that

(a)   transition and elections will not lead to victory for "maximalist" opponents,

(b)   revenge trials will not be conducted, and

(c)   refusal to initiate a transition would lead to more instability in the long run.

Where such evaluations (and their closely associated preferences) are lacking, formal negotiations or implicit cooperative strategies based on concessions become blocked. In Brazil, these six perceptions were present, whereas in both Argentina and Chile they were either clearly lacking or only ambiguously held.

Parties are far more unstable and opportunistic in Brazil than in Uruguay, but they turned out to be no less central to the path of the transition, despite that fact.[9] The generals' success in creating a pro-regime party in Brazil produced a different configuration of interests in the transition, but its split into two parties partially undermined the most ambitious military plans for guiding the redemocratization from above. The serious tactical error of the ruling party in failing to nominate a popular and moderate candidate for the presidency contrasted the opposition's clever choice of veteran centrist Tancredo Neves.[10] The six conditions for a convergence of interests between a majority of the opposition and sectors of the regime were all met. Thus, even without formal negotiations, the transition was ultimately somewhat akin to that which occurred in Uruguay, as Neves campaigned ceaselessly to reassure the armed forces, while retaining the support of all but the radical opposition.[11]

In Argentina, greater fear of reprisals and disorder prevented the military from proposing a deal similar to that which emerged in Uruguay until it was much too late to be accepted. The quite different nature of Argentine parties was a crucial factor, as was their historic distrust of manipulation by the military. The Perónists, assumed by everyone still to be the majority party, had far stronger links to former guerrilla movements and a greater capacity to paralyze the country with strikes than did any Uruguayan party. The dynamic of opposition unity with the radicals was one of intransigence, not negotiation. Ultimately, Argentina's return to democracy in 1983 was made possible by an internal crisis of the military, following the defeat in the South Atlantic War that forced them to abdicate.

---

9   Lamounier and Meneguello (1985).
10   See Skidmore (1988) and the essays in Stepan (1989).
11   The military did, however, remain far more powerful in Brazil. See Stepan (1988).

In Chile in the mid-1980s, the obstacles to negotiation were the greater strength of the Left, the ideologically polarized split in the opposition, and Pinochet's relatively greater retention of support among social elites. Chile's parties remained stuck in competing center and left alliances during the important 1984 talks. The cleavage between center and right also hampered efforts to create a united opposition front to the regime, whereas in Uruguay right-wing Colorados (who had been close to the military) did not constitute such a "bottleneck," providing not only votes but also ministers for the democratic government of Julio María Sanguinetti. The difficulties of unifying the opposition have been ascribed to the degree to which the ideologies and political projects of rival parties were mutually exclusive.[12] Pinochet recovered his balance and managed to save his slow timetable for a closely guided return to restrictive elections.[13] Though relations between the center and the Left improved by the end of the decade, Chile's transition was much slower and less complete than that of Uruguay.

Comparison of the Uruguayan and Chilean cases suggests that historical and structural factors may weigh heavily on political parties' strategies. We saw how the alternative of a hard-line alliance of the Left and radical Blancos, similar to Chile's "democratic movement," did not arise in Uruguay. Above all, the difficulties of Chile's opposition in developing a united strategy stemmed from its historically polarized party system. As González argues, that is the product of Chile's somewhat more stratified social structure, but also its *relatively later expansion of the franchise* than in Uruguay.[14] Just as in the United States early adoption of universal suffrage before industrialization (and longer still before the birth of organized labor) blocked the emergence of strong leftist parties, in Uruguay the Colorados and Blancos managed to survive precisely because of a uniquely successful transition from oligarchic to mass democracy at the beginning of this century. Voting does not follow class lines in Uruguay to any great extent.

Future comparisons of regime changes in Latin American polities must focus not only on the choices made by political actors but also on the constraints placed on those choices by the historic legacies shaping political institutions.[15] Crucial to this effort will be detailed configurative analysis

---

12 Muñoz (n.d.); Garretón (1984).
13 Of course, parties are not exclusively "to blame" for the persistence of authoritarianism in Chile. Pinochet's resilience also stemmed from his role as arbiter in a complex and heterogeneous coalition, the concentration of his personal power promoted by his fusion of the offices of president and commander in chief, and his stubborn opposition to early elections (Huneeus 1985).
14 González (1985b, p. 23).
15 As March and Olsen (1984) argue, though political institutions such as party systems are structurally constrained by social forces and by historical legacies, they nevertheless possess relative

of the historical genesis, evolution, and decay of political parties and party systems.[16] The structuring of the political incorporation at the moment of the extension of the effective franchise to include the entire population of a nation will have profound consequences for its subsequent political experience. Though not immutable, these parameters are resistant to change, as demonstrated by the "molding" of Argentine politics by the Peronist–radical split, and the very different tripolar party system of Chile. The current attempts at consolidation of a party system in Brazil, for the first time on the basis of universal suffrage, constitute just such a crucial historical moment. Yet, contrary to what might be called the "freezing hypothesis," party systems do not necessarily survive unchanged forever. After one and a half centuries, Uruguay has evolved from a two-party system to one of three to four parties.[17] The implications of this evolution for democratic consolidation are liable to be profound, although they lie beyond the scope of this book.

The comparative costs and benefits of Uruguay's path to democracy

For the sake of argument, suppose that Uruguay had chosen a different route back to democracy. The great questions would remain: What might have been gained? How much would have been sacrificed in terms of the resulting quality of democracy? Clearly, interests were sacrificed in the transitional election (those of the Blancos above all). But was more lost as well? Is government by elite conflict management, to the extent that it occurred in Uruguay, truly democratic?

Certainly, Uruguayans now benefit once more from all the formal freedoms demanded and guaranteed by liberal democracy. Social groups are now free to seek to secure their interests. Leaders are once more accountable. Granted that redemocratization may not have had much social content in Uruguay in terms of concrete advances, but it has had some. A report by the United Nations Economic Commission for Latin America praised Uruguay for reducing poverty in the second half of the 1980s. Labor unions have returned to defend working people; the health and education systems are emerging from the dark ages; cultural and

autonomy. I am grateful to Patrick Barrett for drawing my attention to this essay and to the need to strike a balance between the extremes of determinism and voluntarism in political analysis.

16 For a collection of essays that begin this important task, see Cavarozzi and Garretón (1989).

17 The departure of the moderate parties from the Broad Front early in 1989 led to the creation of a fourth major political option in Uruguayan politics, aptly christened the "New Space." However, that new alliance of "List 99" (renamed the Party for People's Government) and the Christian Democrats fared poorly in the November elections. It therefore remained unclear whether a tripolar or quadripolar party system would crystallize.

artistic expressions have flowered once more. The fact that democracies are constrained by scarcity and imperfections does not make them worthless. One cannot justly compare the actual performance of democracy to the potential performance of some hypothetical alternative. What matters is its performance vis-à-vis the concrete experience of authoritarian rule.

Democratic consolidation requires not the abolition of political conflict, but its successful management. In this study, three potential arenas for such conflict management and conflict-regulating mechanisms have been considered:

1 negotiations between opposition parties and the military,
2 negotiations between parties only, and
3 negotiations between parties and representatives of social movements and interest associations.

Whereas the Uruguayan example proved relatively successful with respect to the first type of negotiation, other countries going through democratic transitions and attempted consolidation have shown greater success in achieving the latter two types of conflict regulation, with more favorable implications for the future. Spain's transition to democracy, for example, led to implicit or explicit pacts in all these areas. However, one of the findings illustrated by this study is that such levels of conflict management can turn out to be in conflict themselves. In other words, there are no easy trade-offs between the military, the political, and the social questions.

There is clearly a relation between a nation's path of transition from authoritarian rule and its prospects for democratic consolidation. Uruguay may be more fortunate than some of its near neighbors, where evidence of political learning has seemed less profound. Unlike Argentina, Uruguay avoided the syndrome of a seething and vanquished military anxious to see democracy fail. Compared with Brazil, Uruguay had the advantage of a strong and stable party system, immune to populist surges and resting on a tradition of legitimacy that has been much restored by the military regime's actions, both intentional and unintentional. In contrast to Chile, Uruguay's parties were able to avoid ideological polarization. All of these comparative benefits may be traced back to the path of Uruguay's transition, which seems to have both required and nurtured a relatively high level of political learning. This may be defined as an increase in the capacity of politicians to perceive the consequences of all potential strategies open to them, particularly in terms of the responses of other actors.

In comparative terms, Uruguay's parties made the most explicit attempt yet seen to strike a deal with their military opponents that might lead to their mutual benefit. The persistence of bitter conflicts among the parties over the question of military trials suggests that there may have been hidden costs in such a deal. However, the final proof of the responsible behavior of the National party came in late 1986 when its majority sector at last agreed to propose the law closing the book of past violations of human rights. Nothing obliged the Blancos to accept the terms of the transition or the Colorado electoral victory, however convincing it may have been. Nothing obliged them to stand by the terms of the Naval Club pact or introduce the bill for a statute of limitations. However, as Wilson Ferreira argued, a certain route to democracy had been taken, and the price was amnesty.[18] The important thing for all concerned was that the past was the past, not just for the military, but for the Blancos as well.

A curious epilogue proves that nothing in politics is ever really final. Though our analysis of the transition ends with the enactment of the amnesty for the military, the Broad Front and sectors of the Blanco party at once initiated a campaign to collect over half a million signatures to force a referendum on repealing the statute of limitations. With great reluctance the traditional parties (which dominated the Electoral Court) eventually allowed that to go ahead in April 1989.[19] Uruguay's citizenry was thus given one more opportunity to challenge the compromise that underlay the return to democracy. In the event, the margin of victory for those who favored retaining the law − 55.4% nationwide − was large enough to lay the matter to rest once and for all, but not so great as to suggest that the military could in the future afford to act with impunity.[20] The democratic consensus thus again legitimized the concessions that the politicians had been willing to make to the military in the interest of democracy as an end in itself.

18 On 15 March 1988, Wilson Ferreira succumbed to cancer. He thus never lived to see the victory of his party in the November 1989 elections that brought his former conservative ally, Luis Alberto Lacalle, to power.

19 For a detailed analysis of the debate that raged over whether to bury the past or uphold the principle of human rights, see Weschler (1990).

20 In Montevideo, only 42.5% of those who voted chose to call for retention of the law, granting human-rights campaigners an important symbolic victory. In the rest of the country, however, 67.3% voted for the military's amnesty, ensuring the failure of the repeal effort. See *Búsqueda*, No. 481, 20–26 April 1989, p. 4.

Appendix: Interviewees responding to questionnaire

Broad Front

Mariano Arana
José Bayardi (IDI)
Oscar Botinelli
Carlos Cassina (99)
Guillermo Chifflet (PS)
Carlos Coitiño (IDI)
Carlos Durán (IDI)
Eduardo Jaurena (Movimiento Socialista)
Eduardo León (PS)

Héctor Lescano (PDC)
Víctor Manuel Licandro
José Luis Massera (PC)
Rafael Michelini (99)
Pablo Mieres (PDC)
Wilfredo Penco (DA)
Romeo Pérez (PDC)
Juan Pablo Terra (PDC)
Colonel Zufriategui

Blancos

Gonzalo Aguirre (MNR)
Amalia Alonso (CPN)
Javier Barrios Anza (MNR)
Wáshington Beltrán
Enrique Cadenas Boix (CNH)
Miguel Cecilio (PLP)
Juan Pablo Croce (PLP)
Eladio Fernández Menéndez (MNR)
Raúl Gadea (PLP)
Jorge Gandini (PLP)
Pablo García Pintos (CNH)
Angel María Gianola
Wáshington Guadalupe (H)
Luis Ituño (PLP)
Luis Alberto Lacalle (CNH)

José Pedro Lafitte (PLP)
Héctor Lorenzo Ríos (PLP)
Carminillo Mederos (MNR)
León Morelli (PLP)
Horacio Muniz Durand (PLP)
Walter Pagés (PLP)
Héctor Paysée Reyes
Ariel Pereira (H, Herrerista)
Ana Lía Piñeyrúa
Juan Martín Posadas (PLP)
C. Rodríguez Labruna (MNR)
Rodolfo Saldain (PLP)
Horacio Terra (PLP)
Uruguay Tournée (PLP)

Colorados

Wáshington Abdala (15)
Jorge Batlle (15)
Altivo Esteves (85)
Juan Carlos Fa Robaina (15)
Eduardo Fazzio (15)

Hugo Fernández Faingold (15)
Manuel Flores Mora
Manuel Flores Silva (89)
Francisco Forteza (15)
Hugo Granucci (85)

Luis Hierro Gambardella
Luis Hierro López (85)
Diego Lamas (89)
Ricardo Lombardo (85)
Carlos Manini Ríos (UCB)
Antonio Marchesano (15)
Horacio Martorelli (85)
Jorge Otero

Ope Pasquet (85)
Miguel Petit (89)
Bernardo Pozzolo (15)
Jorge Sapelli
Brigadier Danilo Sena (UCB)
Alfredo Traversoni (85)
Amílcar Vasconcellos
Juan José Zorrilla (15)

Civic Union

Juan Vicente Chiarino
Julio Daverede

Eduardo Pérez del Castillo

Bibliography

1. Quoted interviews

Gonzalo Aguirre, 15 March 1984
Amalia Alonso, 3 July 1984
María del Huerto Amarillo, 22 February 1984
Mariano Arana, 14 December 1984 and 17 April 1985
General Arturo Baliñas, 16 October 1984
Hugo Batalla, 21 March 1985
Jorge Batlle, 23 June 1984
José Bayardi, 30 April 1985
Enrique Beltrán, 8 November 1984
Wáshington Beltrán, 31 October 1984
Bernardo Berro, 4 September 1983 (in Washington)
Néstor Bolentini, 31 October 1984
Leopoldo Bruera, 18 April 1985
Oscar Bruschera, 6 November 1984
Gonzalo Carámbula, April 1985
José Pedro Cardoso, 5 October 1984
Juan Vicente Chiarino, September 1984
Guillermo Chifflet, 26 April 1985
Humberto Ciganda, 13 April 1985
Alba Clavijo, 17 November 1984
Carlos Coitiño, 10 November 1984
Fernándo Crispo Capurro, 28 August 1984
Juan Pablo Croce, 13 July 1984
José Diáz, 27 September 1984
Carlos Duran Mattos, 3 May 1985
José D'Elía, 9 May 1985
Juan Carlos Fa Robaina, 13 July 1984
Luis Faroppa, 6 December 1984
Eladio Fernández Menéndez, 23 November 1984 (in San José)
Wilson Ferreira Aldunate, 4 January 1983 (in Washington)
Manuel Flores Mora, 31 August 1984
Manuel Flores Silva, April 1985 and (in Washington) 4 September 1983
Carlos Folle, August 1981
Francisco Forteza, 2 October 1984
Raúl Gadea, 5 March 1984 and 2 May 1984
Colonel Daniel García, November 1984

251

Guillermo García Costa, 11 July 1984
Pablo García Pintos, 12 December 1984
Reynaldo Gargano, November 1984
Angel María Gianola, 4 October 1984
Wáshington Guadalupe, 13 December 1984
Luis Hierro López, 12 July 1984
Luis Ituño, 4 September 1984
Eduardo Jaurena, 29 March 1985
Carlos Jones, 11 June 1984
Luis Alberto Lacalle, 31 August 1984
José Pedro Lafitte, 20 November 1984
Eduardo de León, 10 May 1985
Alfredo Lepro, November 1984
General Víctor Manuel Licandro, 21 December 1984
Rodolfo Lutegui, 12 December 1984
Cristina Maeso, 26 June 1984
Carlos Manini Ríos, 22 and 28 August and 26 September 1984
Colonel Jorge Martínez, 23 November and 14 December 1984; 15 and 24 April 1985
Enrique Martínez Moreno, 5 November 1984
José Luis Massera, 17 November 1984
General Hugo Medina, 27 March 1987 (in Columbia, SC)
Rafael Michelini, 5 December 1984
Zelmar Michelini, Jr., 24 July 1985 (in Paris)
Dardo Ortiz, 13 December 1984
Walter Pagés, August 1981
Ope Pasquet, 2 May 1984
Héctor Paysée Reyes, 20 November 1984
Eduardo Paz Aguirre, 24 September and 29 November 1984
Wilfredo Penco, 23 November 1984
Ulíses Pereira Reverbel, 29 November 1984
Carlos Julio Pereyra, 12 December 1984
Jaime Pérez, 7 November 1984
Brigadier Pérez Caldas, 13 December 1984
Colonel Pomoli, 3 April 1984
Bernardo Pozzolo, 3 May 1984
General Ramagli, April 1984
Américo Ricaldoni, 15 March 1984
Renán Rodríguez, 7 March and 10 July 1984
Carlos Rodríguez Labruna, 28 September 1984
Jorge Sapelli, 17 July and 29 September 1984 and 9 May 1985
Nelson Sapelli, 11 August 1981
Brigadier Danilo Sena, 4 December 1984
General Líber Seregni, 30 April 1985
Enrique Tarigo, 14 December 1984
Horacio Terra Gallinal, 31 August and 6 December 1984
Uruguay Tournée, 10 and 14 July 1984
Amílcar Vasconcellos, 29 August 1984
Alejandro Végh Villegas, 4 April 1984 (in New Haven)
José Claudio Williman, 4 May 1984
Juan Young, 27 March and 7 May 1985
Colonel Zufriategui, 29 November 1984

2. Newspapers (published in Montevideo unless otherwise noted)

Cinco Días (ceased publication)
Clarín (Buenos Aires)
El Día
Financial Times (London)
The Guardian (London)
International Herald Tribune (Paris)
Jornal do Brasil (Rio de Janeiro)
La Mañana
Le Monde (Paris)
Mundo Color
El País
El País (Madrid)
Tiempo de Cambio (ceased publication)
The Times (London)
El Nuevo Tiempo (ceased publication)
Ultimas Noticias

3. Periodicals (published in Montevideo unless otherwise noted)

Aquí
Asamblea
Las Bases
Búsqueda
Carta Política (Buenos Aires)
Compromiso (Buenos Aires)
Concertación
Convicción
Correo de los Viernes
Cuestión (Stockholm)
El Debate
La Democracia
Desde Uruguay (Mexico)
Dignidad
El Frentista
Guambia
La Hora
Jaque
Keesings Contemporary Archives (London)
Latin American Weekly Report (London)
El Marcador
Le Monde Diplomatique (Paris)
Opinar (ceased publication)
La Semana Uruguaya (ceased publication)
Sincensura
Somos Idea

4. Articles, chapters, dissertations, and unpublished essays

n.a. 1983. "Uruguay 1982: Les résultats des élections internes." *Problèmes d'Amérique Latine*, No. 67, *Notes et Etudes Documentaires*, 4707–8 (February).

Aguiar, César. 1985. "Perspectivas de democratización en el Uruguay actual." In César Aguiar et al., eds., *Apertura y Concertación* (pp. 7–58). Montevideo: Banda Oriental.

Amarillo, María del Huerto. 1981. "El proceso de militarización del estado del Uruguay." M.A. thesis, Madrid.

1985. *El ascenso al poder de las Fuerzas Armadas*. Montevideo: *Cuadernos Paz y Justica*, Servicio Paz y Justica, 64 pp.

Arregui, Miguel, and Charles Gillespie. 1988. "Uruguay." In Abraham Lowenthal, ed., *Latin America and Caribbean Contemporary Record, Vol. V, 1985–6* (pp. B205–30). New York: Holmes & Meier.

Arriagada, Genaro. 1980. "Ideology and Politics in the South American Military: Argentina, Brazil, Chile, Uruguay." Wilson Center Latin American Program working paper No. 55, Washington, DC.

Biles, Robert E. 1972. "Patronage Politics: Electoral Behavior in Uruguay." Ph.D. dissertation, Johns Hopkins University.

Cavarozzi, Marcelo. 1978. "Elementos para una caracterización del capitalismo oligárquico." *Revista Mexicana de Sociología*, 4:1327–51.

1986. "Political Cycles in Argentina since 1955." In Guillermo O'Donnell, Philippe C. Schmitter, and Laurence Whitehead, eds., *Transitions from Authoritarian Rule: Latin America* (pp. 19–48). Baltimore: Johns Hopkins University Press.

Cocchi, Angel, and Jaime Klaczko, 1985. "Notas sobre democracia política y ideología en Uruguay." In Charles Gillespie et al., eds., *Uruguay y la Democracia, Vol. 3* (pp. 9–41). Montevideo: Banda Oriental.

Corlazzoli, Juan Pablo. 1984. "Les élections primaires en Uruguay de novembre 1982." In Dieter Nohlen, ed., *Wahlen und Wahlpolitik in Lateinamerika* (pp. 215–43). Heidelberg: Verlag Heidelberg GmbH.

Cosse, Gustavo. 1984. "Notas acerca de la clase obrera, la democracia y el autoritarismo en el caso uruguayo." In Charles Gillespie et al., eds., *Uruguay y la democracia, Vol. 1* (pp. 87–107). Montevideo: Banda Oriental.

Díaz-Alejandro, Carlos. 1981. "Open Economy, Closed Polity?" Yale University Economic Growth Center discussion paper No. 390.

Filgueira, Carlos H. 1976. "Indicadores comparativos de los departamentos del Uruguay." CIESU Documento de Trabajo No. 13, Montevideo: Centro de Informaciones y Estudios del Uruguay.

Finch, Henry. 1985. "The Military Regime and Dominant Class Interests in Uruguay." In Paul Cammack and Phil O'Brien, eds., *Generals in Retreat* (pp. 89–114). Manchester, UK: Manchester University Press.

Finch, M. H. J. 1979. "Stabilization Policy in Uruguay since the 1950's." In Rosemary Thorp and Laurence Whitehead, eds., *Inflation and Stabilization Policy in Latin America* (pp. 144–80). London: Macmillan.

Finer, Samuel E. 1985. "The Retreat to the Barracks." *Third World Quarterly*, 7(1):16–30.

Flisfisch, Angel. 1984. "Partidos y dualismo en la transición." Paper presented to the conference Procesos de Democratización y Consolidación de la Democracia, Santiago, 9–12 April.

Fontana, Andrés. 1984. "Fuerzas Armadas, partidos políticos y transición a la democracia en Argentina." In Augusto Varas, ed., *Transición a la Democracia* (pp. 113–29). Santiago: Asociación Chilena de Investigaciones para la Paz-Ainavillo.

Garretón, Manuel Antonio. 1979. "En torno a la discusión de los nuevos regímenes autoritarios en América Latina." Wilson Center Latin American Program working paper No. 52, Washington, DC.

1981. "Transformación social y refundación política." *Materiales de Discusión*, No. 12 (March), FLACSO, Santiago.

Gillespie, Charles. 1985. "Uruguayan Communism: Dilemmas of Tactics and Strategy." *Journal of Communist Studies*, 1:3/4.

1986a. "Uruguay's Transition from Collegial Military-Technocratic Rule." In Guillermo O'Donnell, Philippe C. Schmitter, and Laurence Whitehead, eds., *Transitions from Authoritarian Rule: Latin America* (pp. 173–95). Baltimore: Johns Hopkins University Press.

1986b. "Activists and the Floating Voters: The Unheeded Lessons of Uruguay's 1982 Primaries." In Paul W. Drake and Eduardo Silva, eds., *Elections and Democratization in Latin America, 1980–85* (pp. 215–44). La Jolla: CILAS–University of California, San Diego.

1987a. "Party Strategies and Redemocratization: Theoretical and Comparative Perspectives on the Uruguayan Case." Ph.D. dissertation, Yale University (May).

1987b. "Presidential–Parliamentary Relations and the Problem of Democratic Stability: The Case of Uruguay." Paper presented to the American Political Science Association, Chicago (September).

Gillespie, Charles, and Luis Eduardo González. 1989. "Uruguay: The Survival of Old and Autonomous Institutions." In Larry Diamond, Juan J. Linz, and Seymour Martin Lipset, eds., *Democracy in Developing Countries. Vol. 4: Latin America* (pp. 207–45). Boulder, CO: Lynne Rienner.

Gillespie, Richard. 1980. "A Critique of the Urban Guerilla." *Conflict Quarterly*, 1(2):39–53.

González, Luis E. 1976. "La Transformación del sistema político uruguayo." Master's thesis, Fundación Bariloche, Argentina.

1983a. "The Legitimation Problems of Bureaucratic Authoritarian Regimes: The Cases of Chile and Uruguay." Manuscript, Yale University.

1983b. "Uruguay 1980–81: An Unexpected Opening." *Latin American Research Review*, 18(3):63–76.

1985a. "Political Parties and Redemocratization in Uruguay." Wilson Center Latin American Program working paper No. 163, Washington, DC.

1985b. "Transición y partidos en Uruguay y Chile." CIESU Documento de Trabajo No. 93, Montevideo: Centro de Informaciones y Estudios del Uruguay.

1985c. "Transición y restauración democrática." In Charles Gillespie et al., eds., *Uruguay y la Democracia, Vol. 3* (pp. 101–20). Montevideo: Banda Oriental.

1988. "Political Structures and the Prospects for Democracy in Uruguay." Ph.D. dissertation, Yale University (May).

González, Luis Eduardo, and Andrés Rius. 1989. "La opinión pública montevideana a cuatro años de la restauración democrática." Manuscript, Montevideo.

Graceras, Ulíses. 1977. "Intergenerational Cleavages and Political Behavior: A Study of the 1971 Presidential Election in Uruguay." Ph.D. dissertation, Michigan State University.

Guidobono, Alberto. 1972. "Consideraciones metodológicas sobre tres encuestas electorales." *Revista Uruguaya de Ciencias Sociales*, 1(1):15–23.

Handelman, Howard. 1981. "Labor–Industrial Conflict and the Collapse of Uruguayan Democracy." *Journal of Interamerican Studies and World Affairs*, 23(4):371–94.

Huneeus, Carlos. 1985. "La política de la apertura y sus implicancias para la inauguración de la democracia en Chile." *Revista de Ciencia Política*, 7(1):66.

Iklé, Fred, and Nathan Leites. 1962. "Political Negotiation as a Process of Modifying Utilities." *Journal of Conflict Resolution*, 6(1):19–28.

Janda, Kenneth, and Desmond S. King. 1985. "Formalizing and Testing Duverger's Theories on Political Parties." *Comparative Political Studies*, 18(2):139–69.

Kerbusch, Ernst J. 1969. "Uruguay in der Verfassungskrise." *Verfassung und Verfassungswirklichkeit*, 4:195–218.

Lamounier, Bolivar, and Rachel Meneguello. 1985. "Political Parties and Democratic Consolidation: The Brazilian Case." Wilson Center Latin American Program working paper No. 165, Washington, DC.

Lanzaro, Jorge. 1980. "La Constitución nonata." *Cuadernos de Marcha*, New Series, No. 9 (Mexico).

Lérin, François, and Cristina Torres. 1978. "Les Transformations institutionelles de l'Uruguay (1973–1978)." *Problèmes d'Amérique Latine*, No. 42, Notes et Etudes Documentaires, 4485–6 (November).

Lijphart, Arend. 1969. "Consociational Democracy." *World Politics*, 21(2):207–25.

Linz, Juan. 1971. "The Future of an Authoritarian Situation, or the Institutionalization of an Authoritarian Regime: The Case of Brazil." In Alfred Stepan, ed., *Authoritarian Brazil* (pp. 233–54). New Haven, CT: Yale University Press.

——— 1982. "The Transition from Authoritarian Regimes to Democratic Political Systems and the Problems of Consolidation of Political Democracy." Paper presented to the Tokyo Round Table of the International Political Science Association (March 29–April 1).

——— 1985. "Time and Regime Change." Manuscript, Yale University.

——— n.d. "Spain: A Consolidated Democracy." Manuscript, Yale University.

Mann, Arthur J., and Carlos E. Sánchez. 1985. "Labor Market Responses to Southern Cone Stabilization Policies." *Inter-American Economic Affairs*, 38(4):19–39.

March, James G., and Johan P. Olsen. 1984. "The New Institutionalism: Organizational Factors in Political Life." *American Political Science Review*, 78(3):734–49.

Muñoz, Heraldo. 1983. "Ideologías y redemocratización." *Alternativas* (Santiago: Centro de Estudios de la Realidad Contemporaneo), 1:48–66.

Noya, Nelson. 1986. "Tres problemas para la política económica." *SUMA*, 1:41–58.

O'Donnell, Guillermo. 1978. "Reflections on the Patterns of Change in the Bureaucratic-Authoritarian State." *Latin American Research Review*, 13(1):3–38.

——— 1979a. "Notas para el estudio de los procesos de democratización a partir del estado burocrático-autoritario." *Estudios CEDES*, 2(5):3–27. Reprinted 1981 in José Molero, ed., *El Análisis Estructural en Economía* (pp. 325–49). Mexico City: Fondo de Cultura Económica.

——— 1979b. "Tensions in the Bureaucratic-Authoritarian State and the Question of Democracy." In David Collier, ed., *The New Authoritarianism in Latin America* (pp. 285–318). Princeton, NJ: Princeton University Press.

O'Donnell, Guillermo, and Philippe Schmitter. 1986. *Transitions from Authoritarian Rule: Tentative Conclusions about Uncertain Democracies*. Baltimore: Johns Hopkins University Press.

Przeworski, Adam. 1986. "Some Problems in the Study of the Transition to Democracy." In Guillermo O'Donnell, Philippe C. Schmitter, and Laurence Whitehead, eds., *Transitions from Authoritarian Rule: Comparative Perspectives* (pp. 47–63). Baltimore: Johns Hopkins University Press.

Remmer, Karen L. 1985. "Redemocratization and the Impact of Authoritarian Rule in Latin America." *Comparative Politics*, 17(3):253–75.

Remmer, Karen L., and Gilbert W. Merkx. 1982. "Bureaucratic Authoritarianism Revisited." *Latin American Research Review*, 17(2):3–40.

Rustow, Dankwart. 1970. "Transitions to Democracy: Toward a Dynamic Model." *Comparative Politics*, 2(3, April):337–63.

Schneider, Ben Ross. 1987. "Framing the State." In John D. Wirth, Edson de Oliveira Nunes, and Thomas E. Bogenschild, eds., *State and Society in Brazil: Continuity and Change* (pp. 213–55). Boulder, CO: Westview Press.

Share, Donald, and Scott Mainwaring. 1986. "Transitions Through Transaction: Democratization in Brazil and Spain." In Wayne Selcher, ed., *Political Liberalization in Brazil* (pp. 175–215). Boulder, CO: Westview Press.

Shefter, Martin. 1977. "Party and Patronage." *Politics and Society* 7(4):403–51.

Stepan, Alfred. 1980. "Authoritarian Regimes and Democratic Oppositions." Manuscript, Yale University.

1985a. "State Power and the Strength of Civil Society in the Southern Cone of Latin America." In Peter Evans, Dietrich Rueschemeyer, and Theda Skocpol, eds., *Bringing the State Back In* (pp. 317–43). Cambridge University Press.

1985b. "Civil Society and the State: Patterns of Resistance to Domination in the Southern Cone of Latin America." Paper presented at a conference of the Social Science Research Council, April 1982.

1986. "Paths Toward Redemocratization: Theoretical and Comparative Considerations." In Guillermo O'Donnell, Philippe C. Schmitter, and Laurence Whitehead, eds., *Transitions from Authoritarian Rule: Comparative Perspectives* (pp. 64–84). Baltimore: Johns Hopkins University Press.

Taylor, Philip B. 1955. "The Electoral System in Uruguay." *Journal of Politics*, 17(1):19–42.

Torres, Cristina. 1981. "L'Echec de la tentative d'institutionalisation du régime." *Problèmes d'Amérique Latine, No. 64, Notes et Etudes Documentaires*, 4663–4.

5. Books, pamphlets, and government publications

n.a. 1984. *Actos Institucionales (1 al 17)*. Montevideo: Editorial Técnica.

Aguiar, César. 1984. *Elecciones y Partidos. Uruguay Hoy, No. 7*. Montevideo: CIEDUR.

Aguiar, César, et al. 1985. *Apertura y Concertación*. Montevideo: Ediciones de la Banda Oriental.

Arismendi, Rodney. 1971. *Lenin y la Revolución en América Latina*. Montevideo: Ediciones Pueblo Unido.

Barrán, José Pedro, and Benjamín Nahum. Various years. *Historia del Uruguay rural*. Montevideo: Banda Oriental.

Benvenuto, Luis C., et al. 1971. *Uruguay Hoy*. Buenos Aires: Siglo Veintiuno.

Boeker, Paul H. 1990. *Lost Illusions: Latin America's Struggle for Democracy as Recounted by Its Leaders*. New York: Markus Wiener.

Bruschera, Oscar. 1986. *Las Décadas Infamas*. Montevideo: Banda Oriental.

Cammack, Paul, and Phil O'Brien, eds. 1985. *Generals in Retreat*. Manchester, UK: Manchester University Press.

Cavarozzi, Marcelo, and Manuel Antonio Garretón, eds. 1989. *Muerte y Resurrección*. Santiago: FLACSO.

Collier, David, ed. 1979. *The New Authoritarianism in Latin America*. Princeton, NJ: Princeton University Press.

Comblin, Joseph. 1977. *Le pouvoir militaire en Amérique Latine*. Paris: Jean-Pierre Delarge.

Convergencia Democrática en Uruguay. 1984. *Documentos Políticos*. Mexico: n.p.

Costa Bonino, Luis. 1985. *Crisis de los Partidos Tradicionales y Movimiento Revolucionario en el Uruguay*. Montevideo: Banda Oriental.

Dahl, Robert. 1971. *Polyarchy*. New Haven, CT: Yale University Press.

1985. *A Preface to Economic Democracy*. Berkeley: University of California Press.

D'Elía, Germán. 1969. *El Movimiento Sindical. Nuestro Tiempo No. 4*. Montevideo: Editorial Nuestro Tiempo.

Drake, Paul, and Eduardo Silva, eds. 1986. *Elections and Democratization in Latin America, 1980–85*. La Jolla: CILAS-UCSD.

Duff, E. A., and J. F. McCamant. 1976. *Violence and Repression in Latin America: A Quantitative and Historical Analysis*. New York: Free Press.

Equipos Consultores. 1984–5a. *Informe Mensual*.

1984–5b. *Notas de Opinión Pública*.

Fa Robaina, Juan Carlos. 1972. *Cartas a un Diputado*. Montevideo: Alfa.

Ferreira Aldunate, Wilson. 1984. *Vamos a Sumarnos a un Gran Esfuerzo nacional* (pamphlet). Montevideo: Por la Patria.

1986. *El Exilio y la Lucha*. Montevideo: Banda Oriental.

n.d. *Discursos, Conferencias y Entrevistas*. Montevideo: n.p.

Finch, M. H. J. 1981. *A Political Economy of Uruguay Since 1870*. New York: St. Martin's Press.

Fitzgibbon, Russell H. 1954. *Uruguay: Portrait of a Democracy*. New Brunswick, NJ: Rutgers University Press.

Franco, Rolando. 1984. *Democracia "a la Uruguaya."* Montevideo: Editorial El Libro Libre.

Gallup Uruguay. Various years. *Informe de Opinión Pública*.

Various years. *Indice Gallup*.

Garretón, Manuel Antonio. 1984. *Dictaduras y Democratización*. Santiago: FLACSO.

Gilio, María Esther. 1972. *The Tupamaros Guerrillas*. New York: Saturday Review Press.

1986. *Wilson Ferreira Aldunate*. Montevideo: Ediciones Trilce.

Gillespie, Charles, et al., eds. 1984–5. *Uruguay y la Democracia* (3 vol.). Montevideo: Banda Oriental.

Hirschman, Albert. 1965. *Journeys Toward Progress*. New York: Anchor Books.

1969. *A Bias for Hope*. New Haven, CT: Yale University Press.

Huntington, Samuel. 1968. *Political Order in Changing Societies*. New Haven, CT: Yale University Press.

Inter-American Development Bank. 1986. *Economic and Social Progress in Latin America: Inter-American Development Bank 1986 Report*. Washington: IDB.

Kaufman, Edy. 1978. *Uruguay in Transition*. New Brunswick, NJ: Transaction Books.

Labrousse, Alain. 1973. *The Tupamaros*. Harmondsworth, UK: Penguin.

Langguth, A. J. 1978. *Hidden Terrors*. New York: Pantheon Books.

Latin America Bureau. 1979. *Uruguay: Generals Rule*. London: LAB Books.

Linz, Juan, and Alfred Stepan, eds. 1978. *The Breakdown of Democratic Regimes: Crisis, Breakdown, and Reequilibration*. Baltimore: Johns Hopkins University Press.

López Chirico, Selva. 1985. *Estado y Fuerzas Armadas en el Uruguay del Siglo XX*. Montevideo: Banda Oriental.

Macadar, Luis. 1982. *Uruguay 1974–1980: Un Nuevo Ensayo De Reajuste Economico?* Montevideo: Centro de Investigaciones Economicas, Ediciones de la Banda Oriental.

Mieres, Pablo. 1984. *El Comportamiento Electoral de los Uruguayos. Estudios CLAEH No. 39*. Montevideo: CLAEH.

Millot, Julio, Carlos Silva, and Lindor Silva. 1973. *El Desarrollo Industrial del Uruguay*. Montevideo: Universidad de la República, Departamento de Publicaciones.

Nohlen, Dieter, ed. 1984. *Wahlen und Wahlpolitik in Lateinamerika*. Heidelberg: Verlag Heidelberg GmbH.

O'Donnell, Guillermo. 1973. *Modernization and Bureaucratic-Authoritarianism*. Berkeley: University of California Institute of International Studies.

O'Donnell, Guillermo, Philippe C. Schmitter, and Laurence Whitehead, eds. 1986. *Transitions from Authoritarian Rule* (4 vols.). Baltimore: Johns Hopkins University Press.

Partido Colorado. 1984. *Por un Uruguay para Todos. Programa de Principios y Carta Orgánica del Partido Colorado*. Montevideo: El Día.

Pérez Pérez, Alberto. 1971. *La Ley de Lemas*. Montevideo: Fundación de Cultura Universitaria.

Porzecanski, Arturo C. 1973. *Uruguay's Tupamaros.* New York: Praeger.

Rama, Germán. 1971. *El Club Político.* Montevideo: Arca.

Real de Azúa, Carlos. 1964. *El Impulso y su Freno.* Montevideo: Ediciones de la Banda Oriental.

1984. *Uruguay, Una Sociedad Amortiguadora?* Montevideo: Banda Oriental.

Selcher, Wayne, ed. 1986. *Political Liberalization in Brazil.* Boulder, CO: Westview Press.

Silvert, Kalman. 1967. *Expectant Peoples.* New York: Vintage.

Skidmore, Thomas. 1988. *The Politics of Military Rule in Brazil, 1964–1985.* New York: Oxford University Press.

Stallings, Barbara, and Robert Kaufman, eds. 1989. *Debt and Democracy in Latin America.* Boulder, CO: Westview Press.

Stepan, Alfred, ed. 1971. *Authoritarian Brazil.* New Haven, CT: Yale University Press.

1988. *Rethinking Military Politics.* Princeton, NJ: Princeton University Press.

ed. 1989. *Democratizing Brazil.* New York: Oxford University Press.

Tarigo, Enrique. 1982. *Articulos y Discursos por el "No."* Montevideo: Editorial Nuestro Tiempo.

Thorp, Rosemary, and Laurence Whitehead, eds. 1979. *Inflation and Stabilization Policy in Latin America.* London: Macmillan.

United Nations Economic Commission for Latin America. 1986. *Debt Adjustment and Renegotiation in Latin America.* Boulder, CO: Lynne Rienner.

United States Congress. 1976. *Human Rights in Uruguay and Paraguay.* Washington, DC: U.S. Government Printing Office.

Uruguay, Presidencia de la República. 1983. *Palabras Pronunciadas por el Señor President de la República Teniente General Gregorio C. Alvarez el día 24 de marzo en Aceguá, Departamento de Cerro Largo* (pamphlet). Montevideo.

Uruguay. Various years. *Diario Oficial.* Montevideo.

Uruguay, Asamblea General. Various years. *Diario de Sesiones.* Montevideo.

Uruguay, Camara de Senadores. Various years. *Diario de Sesiones.* Montevideo.

Uruguay, Consejo de la Nación. 1981. *Discurso del Señor Presidente de la República Teniente General (Retirado) Gregorio C. Alvarez en Ocasión de Asumir el Compromiso de Honor ante el Consejo de la Nación. 1 de setiembre de 1981, Montevideo* (pamphlet). Montevideo.

Uruguay, Junta de Comandantes en Jefe. 1978. *Las Fuerzas Armadas al Pueblo Oriental* (2 vols., rev. ed.). Montevideo.

Valenzuela, Arturo. 1978. *The Breakdown of Democratic Regimes: Chile.* Baltimore: Johns Hopkins University Press.

Vanger, Milton. 1963. *José Batlle y Ordoñez of Uruguay, Creator of His Times.* Cambridge, MA: Harvard University Press.

1980. *The Model Country.* Hanover, NH: University Press of New England.

Varas, Augusto, ed. 1984. *Transición a la Democracia.* Santiago: ACHIP-Ainavillo.

Vasconcellos, Amílcar. 1973. *Febrero Amargo.* Montevideo: n.p.

Végh Villegas, Alejandro. 1977. *Economía Política: Teoría y Acción.* Montevideo: Polo.

Weinstein, Martin. 1975. *Uruguay: The Politics of Failure.* Westport, CT: Greenwood Press.

Weschler, Lawrence. 1989. *Uruguay: Democracy at the Crossroads.* Boulder, CO: Westview Press.

1990. *A Miracle, A Universe: Settling Accounts with Torturers.* New York: Random House.

Wirth, John D., Edson De Oliveira Nunes, and Thomas E. Bogenschild, eds. 1987. *State and Society in Brazil: Continuity and Change.* Boulder, CO: Westview Press.

World Bank. 1979. *Uruguay Economic Memorandum.* Washington: IBRD.

Zum Felde, Alberto. 1967. *Proceso Histórico del Uruguay.* Montevideo: Arca (1st ed. 1920).

Index

261

CAMBRIDGE LATIN AMERICAN STUDIES

Cambridge Latin American Studies